PREACHING MARK

PREACHING MARK

ROBERT STEPHEN REID

St. Louis, Missouri

© Copyright 1999 by Robert Stephen Reid.

All rights reserved. No part of this book may be reproduced without written permission from Chalice Press, P.O. Box 179, St. Louis, MO 63166-0179.

Biblical quotations, unless otherwise noted, are from the *New Revised Standard Version Bible*, copyright 1989, Division of Christian Education of the National Council of Churches of Christ in the USA. Used by permission.

Cover design and art: Bob Watkins
Interior design: Elizabeth Wright
Art direction: Michael Domínguez

This book is printed on acid-free, recycled paper.

Visit Chalice Press on the World Wide Web at
www.chalicepress.com

10 9 8 7 6 5 4 3 2 1   99 00 01 02 03

Library of Congress Cataloging–in–Publication Data

Reid, Robert Stephen.
   Preaching Mark / by Robert Stephen Reid.
      p.   cm.
   Includes bibliographical references.
   ISBN 0-8272-2958-5
   1. Bible. N.T. Mark--Homiletical use. 2. Bible. N.T. Mark Commentaries. I. Title.
   BS2585.5.R45   1999   99–37930
   226.3'06--dc21   CIP

Printed in the United States of America

Contents

List of Contributors	vii
Preface	ix
Introduction	1
Mark 1:1–15: The First Narrative Complex	18
Mark 1:16—2:14: The Second Narrative Complex	23
"He Came to Proclaim a Message" *A sermon by Judith M. McDaniel*	30
Mark 2:15—3:6: The Third Narrative Complex	34
Mark 3:7—4:1: The Fourth Narrative Complex	39
"Room in the Family" *A sermon by Stephen Farris*	45
Mark 4:2–34: The Fifth Narrative Complex	50
Mark 4:35—5:43: The Sixth Narrative Complex	56
"Hope at the Center" *A sermon by Robert S. Reid*	63
Mark 6:1–52: The Seventh Narrative Complex	68
Mark 6:53—7:31: The Eighth Narrative Complex	75
Mark 7:32—8:27: The Ninth Narrative Complex	81

Mark 8:27—9:29: The Tenth Narrative Complex	87
"Who Is He—And So What If He Is?" *A sermon by James E. Mead*	94
Mark 9:30—10:45: The Eleventh Narrative Complex	100
"The State of Our Spiritual Pantry" *A sermon by Paul Scott Wilson*	108
Mark 10:46—11:25: The Twelfth Narrative Complex	115
Mark 11:27—12:12: The Thirteenth Narrative Complex	121
Mark 12:13–44: The Fourteenth Narrative Complex	126
Mark 13:1–37: The Fifteenth Narrative Complex	133
Mark 14:1–53: The Sixteenth Narrative Complex	140
"While the Church Is Sleeping" *A sermon by Ronald J. Allen*	148
Mark 14:54—15:20: The Seventeenth Narrative Complex	154
Mark 15:21–39: The Eighteenth Narrative Complex	160
Mark 15:40—16:8: The Nineteenth Narrative Complex	165
"Tell All to Everyone" *A sermon by Lucy Lind Hogan*	171
Conclusion	176
Bibliography	183
Notes	188

List of Contributors

Ronald J. Allen is professor of preaching and New Testament, Christian Theological Seminary, Indianapolis, Indiana

Stephen Farris is professor of homiletics, Knox College, Toronto, Ontario, Canada

Lucy Lind Hogan is associate professor of homiletics, Wesley Theological Seminary, Washington, D.C.

Judith M. McDaniel is professor of homiletics, Virginia Theological Seminary, Alexandria, Virginia; and president of the International Society of Homiletics, Societas Homiletica

James E. Mead is executive presbyter of the Pittsburgh Presbytery, Presbyterian Church (USA), and vice-moderator of the PC(USA), 1998–99

Robert Stephen Reid is an ordained American Baptist minister serving as scholar-in-residence, University Place Presbyterian Church, Tacoma, Washington; senior lecturer, St. Martin's College; and adjunct faculty, the University of Washington

Paul Scott Wilson is professor of homiletics, Emmanuel College, University of Toronto, Ontario, Canada

Preface

The writing of *Preaching Mark* has been at the heart of my theological and homiletical journey for much of the last quarter of the twentieth century. The expedition began in the mid-seventies during an InterVarsity Mark Manuscript Study. Together with other college students, I spent a week working through the text of Mark, circling and reflecting on the implications of repeated words. During that study I saw more than just a way to discover key themes in Mark. And I would know, for I brought a trained eye to that experience. I saw patterns of relationships like those I had been trained to see while working for Army intelligence as a code-breaker in Southeast Asia during the early 1970s. I was probably one of the last to receive extensive training in this art, since computers were already displacing the need for field operatives. What I saw fueled questions I brought to seminary in 1976.

In my second quarter at Fuller Seminary, Dr. Ralph P. Martin assigned students in his New Testament Introduction course to make use of critical resources in writing a brief paper, a running commentary on the traditional group of "five conflict narratives" at the outset of Mark's Gospel. With the temerity of a student who knew not the monolith he was challenging, I argued that, chiastically, there were only four stories. It seemed that the form critics were including a story that was outside the implicit structural relationships of the other four stories. These critics, I imperiously announced, were reading Mark's narrative through their form filters rather than letting the narrative yield its own form. Dr. Martin took note of the paper, commending my attention to Joanna Dewey's essay, "The Literary

Structure of the Controversy Stories in Mark 2:1—3:6." Two years later, in late spring of 1979, Dr. Martin commended my attention to a book. Frank Kermode's *The Genesis of Secrecy* had just been published. Dr. Martin said, "You may want to take a look at this book. I think it is taking biblical studies in a direction you are going." Prescient words in the halls of a seminary in 1979. However, the mysteries of using formal literary and rhetorical theory as a critical tool in my biblical inquiry were still more than a decade away, for I was off to pastoral ministry.

Wrestling with the text of Mark became a joy during those first years as the pastor of First Baptist Church of Prosser, Washington. Wednesday nights for more than a year, people turned out to engage my visualized proposals for the structure of Mark's argument in the text. They stared at my overhead projections of the text, and together we explored how looking at the text in this way helped to see what Mark may have been emphasizing by the way he wrote the story. To my surprise and delight, most of the people who attended these studies were intrigued rather than put off by this way of looking at the text. I eventually came to realize that it was a kind of critical viewing of the text, whose rhythms were intuitive. It was as basic as:

> Hickory Dickory Dock
>   the mouse ran up the clock.
>   The clock struck one
>   and down he run
> Hickory Dickory Dock.

If this was a way of knowing that every child finds fascinating, it was equally intriguing to think that much of the power and memorableness of Jesus' story might have been communicated with similar techniques. I also discovered that, like students of the InterVarsity Manuscript Study, this kind of study provided those Wednesday night study participants with a tool to help them get at the "intention" of the text. Far from detracting from the authority of scripture, it took people deeply into the text, exploring a hands-on way of arriving at new meanings for familiar stories. It was a discovery born out in my next pastorate, at Sixth Avenue Baptist Church in Tacoma, Washington, and in my preaching during subsequent interim pastorates. Thanks to the people in all these congregations who helped me continue this inquiry.

While still at Prosser, a colleague, Rev. Alvin Lustie, and I decided to put our hands to writing a book on Mark's compositional artistry. Even after Al moved to Colorado, we took turns flying to one another's homes to work out the proposals for the structures. Many of the construals in this present version were born out of those days of study, as Al and I first began making use of what computers allowed us to do in moving text about to see alternative construals. The argument of this study was born out of conversations with Al and our first efforts to put that argument to words. Although the responsibility for what follows must lie with me, Al Lustie's biblical and pastoral reflections prod my reasoning at many points. Changes in both of our vocations brought an end to the joint project as both of us headed off for education. Al began to teach, while I went on for further graduate education.

While studying rhetoric and literary theory at the University of Washington, I had the privilege of exploring this question about Mark's "audience-entered rhetoric" in my M.A. thesis. The commentary in this volume is a much abbreviated version of that document. I was satisfied with my work on Mark but unsatisfied with efforts to locate this phenomenon of composition in the classical rhetorical tradition. Hence, my doctoral studies went in search of the justification of using parallelism as a "literate" technique of composition in the first centuries B.C. and A.D. The results of that inquiry, for which I received the American Society of the History of Rhetoric's "Outstanding Dissertation of the Year" award for 1994–95, strongly shape the argument of the Introduction in this present volume. For their patience and encouragement in helping to shape me as a rhetorician and for allowing me to pursue this inquiry through ancient and contemporary theories of rhetoric I thank John Campbell, my chair for both my M.A. and Ph.D. studies, as well as committee members Barbara Warnick, William Purcell, and David McCracken.

The final piece on the journey of this inquiry from question to text comes from four quarters. The first came through continued pursuit of what ancient rhetoricians meant by the idea of the "prose economy" of a treatise in various published essays. The second came through the willingness of fellow homileticians in the Academy of Homiletics to discuss the merit of this approach for preaching in the Rhetoric and Hermeneutics Working Group. For the insights of this group and the encouragement of David Fleer, of Michigan Christian College, I am grateful. The third quarter came from the efforts of two ministers who were willing to take this study and use it to frame a season of preaching their way through the Gospel of Mark. These include Rev. Jeff Bullock, who at the time was pastor of Queen Anne

Presbyterian Church in Seattle and is now President of Dubuque Theological Seminary. Jeff's administrative duties precluded his offering one of his sermons for this book, but his assessment and insights on the value of the work in preaching were excellent. The second pastor was Rev. Jim Mead, who was then pastor of University Place Presbyterian Church in Tacoma and is now Executive Presbyter of the Pittsburgh Presbytery of the PC (USA). While Jim was at University Place, he preached his way through a draft of this book while I, in my capacity as scholar-in-residence for this congregation, taught the same sermon texts for groups of adult learners who had either heard the sermon in one service or would hear it in the next. Jim and I discovered that, far from being repetitive, one experience fed the other. I owe a debt to both Jim and the participants of that class in the final efforts to refine this study. The last quarter came from those who, like Jim Mead, help complete the task of the study by using the analysis to compose a sermon. Here thanks go to Ron Allen, Stephen Farris, Lucy Hogan, Judith McDaniel, and Paul Scott Wilson.

Like all books, this one is a journey—in this case, one that can be read across the choices of my professional life. To each of the people who have contributed to this study named here, and those who are here but unnamed, I say thank you. I give special thanks to my spouse, Barbara, for her unfailing support and to my grown children, who spent much of their childhood watching their dad bent over a computer working on Mark. All three of these people have weathered the personal and professional vicissitudes of this journey with me. Appreciation is also extended to Jon L. Berquist of Chalice Press for the encouragement of his first response on reading an altogether unusual manuscript, for always being only a thoughtful e-mail message away, and for his effort in carrying the ball once it left my hands. My hope is that *Preaching Mark* will continue its journey in the preaching and teaching of those who would use this book as a means to encounter the *voice* of Mark, and the story of Jesus he tells, and to discover new ways to make that story relevant for another generation of listeners. For it is Mark's vision of Jesus and the urgency of his call to respond to Jesus' message of the kingdom come that has held my attention, amazement, affection, and allegiance throughout this journey.

Introduction

> *"When I came to you, brothers and sisters, I did not come proclaiming the mystery of God to you in lofty words or wisdom. For I decided to know nothing among you except Jesus Christ, and him crucified. And I came to you in weakness and in fear and in much trembling. My speech and my proclamation were not with plausible words of wisdom, but with a demonstration of the Spirit and of power, so that your faith might rest not on human wisdom but on the power of God."*
>
> —Paul of Tarsus, 1 Cor. 2:1–5; ca. 52–56 A.D.

Ancient customs of persuading audiences were as constrained by culturally legitimate ways of making a case then as they are today. We understand that a talk that begins with the words "Ladies and gentlemen of the jury, the case before you is about…" will be bound by current, culturally acceptable ways of presenting forensic argument, much as we understand that Jesus' words, "You've heard it said…, but I say unto you…," represent a similar, culturally meaningful way of contrasting the binding law of halakah interpretation with the moral ideal of aggadah reasoning. What made Jesus' pronouncements radical was not that he created unheard-of ways to proclaim the "gospel" as much as his audacity in the use of existing forms of persuasion; for example, he was even willing to challenge halakah teaching with aggadah preaching.[1]

In the same way, Paul was an effective spokesman for "gospel" because he was apparently as schooled in his use of Greco-Roman argument theory as he was in rabbinic logic. We can assume this schooling because in the first century B.C., rhetoric was the basis upon which all higher education was predicated in the Roman Empire. Students were literally drilled in ways to make "plausible" arguments and ways to embroider and stylize phrases if the occasion called for it.[2] Thus, Paul's disclaimer concerning his rejection of rhetoric's "plausible wisdom," heartfelt as it may have been, should not be accepted at face value. Rhetorically, demonstration was always considered a proof that carried more conviction for an audience than the *plausibility* of persuasive argument (Aristotle, *Rhetoric* 1.1.11; 1355a). And in the portion of the epistle cited in the headpiece, Paul is actually making a *plausible* argument—directed to the religious sensibilities of his audience—for why his authority should not be discounted simply because orators more eloquent than he had arrived on the scene. In other words, Paul could no more escape the influence of his education than people who have become literate can escape the effect of literacy on their ability to reason with greater complexity. His kind of talk gives him away. And for their part, the kind of audiences who read or heard such discourse, whether in Corinth or Capernaum, intuitively understood and gave credence to such strategies of reasoning. The strategies represented the customary art of "plausible wisdom" among audiences in their day and culture.

This attention to what audiences would count as *plausible* argument has been the defining feature of rhetoric from the Greek preclassical period until well after the Hellenistic era, throughout the period in which, as Havelock has described it, the Muse learned to write.[3] And even though the rabbis and scribes held little interest in documenting the nuance of their poetic technique or the rhetoric of their narratives *as such*, their storytellers still had a marvelous capacity for interweaving just the right disequilibriums and resolutions of emplotment necessary to capture the imaginations of audiences.[4]

The ancient Greek preoccupation with understanding the effect of persuasion for an audience is often discriminated from modern interest in how audiences respond. The ancients, we are told, were primarily concerned with technique, while we moderns are primarily concerned with signification and meaning.[5] But this distinction draws heavily on Aristotle (*Poetics* 1462b), and increasingly we have become aware that he is a biased source in this debate.[6] For when it comes to narrative, form has always been at the essence of argument.

Plot can never be fully reduced to the constituent elements of its technique, yet it can move and persuade an audience to take action with eloquence equal to that of any civic discourse. This is nowhere more evident than in the first-century gospel narratives, and especially the Gospel of Mark.

In this study, my purpose is to offer a visualization and analysis of Mark's use of a culturally legitimate way of structuring his argument while also telling a story. My interest is to explore the voice beyond the occasional parenthetical asides, to discover how Mark uses the story of Jesus to preach to his own community. By examining the way he makes literate use of parallelism and antithesis, my intention is to recover some sense of his narrative voice in order to assist contemporary preachers who see their own interpretive and homiletic task as attempting to perform *intentions* aligned with the argument strategies of a biblical text.

For many preachers this phenomenon of composition is familiar. They have seen it used increasingly in commentaries and other preaching resources.[7] For some, however, there is a need to justify its rhetorical provenance, its significance, and the hermeneutic of preaching intentions aligned with a text. Let me sketch these issues by posing three sets of questions:

(1) If Mark is really composed with all this symmetry and parallelism, are there any ancient references to this? Is there an awareness of this way of composing in the ancient handbooks concerned with the use of persuasive argument in narratives?

(2) Why look at extended chiasm? Is it an interesting but largely irrelevant artifact of gospel composition or something essential to the gospel argument?

(3) What about the problem of committing, what critics call the "intentional fallacy"? If the purpose of this study is to assist preachers in seeing how Mark may have used the Jesus story to preach to his own community, doesn't that assume we can know what Mark's "intention" was? For that matter, if preachers preach intentions, doesn't this just doubly complicate the problem of committing the "intentional fallacy"?

Responses to these three questions will guide most of the discussion in the remainder of this introduction. Readers uninterested in these preliminary questions are encouraged to move to the study itself. It is designed pedagogically so that necessary methodological explanations are developed as needed in the discussion of the text.

With practice, seeing the connections becomes intuitive, much as it probably was for those who first composed and read text in this way. Issues regarding differences in approaches to the practice of rhetorical criticism and my use of specific terminology in this study are taken up at the concluding section of this chapter.

My proposal for the overarching meta-arrangement of the gospel can be found in the conclusion of this study. Where commentaries put such matters up front, I think the force of that proposal is best found after the reader has engaged in the push and pull of thinking through the rhetorical design of the individual narrative complexes of the Marcan text.

Preliminary Concerns

If you are among a growing number of readers who want to know where this way of composing comes from, what difference it makes, and how it affects preaching, let me respond to the questions I posed above in turn. The responses, though occasionally technical, are important because they permit me to raise the fundamental question of what difference this kind of study can make in assisting preachers who see their interpretive and homiletic task as attempting to perform *intentions* aligned with the argument strategies of a biblical text.

Mark's "Finished" Prose Economy

The overall arrangement of Mark's Gospel has puzzled interpreters from the earliest period. By the middle of the second century a debate arose between Justin Martyr and Papias of Hierapolis about whether Mark's work was even artistically arranged and whether it was simply a collection of anecdotes or a *finished* composition (*autotel syntaxis*). Justin did not hesitate to describe the Gospel as a finished work, but Papias appeared to be willing to diminish Mark's contribution to its arrangement in order to attribute the authority of the work to the oral reminiscences of the apostle Peter.[8] That the difference of opinion could even occur indicates that the conception of a finished narrative composition was already changing from the common view held by historians. In fact, for reasons that served the church, it was Papias' opinion concerning the Gospel of Mark that prevailed. The notion that Mark's Gospel was composed as a finished narrative lost currency in the later ages, but in the first century A.D., it would have been surprising if a narrative work composed in koiné Greek would have been organized in anything other than a finished style.[9]

The finished narrative style is described by the historian Diodorus Siculus (ca. first century B.C.) as part of a writer's compositional task in sustaining a balanced continuity in telling the story (*Universal History*, Book XVI). I have drawn attention to Diodorus Siculus' technical use of this term in describing narratives as either *finished* (*autoteleis*) or *half-finished* (*hēmiteleis*) elsewhere.[10] Here we need only note that Diodorus, like most historians in his day, arranged the events of his history thematically with a view toward instigating civic virtue in his audience. From time immemorial, singers and prophets told histories and heritage sagas by using ring-composition's narrative mnemonic of paralleling sequence: the initial problematizing stories, followed by the central climax, followed by the systematic resolution of each of the initial problematizing stories.[11] During the time of transition, before a linearity born of literacy, literate historians still told narratives according to the conventions inherited from orality. Diodorus was one of these old school historians. His distinction between finished narrative, which brings a collection of episodes naturally to its conclusion, and the newfangled notion of telling histories as linear progressions that provide sequence without balancing resolution (a *hēmiteleis* narrative) is the most methodologically aware description of the compositional convention of overarching architectonic parallelism in prose narrative we possess.

It is seconded by Dionysius of Halicarnassus, who employs the same set of phrases in expressing his frustration with the arrangement of Thucydides' *History* and his departure from the customary arrangement of a proper history. Dionysius argues that the majority of historians in his day (ca. the second half of the first century B.C.) would agree with him that a history should be arranged to "begin where nothing can be imagined as preceding it, and end where nothing further is felt to be required" (*On Thuc.* 9). Of course, he is arguing that thematic unity should be the organizing criterion for telling a history. Good histories, according to Dionysius, offer a moralizing narrative with an appropriate beginning, middle, and end.[12]

As indicated above, this stylistic preference concerning the appropriate way to tell a moralizing history was already giving way in the centuries before and after Christ to a more linear approach. For example, half a century earlier, Polybius (ca. 202–120 B.C.) had already announced his distaste for the stock approach to composition (*History*, Book XXXVIII:5): "Some readers will criticize my work on the ground that I have given an incomplete (*atelê*) and disjointed narrative of events" and that "serious students, I am told, demand continuity and desire to follow a subject to its conclusion (*to telos*)—the method which procures the maximum amount of gratification and instruction to the attentive reader." For his part, Polybius states, "I not only dissent from this view, but cherish the opposite" (*History*, Book XXXVIII:5).[13] Polybius' method is much preferred to that of Diodorus and Dionysius by most modern historians, but in antiquity, Polybius was the eccentric, flying in the face of convention.

For their part, Dionysius and Diodorus represent the "old school" approach to establishing finished balance in the overall subject matter arrangement of one's *prose economy*. They would have recognized Mark's Gospel as an instance of the finished style of what Dionysius refers to as the prose economy of a work's narrative composition. But Dionysius would also have been quick to express his utter disdain for the "juvenile affectation" of using parallelism and antitheses at the level of the subject matter composition. He thoroughly disapproved of cyclic construction of the period because "the thought often becomes slave to the rhythm of the words, and realism is sacrificed to elegance" (*Isoc.* 12). Although he never would have considered Mark's compositional style as elegant, he still undoubtedly would have accused him, as he did Isocrates, of "inundating [readers] with floods of parallelism" (*Isoc.* 14).

It is a commonplace among scholars that ring-composition was the most prevalent compositional technique employed in structuring the arrangement of words in ancient poetics.[14] Cairns as well as Rudd have identified the parameters for identifying and schematizing the technique of ring-composition as a way of arranging words.[15] Strange as it may sound to our twentieth century ears, histories and biographies in antiquity were considered a subset of poetics (Aristotle, *Poetics* 1451a35–b6 and 1459a17–29). So we need only extend and apply these principles to prose poetics as readily as they have been applied to odes and lyric poetry. What remains is to ask why, in the middle of the second century, did Justin Martyr have to defend the notion that Mark's Gospel was artistically arranged? If this method of composition was both common and well-recognized, why did it suddenly become unrecognizable? Given the position Justin took in the debate, it appears that he was still aware of the convention of composing narrative in this manner. But it also appears that assumptions concerning what counted as a literately finished compositional style were giving way in the period we know as the Second Sophistic to other notions of what made for good organization.

Perhaps the clearest explanation of this shift is that it was representative of the general changes in compositional theory occurring during the first and second centuries A.D.[16] Not only were avant-garde historians ridiculing the "old school" notions of rhetorical historiography (cf. Lucien, *How to Write History,* ca. second century A.D.), but Quintilian, writing in the last quarter of the first century A.D., indicates there was a good reason for the absence of any substantive discussion of subject-matter arrangement (prose economy). He states that the Greek rhetorician Hermagoras (ca. second century B.C.) "places *judgment, division, order* and everything relating to expression under the heading of *economy* [*oikonomia*], a Greek word meaning the management of domestic affairs which is applied metaphorically to oratory and has no Latin equivalent" (3.3.9).[17] In other words, even as the Greek language provided the *ethos* of the intellectual tradition during the Second Sophistic, it was also giving way to an emerging Latin literate consciousness. The self-consciously literate style of composition that, in the words of Dionysius, represented "not mere writing but chiseling and turning" as if the writers were sculptors of words and works (*On Arr.* 25 and *On Dem.* 51) was inevitably giving way to a less affected style of composition.[18]

Only recently have critics returned to Mark's Gospel and sensed that it holds some structural secret that, if it could be unlocked, might open hermeneutical windows on the very nature and necessity of narrative ambiguity. In *The Genesis of Secrecy: On the Interpretation of Narrative*, Frank Kermode finds that

> Perhaps…there is a secret at the heart of Mark which is not a theology and perhaps not even really a secret; but rather some habit of narrative paradox or conjunction that might, in the end, be best represented without the use of words, in a diagram or by algebra. Strictly formalized, intercalation might be the clue to the whole, from the small part under consideration to the entire gospel as it stands in the larger book.[19]

I believe that one step in the direction of revealing the secret of Mark's habit of narrative emplotment (and thereby his creation of narrative ambiguity) is made possible by the assumption that he could presume readers and hearers who expected finished narratives to be worked out in literate narrative complexes.

The Recovery of Mark's Voice for Preaching

Scholars have noted the existence of parallelism in the compositional structure of Mark's Gospel account for centuries. For example, Bengel offers a simplified proposal for the structure in his *Gnomon* in the eighteenth century, and, more recently, Dewey and Tolbert have offered some sophisticated proposals concerning specific narrative collections within the Gospel.[20] Extended chiasm is too well documented in New Testament literature to need extensive justification here.[21] However, there are still good critics who hesitate to accept the value of its utility in interpreting the New Testament, fearing that too often it has become something akin to looking for hidden meaning in the "patterns of the carpet."

For example, Robert Fowler has recently argued that he is suspicious of the "current critical zeal for chiasm" in gospel studies because of the silence concerning it in the rhetorical handbook tradition and because he finds its visually literate complexity too much to expect of the original oral-aural audiences.[22] Yet studies like that of Dewey's lead him to assert that he wants to keep an open mind about the subject.[23] Perhaps more to the point, Fowler notes that most critics who make reference to the phenomenon tend to define chiasm more in terms of story content rather than in terms of narrative strategy or discourse. In other words, if the phenomenon is considered as a narrative strategy, the question should be to discover its rhetorical function at the level of discourse and not just at the level of story. This leads Fowler to conclude, "If attention can be shifted from neat diagrams and architectural symmetry visually apprehended, to the progressive, temporal encounter that every hearer and reader of the Gospel experiences, then we may better understand not what chiastic structures are visually but how they function temporally."[24] This comment represents a justifiable critique of much that passes for chiastic analysis in gospel studies, but the critique is still flawed because it makes temporality the defining feature of narrative. As indicated in the previous section, the urge to create a sense of thematic unity out of the stuff of "what happened" still controlled narrative design more than the literate urge to submit plot to the control of temporal linearity. I have defined this overlapping middle stage between a fully oral and a fully literate consciousness in ancient compositional theory elsewhere.[25] In this study, rather than focusing on chiasm's relationship to the temporal story, I am examining chiasm (and other forms of parallelism) as a means of recovering the rhetoric of Mark's compositional strategy in direct juxtaposition to the one-thing-after-another of the story's dramatic plot. More important than its temporal implications, the question is to discover how chiasm *functions* as argument.[26]

The claim of this study is that chiasm *is* the argument strategy that structures Mark's nineteen narrative collections. It serves as the *glue* that sustains the connections within the narrative complexes. Clearly, Mark unfolds the Jesus narrative, but the order in which he presents it tells us a great deal about his concerns for the community to whom he writes. The primary means we have to discover those concerns is by understanding the argument conducted in the juxtaposition of the stories. Studying chiastic construals of that argument can assist contemporary preachers in gaining insight into the strategy by which the gospel author rhetorically "constructs" his audience. Said another way, by focusing on the argument that sustains the integrity of individual narratives in the particular way in which Mark chiastically structures their telling, contemporary preachers are permitted rhetorical access to the original preacher's voice. Rather than looking for his literary voice in the one-thing-after-another of the story, Mark's voice is found in the reasons why he orders the stories in relationship to one another. That order, as it becomes obvious in this study, is found in the rhetoric of his compositional strategy. This point is significant for preachers who strive to perform intentions aligned with a biblical writer's argument strategies.

On Interpreting and Preaching Intentions Aligned with Argument Strategies

The purpose of this study is to assist contemporary preachers in the task of exegeting the intention of Mark's argument strategies, at least to the degree that it can be recovered from an analysis of the rhetorical form, and to provide an analysis that hopefully proves suggestive for preaching these texts. Anyone familiar with contemporary literary or hermeneutic theory recognizes this statement is problematic. In contemporary literary theory, it is generally considered bad form to discuss texts as if we can get at *authorial* intent, as if our inquiries somehow permitted us access to the mind of the author or the psychological intentions that reside within the text.[27] Similarly, contemporary hermeneutic theory regards the notion that we can get at intention behind the text or discover what a text "means" through exacting grammatical-historical exegesis as a version of "Romanticist hermeneutics."[28] But what cannot and should not be overlooked in this discussion is that preachers by profession are called to perform the interpretation of texts for communities. Like legal scholars, they cannot escape the necessity of interpreting historically situated texts to arrive at some sense of meaning, especially as it applies to contemporary life.[29] It may be problematic to hold the author's original intention as the criterion of a "valid" interpretation, but it would be equally problematic to treat a text as if it were authorless. The text has an author even if we have no idea who he was and only have access to the implied author of the text's *language*.

One way that contemporary homileticians have responded to this issue is to shift attention away from authorial intention to textual intention. For example, Buttrick states that a preacher's attention should be directed to the "intending in the *language* itself" and that in this sense "biblical language is intentional and, therefore, performative."[30] The focus in much contemporary preaching theory is shifted away from trying to discern authorial intentions toward the "performative" nature of language itself. So, rather than looking for "intentions," contemporary homileticians are more likely to be looking for the "intending-to-do" of the text's language.[31] As a result, close attention is given to the genre and the rhetorical strategy of the text with a goal to perform, if not the intention of the text, at least an intention that is aligned with the text.[32]

In this study I am purposefully focusing attention on recovering Mark's voice as it is found in the strategy of his fictive argument. Narrowly defined, *voice* is a term literary theorists use that answers the question "Who speaks?" as opposed to point-of-view, which answers the question "What perspective is taken?" The difference between these two concepts may help us to understand the significance of the former. Point-of-view is a perspective presented as an aspect of composition, while voice represents the traces of the implied author's argument addressed to the reader. We can speak of the various points-of-view found among the characters of a narrative, but voice refers to the textual traces of the one who offers the text to be read, of the strategy of persuasion of a text's implied author.[33] In the previous section, I argued that Mark's voice is found in the reasons why he tells the various stories in the order in which he tells them. And this, I argue, is another way we can pay attention to the "intending" of the language of the text. We do not know the intentions of the writer of Mark, but Mark is written according to the conventions of a strategy of discourse that allows us to discover the intentions of its implied author in the fictive argument of the author's narrative voice.

In my analysis, I attempt to determine the essential motif that constitutes the *persuasive strategy* that binds together the stories in the particular manner in which they are told in each of the Gospel's nineteen narrative complexes. I assume that audiences for this kind of argument, like Diodorus and Dionysius, would have understood this moralizing way of organizing and composing a narrative. Thus, my approach in this study is similar to that of the reader-response critic, who, in Stephen Moore's succinct summary, "spins out a full-fledged story of reading, one whose hero/ine is the implied reader, and whose plot is made up of this reader's successive attempts to negotiate the gaps, ambiguities, and enigmas of the Gospel text."[34] But I am also keenly aware that what I offer is an interpretation. The episodic construals of parallelism are an interpretation. The determinations of the boundaries of each narrative complex are an interpretation. The reflections offered as the essential motifs are an interpretation. Each of these is controlled as much by the questions I bring to the text as those yielded by the strategy of composition. The burden of the argument is not carried by any one construal, but by the overwhelming burden of the way that Mark has consistently maintained this strategy of discourse throughout the compositional process. The burden of my argument is built on this Gospel's "floods of parallelism" rather than any single instance of it.

According to hermeneutical theorist Paul Ricoeur, the individual who takes on the responsibility of reading and interpreting texts to a larger audience must take the tasks of *understanding* and *explanation* quite seriously. For Ricoeur, the primary task of hermeneutic understanding involves the interpreter's ability to take up in himself or herself the structuring that is performed by the text.[35] Hence, the rigorous interpreter must find the question(s) to which the text offers an answer, to reconstruct its symbolic and cultural codes by attempting to reconstruct the expectations of the text's implied receivers, and to accept that such an inquiry can only be conducted within the constraints of the world of questions and expectations that the reader brings to the text.[36] For this kind of interpreter, "The merely historicizing question—what did the text say?—remains under the control of the properly hermeneutical question—what does the text say to me and what do I say to the text?"[37]

Keeping the balance of this equation is why I speak of preaching intentions *aligned* with the argument strategies of the text. Discovering what a text may have meant is only sought because we are concerned with what meaning we still derive from the text. But both elements are a necessary part of understanding and explanation. Which is why, to preach the stories we find in gospels like Mark, we need to have some idea how the story being told was used to speak to the first audience to whom it was preached. Stated simply, this study is an effort on behalf of contemporary preachers to offer an interpretive analysis of Mark's strategy of discourse design in the form of interpretive "wagers" about how a rhetorical analysis can re-voice the nature of this ancient preacher's concerns for his community. It is intended to be a contribution to the interpretation of one aspect of the genre structures implicit in the compositional form of the text, with a goal to provide contemporary preachers with a suggestive reading of the *preaching motif* implicit in the structures of the text. Beyond this suggestive function, it is the task of the preacher to offer an explanation of the stories as a strategy for listeners of "being-in-the-world."

The sermons included in this study model the task. Space constraints do not permit the inclusion of a sample sermon for each narrative complex of the Gospel of Mark. Our preachers include Judith McDaniel, Stephen Farris, James Mead, Paul Scott Wilson, Ronald J. Allen, Lucy Hogan, and myself. In addition, I have asked our preachers to include a brief set of comments in which they indicate how the historicizing material, the "What did the text say?" provided by this study, assisted them in responding sermonically to the more important question, "What does the text say to me and what do I say to the text?" The preachers were free to adopt their own approach and to address whatever portion of a complex they desired.[38] The purpose was to discover how a variety of preachers, representing a spectrum of confessional traditions, might make use of the access to the Marcan voice that this study permits in the homiletic task of preaching intentions aligned with the argument strategies of the biblical text.

Preaching, Rhetorical Criticism, and the Terminology of This Study

Quite obviously, contemporary biblical studies have shifted away from the emphasis of allowing history and classicism to direct inquiry and have turned self-consciously to literary and rhetorical methodologies to ask about the "meaning" of the text. Stephen Farris recently noted that homileticians have begun to find this kind of inquiry more useful than the arcane observations offered as interpretation according to the "excavation" approach of commentaries engaged in historical-critical exegesis. He observes that by and large the benefits of looking at texts by way of the newer methodologies are still unsystematic and less than accessible to the average preacher. With the beginning of a new millenium, he suggests that the time is right for studies that provide preachers with the insights from reader-response criticism, narrative criticism, architecture analysis, and the like.[39] This study is intended as a response to this call to provide preachers with insights from a methodology that allows them (using Farris' metaphor of Jacob wrestling with an angel) to "limp away" from the engagement with a critical methodology's insight, having been "blessed" for their effort.

This study makes use of rhetorical principles that guide both the way argument is conducted and the strategy by which it is presented in the New Testament, what Farris undoubtedly means by "architectural" methodologies. At present there are a spate of studies available to serve as guides that unlock the ancient mysteries of argument and composition theory in antiquity. However, the preacher unaware of the complexities of the rhetorical tradition may become confused by two quite different ways modern exegetes tend to apply it in these works. At the risk of some reductionism, I think it reasonable to suggest that most of the contemporary appropriations are divided between ones that either make use of rhetorical theory as a means of focusing on the story or reasoning "world" of the text and approaches that make use of rhetorical theory as a means of focusing on the relation between the text and its social and historical context.

Two Approaches? Rhetorical Criticism in Biblical Studies

Exegetes who generally follow the former approach (focusing on the story world of the text) tend to follow James Muilenburg's programmatic call to engage in the "rhetorical criticism" of text. These critics believe that the text yields its own best theory of composition and generally view ancient rhetorical theory as the "art of composition," a combination of ancient Greco-Hebraic rhetoric and poetics. Here the classical and rabbinical traditions of reasoning theory and compositional technique are used primarily to explain structure discovered first by means of close reading. The goal of this kind of inquiry is to explore the story world or reasoning world of the text. From this perspective, the classical tradition simply serves to establish a comparative baseline of normal compositional practice as well as to provide a means to independently establish the norm of audience expectation concerning the limits of a given genre. Excellent evidence of the fruit of this kind of approach can be found in works of Michael Fishbane, Phyllis Trible, and Mary Anne Tolbert.[40]

On the other hand, exegetes who tend to focus on the relation between the text and its social context generally use the classical rhetorical tradition of argument theory as a way to understand how the biblical text would reasonably have been structured for a first century audience. Critics who approach their task in this manner are more apt to refer to George Kennedy's authoritative summary of the classical tradition of "rhetorical theory" or have extensive citations referring to original works within the rhetorical tradition to establish expectation within a given context or genre.[41] From this perspective, the classical tradition of oratorical theory is employed as a way of locating the rhetorical performance of a biblical writer in a larger literary-social environment and to assess the effectiveness of the presentation according to the extrinsic standard of what counted as persuasive argument. Excellent evidence of this kind of approach can be found in the work of Hans Dieter Betz, Burton Mack, and Adela Yarbro Collins.[42]

The preacher who is unaware of these a priori assumptions about how critics and commentators tend to make use of the rhetorical tradition can easily become confused or assume that two different kinds of "rhetoric" are involved. For example, in the excellent *Guides to Biblical Scholarship* series from Fortress Press, two contributions are offered as introductory handbooks to the subject. Burton Mack's *Rhetoric and the New Testament* is in their New Testament series, while Phyllis Trible's *Rhetorical Criticism: Context, Method, and the Book of Jonah* is in their Old Testament series. The presentation of rhetorical theory and criticism in these two books is so different that it would not be surprising to find the average reader assuming that "rhetorical criticism" describes an approach that only applies to reading Old Testament texts, while "rhetorical theory" refers to the process of making a systematic comparison of a text with the descriptive, taxonomic tradition of Greco-Roman rhetoric. The different approaches of these authors are undoubtedly attributable to a number of issues (not the least of which is that both writers are describing the effect of a rhetorical turn in the critical methodologies of his or her particular discipline, i.e., social histories criticism and form criticism). Yet these differences might lead the noninsiders for whom these books are written to assume that the way of applying the tradition should remain different for Old Testament and New Testament texts. Until recently, they largely have.[43]

This study represents a blend of both approaches. I begin with the assumption that rhetorical *method*, whether that of ancient Greco-Roman rhetoricians such as Dionysius of Halicarnassus and Longinus or that of modern rhetoricians such as Wayne Booth or Kenneth Burke, does not intrinsically distinguish the function of persuasion in oratory from that of narratives. As Booth made eminently clear in *The Rhetoric of Fiction*, in their telling, stories create a world that makes us aware of a "value system." In the process of appropriating meaning in the reading of a story, we choose temporarily to suspend any disbelief we may have as we consider the ways of this world. In turn, this textualized world "must fill with its rhetoric the gap made" by the suspension of our beliefs.[44] When Booth first made this argument in the 1960s, it introduced students of literature to a whole new way of conceiving the world of narrative as argument. At the time he saw little difference between the task of communicating meaning in the argument of a novel and the argument of a treatise or speech. After several decades it is reasonable to say that today few critics would treat the rhetoric of narrative as substantively different from the rhetoric of any oral or textualized discourse.

In this study I use Zahava McKeon's phrase *fictive argument* to describe the notion that narrative can embody argument beyond that of its story.[45] Like Booth, she finds little reason to treat the rhetoric of a narrative as different from the rhetoric of a speech. But she also claims that all argument, whether in speeches or novels, creates its own narrative world, no matter how briefly sketched, by constituting the subject matter, the ideas, and movement of that which can be known about the author's concerns. This leads her to claim that all arguments are, therefore, fictive arguments. Obviously, this presses beyond Booth's original claims concerning argument in narrative. But McKeon's discussion of the impossibility of distinguishing novels from nonfiction makes her use of the term *fictive argument* provocative. Behind any argument, whether in the discourse of a speech or the telling of a story, is a narrative voice proposing an understanding of a world we are invited to enter.

In the context of this study, I have appropriated this phrase to draw attention to the argument that can be found in Mark's form and distinguish it from the argument found in the one-thing-after-another temporality of the story itself. My attenuated use of the term *fictive argument* is intended to create a sense of presence for the notion that argument in narrative can be conducted in the structured rhetorical form of text in ways that might be quite different from the explicit argument of the ongoing plot itself.[46] Even though recent preaching theory has capitalized on rediscovering the power of story, in this study I want to suggest ways that a contemporary preacher may attend to the structure of the fictive argument implicit in the Gospel of Mark. To state the case of what I am about in practical terms, I think most preachers would find it valuable in devising sermon strategy to have specific recourse to a way of discovering how gospel writers were using the Jesus stories to preach to their own communities. This is a study in Mark's strategy, his fictive argument embedded in the arrangement of his presentation of the Jesus story.

The Design and Terminology of This Study

Nineteen narrative complexes are schematized and briefly examined in this study. Each collection begins with an artificial proposal for the schematization of the parallelism of Mark's literate compositional design. I say "artificial" because the literately schematized construal makes concrete and visual a literate compositional technique whose roots lay in the mnemonics of oral composition. I say "proposed" because I do not begin to assume that the arrangement of either the individual episodes or the relationship between the episodes offered here is the official or the intended form. The schematization represents a visual heuristic that permits contemporary readers, unaccustomed to this ancient kind of textual "toying with words" (Plato, *Apology* 17c), to be able to visualize the fictive argument specific to the narrative collections that is independent of the imposed chronology of the plot's one-thing-after-another sequence. This is followed by two sections in which I discuss the implications of the presentation. In the first section I discuss the rhetorical design of the collection, its parallels, and the potential for intersignification in the design of Mark's fictive argument. The second section is an effort to draw together the central thematic motif that emerges from intersignifying relationship of the materials that fall within the confines of the clearly delineated collection.

The reader may be tempted to skip past the construals and move directly to the comment. Resist the temptation. The *primary* argument of this study is found in the construal of the text. Spend time examining the parallels. Read a story by matching the parallels and working to the central climax. Look for parallels that surprise. Not all parallels are equal, but sometimes strong parallels force the juxtaposition of segments or stories that would otherwise not be obvious. Wondering why is one of the key steps to homiletic insights.

A brief note on the terminology I employ may be helpful in understanding the distinctions I suggest with regard to Mark's arrangement. The term *extended chiasm* refers to the manner in which a story, episode, or saying is schematized in an A-B-C-C'-B'-A' pattern. *Step-parallelism* refers to an alternate paralleling technique schematized here as 1-2-3-4, 1'-2'-3'-4'. Following Taylor, narrative collections of several such episodes are referred to as *narrative complexes*. The relationship between several narrative complexes is referred to as a *meta-narrative complex*. The relationship between all nineteen narrative complexes, or collections, is discussed in the final section of this study as the Marcan *oikonomia* or the "over-arching narrative structure of the gospel."

Since the purpose of this study is to treat Mark as preacher for contemporary preachers, it is necessarily limited in its focus. My purpose is neither to survey recent attempts at suggesting chiastic arrangements within the Gospel, nor to provide a comprehensive survey of the scholarly consensus concerning any given collection. What notes there are serve to further the pointed objective of clarifying the argument of this study. As a study of a preacher for preachers, the purpose is to provide just enough discussion to stimulate exegetical questions concerning how any one story fits into the larger scheme and how, together, those stories may have been experienced by the audience that first read and pondered them. I turn now to take up the fictive argument of Mark the preacher for people desiring to preach Mark today.

Mark 1:1–15
The First Narrative Complex

I THE BEGINNING OF THE GOSPEL (Mk. 1:1–3)

{1}	1		The beginning of the good news of Jesus Christ, the Son of God.	GOSPEL
{2}			As it is written in the prophet Isaiah,	PROCLAMATION
		2'	"See, I am sending my messenger ahead of you, who will prepare your way;	PREPARATION
{3}	1'		the voice of one crying out in the wilderness:	PROCLAMATION
		2'	'Prepare the way of the Lord, make his paths straight.'"	PREPARATION

II THE PREPARING ONE (Mk. 1:4–8)

{4}	1	John the baptizer appeared in the wilderness,	WHO JOHN WAS
	2	proclaiming a baptism of repentance for the forgiveness of sins.	WHAT HE PROCLAIMED
{5}	3	And people from the whole Judean countryside and all the people of Jerusalem were going out to him, and were baptized by him in the river Jordan, confessing their sins.	WATER BAPTISM
{6}	1'	Now John was clothed with camel's hair, with a leather belt around his waist, and he ate locusts and wild honey.	WHO JOHN WAS
{7}	2'	He proclaimed, "The one who is more powerful than I is coming after me; I am not worthy to stoop down and untie the thong of his sandals.	WHAT HE PROCLAIMED
{8}	3'	I have baptized you with water; but he will baptize you with the Holy Spirit."	SPIRIT BAPTISM

II' THE PREPARED-FOR ONE (Mk. 1:9–11)

{9}	A	In those days Jesus came from Nazareth of Galilee and was baptized by John in the Jordan.	PURIFICATION IN BAPTISM
{10}	B	And just as he was coming up out of the water, he saw the heavens torn apart and the Spirit descending like a dove on him.	SPIRIT
{11}	C	And a voice came from heaven,	VOICE
	C'	"You are my Son, the Beloved; with you I am well pleased."	MESSAGE
{12}	B'	And the Spirit immediately drove him out into the wilderness.	SPIRIT
{13}	A'	He was in the wilderness forty days, tempted by Satan; and he was with the wild beasts; and the angels waited on him.	PURIFICATION IN EXPERIENCE

I' THE BEGINNING OF THE GOSPEL (Mk. 1:14–15)

{14}	1	Now after John was arrested, Jesus came to Galilee,	PREPARATION COMPLETE
	2	proclaiming the good news of God,	PROCLAIM GOSPEL
{15}	1'	and saying, "The time is fulfilled, and the kingdom of God has come near;	PREPARATION COMPLETE
	2'	repent, and believe in the good news."	PROCLAIM GOSPEL

The Rhetorical Shape of the Narrative Complex

We begin with the basic question "How are the boundaries of the narrative determined?"[1] Rhetorically, repetition is the key to discovering the matching bookend episodes. For example, ancient audiences would have immediately noticed the unusual words "good news" in the opening and their repetition (twice over) in verses 14–15. The Gospel begins by announcing "good news" in Jesus Christ, "the Son of God," and reinforces this with Jesus' challenge to "Repent and believe the good news." In this way, the final frame of the narrative complex fills out and defines the meaning of the initial and otherwise ambiguous words "good news."

The framing episodes of the narrative complex are balanced by two episodes within. Episodes II and II' introduce John as the preparing one and then Jesus as the prepared-for one. Notice how Mark continues to employ the strategy of step parallelism (1-2, 1'-2') from Episode I in telling John's story in Episode II. In effect, the story tumbles forward until the momentum is stopped by the inversion in Episode II'. Its circular design invites readers to slow down and ponder a central climactic claim (which just happens to be the divine pronouncement). What Mark has accomplished is to have his story push forward, slowing to a pause only when the main character finally steps on the scene to be divinely authorized. Introducing John as the one who prepares sets the reader up for a beginning. John becomes master of ceremonies, stepping to center ring and proclaiming, "And now, ladies and gentlemen, let the show begin!" The lights shift to the next ring and Jesus arrives, is purified by baptism and temptation, receives the Spirit, and is blessed. The time has come. The kingdom is near. The *good news* is in motion. Everything else was overture. The story begins here.

The juxtaposition of the episodes in the first narrative complex can be visualized thus:

```
 I  THE BEGINNING OF THE GOSPEL            Mk. 1:1–3
    II  THE PREPARING ONE                  Mk. 1:4–8
    II' THE PREPARED-FOR ONE               Mk. 1:9–11
 I' THE BEGINNING OF THE GOSPEL            Mk. 1:14–15
```

The Central Motif of the Complex

Mark's first narrative collection serves the function of an orchestral overture. It collects our attention, offers up pieces of the melodies to be played later at length, but most of all it brings our focus dramatically to bear on the one who is to come: Jesus of Nazareth. If there is one central motif running throughout this first narrative complex, it is an expression of joy that gospel begins as a "Feast of the Word." Whatever former silence of God there may have been, Mark declares it ended. Whatever prior famine of "hearing the words of the Lord" there may have been (Am. 8:11–12), Mark announces good news, worthy of celebration. Famine is replaced with a banquet. This is Word in abundance, a resplendent meal in the variety of its courses. The first course begins in recalling the Word of prophetic promise. This is quickly followed by a course of proclamation in the prophetic Word of John the Baptizer. Then comes the main course, a divine Word of interpretation pronouncing a blessing on Jesus. And not to be outdone, the most important course of all is the Word of good news proclaimed by Jesus of Nazareth. For Mark, it is this abundance of Word that is the performative of his fictive argument. His "Feast of the Word" simultaneously announces the presence of kingdom come even as the narrative structure credentials it. We are all familiar with the beautiful christological hymn to the Word that serves as preamble to the Gospel of John. That hymn is a transcendent paean to the Word become flesh. Yet long before its poetic rhythms were cast, Mark offered a prologue of his own in which a "Feast of the Word" serves as preamble to the fictive argument of his Gospel.

As prologue to the story he will tell, Mark also uses this collection to implicate the end of his Gospel at the outset. He does this in at least three ways. First, the divine voice at the baptism and at the transfiguration is mirrored in the final narrative complex by the divine messenger who provides the interpretation of the empty tomb. With different emphases in each complex, the death-burial-resurrection motif is variously enacted in a literate process of intersignification by which each narrative ends up interpreting the others.[2] I will explore this idea at greater length in the central and final narrative complexes. At this point it is only necessary to point out that these three narrative complexes, in which a divine Word of interpretation is provided, collapse the Gospel into one large, intersignifying chiastic structure.

A second way Mark implicates the end of the matter at the outset is through the introduction of the Spirit. For his part, Mark is unmoved by questions we may ask about who exactly heard the heavenly voice or how we are to visualize the appearance of the Spirit. Instead, these events come together at one moment to credential Jesus in light of Isaiah 42:1–3, "Here is my servant, whom I uphold, my chosen, in whom my soul delights; I have put my spirit upon him; he will bring forth justice to the nations...He will faithfully bring forth justice." This cryptically uttered citation offered as Word of God is the key that unlocks the meaning of Jesus' ministry from the outset. Here, Mark implies something of the self-understanding of his own community in the words of promise from John the Baptist ("He will baptize you with the Holy Spirit"). The Spirit, "put on" Jesus at his baptism, is the Spirit in which his followers would be immersed (1:8, 13:11) and the purpose of this empowerment is to "bring justice to the nations." By having the heavens *rent* in the coming of the Spirit, Mark prefigures the *rending* of the temple curtain at Jesus' death (15:38). This word, *rend*, occurs only twice in Mark. The empowerment in the Spirit, introduced at the outset of the Gospel, is evocatively associated with the declaration of "justice" for the Gentiles announced at its conclusion. As this Gospel develops, it will become obvious how Mark makes repeated allusion to Jesus' authorization of the Gentile mission. The reason? It is the defining raison d'être of Mark's community.

Mark concludes his story at its outset in a third way. With the message of good news he asserts that the appropriate response to this announcement of divine reign is repentance and belief.

The Jewish translators of the Greek Septuagint version of the Hebrew scriptures had used the unusual word *gospel*, or *good news*, to translate several concepts announcing the hope of the inbreaking kingdom of God. In classical usage the word was an accolade to be used at the birth, coming of age, or ascension to the throne of one of the emperors of Rome. It was used to import a mystical God-quality to the emperor-cult.[3] By defining his narrative as *good news*, Mark effectively joins both uses of the idea in one setting. The adoption of the emperor as a son of God at his ascension to the throne is mirrored in this collection in the affirmation of Jesus as the son of God, both in the opening verse and in the point-of-turning act of baptism. The proclamation in the final framing episode interprets the meaning of the preceding narrative as signs of the kingdom come. The appropriate response to such news is repentance. The biblical idea of repentance is not so much a turning away from something as a returning to it. In context it is part of the prophetic call to the people of God to return with one's whole being to commitment to Yahweh.[4] In classical Greek it meant to change one's mind, thus to turn from one's former ideas or choices toward new ideas and choices. Mark's Jesus calls for repentance, without arguing or attempting to persuade listeners of its necessity.

The rhetorician George Kennedy argues that unlike other gospel writers, Mark makes his case for Jesus as an instance of proclamation rather than as argument. For example, Matthew's Jesus says, "Repent, for the Kingdom of Heaven has come near" (Mt. 4:17); phrased this way, in the form of an argument, Matthew's Jesus offers a grounds clause ("for...") as a reason why an individual should repent. Yet Mark's Jesus simply makes four assertions: (1) the time is fulfilled, (2) the kingdom of God has come near, (3) repent, and (4) believe in the good news. Kennedy suggests that this is a "radical Christian rhetoric" characterized by an absolute claim of authoritative truth without evidence or logical argument.[5] He also notes that it is the characteristic form of Jesus' preaching in Mark's Gospel. The distinction is significant, for *preaching* can be proclamation without persuasion, assertions made based on the assumption of truth or the doctrine of grace rather than defended with rational arguments. Augustine makes a similar claim in *De Doctrina Christiana* by reminding preachers that gospel is not apprehended through careful analysis of how to achieve a persuasive rhetorical effect, but in feeling the power of the revealed message itself (4.21). In line with this reasoning, Kennedy notes, "[Gospel] truth must be apprehended by the listener, not proved by the speaker. The reaction of a person in the audience to the [gospel] is like a person's reaction to a miracle, the direct evidence of authority: either that individual believes or chooses not to believe."[6]

Although I concur with Kennedy's assessment of the radical nature of Jesus' rhetoric in Mark's Gospel, I would argue that, to discover Mark's *persuasive purpose*, one must look to the fictive argument embodied in the arrangement of his material. The argument he makes in juxtaposition of his episodes *is* his sermon amidst the story. In the interrelated structure of this first of his sermons, Mark presents a *persuasive* case that all eyes should be focused on this Jesus who came from Nazareth. Extraneous matters must not detract a disciple's attention, for this is the one whom the heavens declare to be the son of God. This Jesus of Nazareth is the hoped-for promise of the ages, the one who will bring justice to the nations. This is the singular melody in the overture to which all else is but counterpoint.

Mark 1:16—2:14
The Second Narrative Complex

I JESUS CALLS FOLLOWERS BY THE SEA (Mk. 1:16–20)

{16}	1	As Jesus passed along the Sea of Galilee,	JESUS BY THE SEA
	2	he saw Simon and his brother Andrew	SEES MEN AT VOCATION
		casting a net into the sea—for they were fishermen.	
{17}	3	And Jesus said to them, "Follow me	CALLS MEN
		and I will make you fish for people."	
{18}	4	And immediately they left their nets	MEN FOLLOW
		and followed him.	
{19}	1'	As he went a little farther,	JESUS BY THE SEA
	2'	he saw James son of Zebedee and his brother John,	SEES MEN AT VOCATION
		who were in their boat mending the nets.	
{20}	3'	Immediately he called them;	CALLS MEN
	4'	and they left their father Zebedee	MEN FOLLOW
		in the boat with the hired men, and followed him.	

II JESUS' AUTHORITY OVER EVIL SPIRITS (Mk. 1:21–28)

{21}	A	They went to Capernaum; and when the sabbath came,	CAPERNAUM
		he entered the synagogue and taught.	
{22}	B	They were astounded at his teaching,	AMAZED AT TEACHING
		for he taught them as one having authority,	WITH AUTHORITY
		and not as the scribes.	
{23}	C	Just then there was in their synagogue	
		a man with an unclean spirit,	UNCLEAN SPIRIT
{24}	D	and he cried out, "What have you to do with us,	
		Jesus of Nazareth? Have you come to destroy us?	DEMON CRIES OUT
	E	I know who you are,	WHO JESUS IS
	E'	the Holy One of God."	WHO JESUS IS
{25}	D'	But Jesus rebuked him, saying, "Be silent,	JESUS DEMANDS SILENCE
		and come out of him!"	
{26}	C'	And the unclean spirit, convulsing him	UNCLEAN SPIRIT
		and crying with a loud voice, came out of him.	
{27}	B'	They were all amazed,	AMAZED / NEW TEACHING
		and they kept on asking one another,	
		"What is this? A new teaching—with authority!	WITH AUTHORITY
		He commands even the unclean spirits, and they obey him."	
{28}	A'	At once his fame began to spread	
		throughout the surrounding region of Galilee.	GALILEE

III THE MINISTRY OR THE MESSAGE? (Mk. 1:29–39)

Scene 1: A Compassionate Healing (1:29–31)

{29}	A	As soon as they left the synagogue,	
		they entered the house of Simon	EXPECTATION OF HOSPITALITY
		and Andrew, with James and John.	
{30}	B	Now Simon's mother-in-law was in bed with a fever,	FEVER
		and they told him about her at once.	
{31}	C	He came and took her by the hand	JESUS TOUCHES
	C'	and lifted her up.	JESUS HEALS
	B'	Then the fever left her,	FEVER
	A'	and she began to serve them.	EXPECTATION MET

24 — Preaching Mark

Scene 2: The Resulting Aftermath (1:32–39)

{32}	1	That evening, at sundown, they brought to him all who were sick or possessed with demons.	EVENING
{33}	2	And the whole city was gathered around the door.	PEOPLE GATHER
{34}	3	And he cured many who were sick with various diseases, and cast out many demons;	MIRACLES
	4	and he would not permit the demons to speak, because they knew him.	SILENCES DEMONS
{35}	1'	In the morning, while it was still very dark, he got up and went out to a deserted place, and there he prayed.	MORNING
{36–37}	2'	And Simon and his companions hunted for him. When they found him, they said to him, "Everyone is searching for you."	DISCIPLES SEARCH
{38}	3'	He answered, "Let us go on to the neighboring towns, so that I may proclaim the message there also; for that is what I came out to do."	MESSAGE
{39}	4'	And he went throughout Galilee, proclaiming the message in their synagogues and casting out demons.	CASTS DEMONS OUT

III' YET COMPASSION COMPELS MINISTRY (Mk. 1:40–45)

Scene 1: A Compassionate Healing (1:40–42)

{40}	A	A leper came to him begging him,	LEPER BEGS
	B	and kneeling he said to him, "If you choose, you can make me clean."	CHOOSE CLEAN
{41}	C	Moved with pity, Jesus stretched out his hand	STRETCHES HAND OUT
	C'	and touched him,	TOUCHES
	B'	and said to him, "I do choose. Be made clean!"	CHOOSE CLEAN
{42}	A'	Immediately the leprosy left him, and he was made clean.	LEPER HEALED

Scene 2: The Resulting Aftermath (1:43–45)

{43}	1	After sternly warning him he sent him away at once,	SENT AWAY
{44}	2	saying to him, "See that you say nothing to anyone;	SILENCE
	3	but go, show yourself to the priest, and offer for your cleansing what Moses commanded, as a testimony to them."	RETURN TO COMMUNITY
{45}	1'	But he went out	WENT OUT
	2'	and began to proclaim it freely, and to spread the word,	PROCLAIM FREELY
	3'	so that Jesus could no longer go into a town openly, but stayed out in the country; and people came to him from every quarter.	EXILED FROM COMMUNITY

II' JESUS' AUTHORITY OVER DISEASE AND SIN (Mk. 2:1–12)

{2:1–2}	A	When he returned to Capernaum after some days, it was reported that he was at home.	CAPERNAUM AGAIN
		So many gathered around that there was no longer room for them, not even in front of the door; and he was speaking the word to them.	MANY GATHER
{3}	B	Then some people came, bringing to him a paralyzed man, carried by four of them.	PARALYTIC CARRIED IN

{4}		And when they could not bring him to Jesus because of the crowd, they removed the roof above him; and after having dug through it, they let down the mat on which the paralytic lay.	
{5}		C When Jesus saw their faith, he said to the paralytic, "Son, your sins are forgiven."	JESUS' PRONOUNCEMENT: FORGIVES SINS
{6}		D Now some of the scribes were sitting there, questioning in their hearts,	
{7}		"Why does this fellow speak in this way? It is blasphemy!	BY WHAT AUTHORITY?
		E Who can forgive sins but God alone?"	SPEAK FORGIVENESS?
{8}		F At once Jesus perceived in his spirit that they were discussing these questions among themselves;	THESE QUESTIONS
		F' and he said to them, "Why do you raise such questions in your hearts?	SUCH QUESTIONS
{9}		E' Which is easier, to say to the paralytic, 'Your sins are forgiven,' or to say, 'Stand up and take your mat and walk'?	SPEAK FORGIVENESS?
{10}		D' But so that you may know that the Son of Man has authority on earth to forgive sins"	BY HIS AUTHORITY
		C' —he said to the paralytic—	
{11}		"I say to you, stand up, take your mat and go to your home."	JESUS' PRONOUNCEMENT: DEMANDS FAITH
{12}	B'	And he stood up, and immediately took the mat and went out before all of them;	PARALYTIC WALKS OUT
	A'	so that they were all amazed and glorified God, saying, "We have never seen anything like this!"	ALL AMAZED AGAIN

I' JESUS CONTINUES TO CALL FOLLOWERS BY THE SEA (Mk. 2:13–14)

{13}	1	Jesus went out again beside the sea; the whole crowd gathered around him, and he taught them.	JESUS BY THE SEA
{14}	2	As he was walking along, he saw Levi son of Alphaeus sitting at the tax booth,	SEES MEN AT VOCATION
	3	and he said to him, "Follow me."	CALLS MEN
	4	And he got up and followed him.	MEN FOLLOW

The Rhetorical Shape of the Narrative Complex

Biblical commentators traditionally summarize this collection of stories as a "specimen day of ministry"[1] or a collection of "the authoritative acts of Jesus,"[2] but my schematic construal according to the ancient conventions of a finished narrative immediately indicates that the complex has far more in common than a mere twenty-four hour period or the simple recognition that it includes several miracle stories.[3] Episodes II, III, III', and II' (Mk. 1:21–28, 29–39, 40–45, and 2:1–12) clearly depict Jesus in a vocational crisis between the demand to produce miracles and his desire to proclaim gospel. Episodes I and I' (Mk. 1:16–20 and 2:13–14) depict Jesus' ministry of calling disciples.[4]

The framing stories of this narrative complex are readily established through the almost rigidly reduplicated calling episodes in 1:16–20 and 2:13–14.[5] These stories gain internal momentum as the action tumbles forward. The nature of a progression does not invite the audience to linger in consideration like an inversion. A progression drives to a linear climax and beyond. However, in this instance, the audience would be forced to linger at the conclusion of Episode I' because it contains no balancing denouement. This last episode stands internally unparalleled, making the final frame of the collection appear *unfinished.* First-century audiences, who either intuitively or formally understood the ethos of this storytelling technique, would have felt as if the collection concluded off-balance, or more accurately, that it had not concluded at all. Their rhetorical conventions for narrative composition demanded something that was not there. So Mark's framing technique forces his audience to ask two intriguing question: "Why do these calling stories form the boundaries of a narrative collection that appears to be preoccupied with Jesus' ministry of miracles?" and "Where is the conclusion of the story?"

In this study I use the term *scene* to indicate a discrete portion of a narrative episode that is self-contained but comprises only a portion of the story developed in the episode. Multistructured episodes often occur as a balanced set. If an integral story breaks down into more than one narrative structure within an episode, then it is highly likely that the balancing episode will have more than one narrative structure. The juxtaposition of the episodes in the second narrative complex can be visualized thus:

```
I   JESUS CALLS FOLLOWERS BY THE SEA              Mk. 1:16–20
  II   JESUS' AUTHORITY OVER EVIL SPIRITS         Mk. 1:21–28
    III   THE MINISTRY OR THE MESSAGE?            Mk. 1:29–39
          Scene 1: A Compassionate Healing        (vv. 29–31)
          Scene 2: The Resulting Aftermath        (vv. 32–39)
    III'  YET COMPASSION COMPELS MINISTRY         Mk. 1:40–45
          Scene 1: A Compassionate Healing        (vv. 40–42)
          Scene 2: The Resulting Aftermath        (vv. 43–45)
  II'  JESUS' AUTHORITY OVER DISEASE AND SIN      Mk. 2:1–12
I'  JESUS CONTINUES TO CALL FOLLOWERS BY THE SEA  Mk. 2:13–14
```

The Central Motif

Mark has composed the narrative development within this complex as his own version of the temptation narrative. His reference to the wilderness temptation in 1:12–13 indicates his familiarity with a version of the tradition reported by Matthew at 4:1–11 and by Luke at 4:1–12. In the Lucan and Matthean accounts of the narratives, each temptation represents a choice to respond to the competing definitions of the role of the "Messiah" current in Jesus' society (the desire for bread, temple leaping, and dominions may be understood as temptations to become a new Mosaic manna provider, a Pharisaic miracle worker, or a Zealot leader). Satan is metaphorically depicted in those Gospels as tempting Jesus to respond to the expectations of one after another of the various pressure groups. In Mark's Gospel it is the demonic spirits who attempt to announce Jesus' messianic identity and Jesus is depicted as subduing and denying them. He portrays Jesus as responding to the temptation to choose the ministry over the message in the solitude of prayer. Mark's temptation is not spiritualized. If he purposefully constructed his narrative complex as a crisis of identity for Jesus, then, instead of extrinsic metaphors for competing vocational expectations, Mark has depicted Jesus as grappling with a dilemma intrinsic to his vocation.

Framing this focused series of episodes about Jesus' vocational crisis (1:21—2:12), Mark offers the rigidly structured calling stories. Their formulaic presentation represents each instance of following as a story of radical choice stripped bare. He portrays Jesus as calling disciples to follow him as he follows God. By structuring the stories in this manner he depicts Christian discipleship as a vocational crisis in which followers must prayerfully reject the temptation to define their relationship in anything less than radical commitment. If human vocation is defined in its classical sense of "calling," then these stories detail the intimate aspects of a "calling" crisis in which Jesus is depicted as choosing to serve the purposes of God rather than the expectations of others, and, by his juxtaposed example, disciples are challenged to do the same. But the challenge is not simply extended to the disciples whom Jesus called. By manipulating the expectations of his own form, Mark draws the reader of his Gospel into an active participation with the narrative. They must choose as well.

Authors in antiquity were overwhelmingly self-conscious of the desired effect that their rhetorical and literary creations were intended to produce.[6] In discussing the stylistic variation of the second person, for example, Longinus cites a travel narrative from Herodotus and states, "You see, friend, how he takes you along with him through the country and turns hearing into sight. All such passages with a direct personal application set the hearer in the center of the action. By appearing to address not the whole audience but a single individual…you will move him more and make him more attentive and full of active interest, if you arouse him by these personal appeals" (195r, XXXVI, 2–3). Attempts to rouse readers of a historical narrative to make similar choices could be effected by jarring their sense of anticipation. Mark achieves this by allowing the final step-progression to remain unparalleled. First-century audiences, who either intuitively or formally understood the ethos of the step-progression as a storytelling technique, would have felt as if the collection concluded off-balance, or more literally, that it had not concluded at all. Their rhetorical conventions demanded something that was not there. In order to experience the *aporia* in Mark's irresolution of finished narrative conventions, consider the following modern-day limerick:

> An elephant went to Seattle
> prepared to engage in a battle.
> The rain doused his trunk,
> which promptly shrunk

Anyone either reading or hearing this feels cheated. Something is missing. Even though we may never have learned them formally, from childhood experience most people in Western culture know that such limericks must have five lines and that the last line should end with a word that rhymes with the concluding words of the first two lines. The cultural drive to "finish" limericks is so strong that the average reader may have already tried to devise a satisfyingly appropriate conclusion. Our stake in the convention of limerick resolution is that strong.[7]

Mark left his audience equally off-balance. They would have searched the collection for the final resolution and in the searching, the awareness would have dawned on them as it does on us: Only they can complete the story. They are not allowed merely to hear how others responded to this radical vocational crisis to leave all and follow Jesus; they must decide for themselves whether they, too, will fulfill the role of the faithful and become the missing disciple who responds. Experiencing the narrative in this way forces the audience to become aware of their own existential necessity to act. Only their response can redeem the balance of the narrative and put the story back on course.

In terms of the overall organizational arrangement of the Gospel, this collection is set in symmetrical juxtaposition to the second to last narrative collection—the story of Jesus' crucifixion and death. Just as Jesus denied himself, took up his cross, and pursued the kingdom of God regardless of consequences, Mark here depicts the response of disciples to the call of the Lord as a similarly radical break with all former expectations. As Jesus says in the central narrative complex (Mk. 8:34),

> If anyone would come after me,
> > he must deny himself,
> > take up his cross,
> and follow me.

From the beginning, following Jesus entailed a radical break with all former societal expectations in the name of serving a kingdom come.

He Came to Proclaim a Message
A sermon by Judith M. McDaniel

Sermon Text: Mark 1:21–28

His teaching made a deep impression on them because he taught them with authority. "Here is a teaching that is new," the people said, "and with authority behind it."

The Bible tells us Jesus' authority was of a different kind from that of the scribes, who sought support for their teaching in tradition. Yet as we examine the scene from this portion of the Gospel, we find few clues about what it was that made Jesus' authority so different, few indications of the marks of his authority.

Oh yes, he cast out demons. But it was his teaching that astounded them. And there is little to identify what it was about his teaching that was so authoritative. All we know is that it had something to do with the man himself.

Mark is almost cryptic in his opening portrayal of Jesus. There is no description of Jesus the individual. There is no elaboration of the figure of this man. There is no development of character in this story. Mark simply states that Jesus is baptized; he goes into the desert, where he is tempted; upon his return, he calls his first four disciples; and then he immediately begins teaching and healing.

Why did those people regard his words as authoritative? What influence was there emanating from his character? What power was there in his bearing that was so arresting?

In the Gospel according to Mark, the question of Jesus' authority is raised repeatedly. In the confrontation over healing a paralytic on the Sabbath, Jesus says, "So that you may know that the Son of man has authority on earth to forgive sins, I say to you, 'Stand up, take your mat, and go to your home.'" Twice Jesus gives authority to his apostles to cast out demons. Toward the close of the Gospel, in an encounter with the chief priests, scribes, and elders, Jesus is asked, "By what authority are you doing these things? Who gave you this authority to do them?" Clearly, understanding the source of this man's authority was as great a challenge to his contemporaries as it is to us. We have yet to fully grasp it. In an attempt to understand, we cast about for examples of authority from our own experience. We look to commonly held models of authority and examples of charismatic leadership around us. But the source of authority is unclear to us.

Customarily, our elected officials are recognized authorities. We expect leadership from our president, our congressmen, our governor, our state and local officials. And we realize that the source of their authority has two components: It is both a vote for them on our part and, on their part, the assumption of this approval, empowering them to act in a very personal way. Customarily, we look to presidents of corporations and leaders of labor unions as authorities. In each instance the capacity to lead is both bestowed on them from outside and dependent on its possessor for development. In law, medicine, the church, and academe there are expectations of leadership from those in positions of authority.

In seminaries, we train future leaders of the church, both lay and ordained. They, in turn, will enter parishes in which they will train members of the congregation. They will train you and they will train me to fulfill our baptismal vows—vows taken for some of us in our infancy or vows taken by others as adults. They will teach us to fulfill the vow to love others in the power of the Spirit, to witness to God's love, and to lead others to Christ. For we want to fulfill our baptismal vows. Whether lay or ordained, we worship in obedience to the command to prepare ourselves to offer leadership in service to high goals. We have been called to equip ourselves, called to witness, called to lead others to Christ. So why is it you and I have so much trouble understanding what it takes to be a leader and to speak with authority?

We are apt to describe a desirable leader as assertive yet accessible, an advocate yet an equal, an example yet a friend. At many levels in the church, we look for leaders who are humble, trustworthy, faithful, compassionate, and receptive. Above all we look for those who will share leadership. We want someone who is a helper, mentor, mediator, someone sensitive to the opinions and needs of others. Those are admirable traits in many situations. But to listen and to ask is not to lead. One who listens and asks solely is outer-directed, process-fixated, and vacillating. And Jesus didn't call us to be either admirable or vacillating. He called us to act, to act in a unique and costly way.

If our moral compass is adrift, perhaps it is because what we really valorize is choice, not cost. We want to leave open as options those high goals we will serve. By force of will, by cleverness of mind, by strength of purpose, *our* ends will be served, *our* power will be solidified, *our* influence will prevail. Besides, voices tell us the time for heroes is past, and there are multitudes hungering for honor without the price.

We equate authority with power, but Jesus tells us authority is not about power, much less power over others. Jesus tells us authority depends on relationship, and that authority involves a costly price; for to be in relationship is to offer oneself with no guarantees. When Jesus describes authority, he uses such terms as servant and even slave; and his disciples respond as you and I might: "I'd love the honor, but I don't want the work."

Still, the voice of Jesus says, "Be slave of all, slave to the One who is other than oneself, the One *for* all." That voice says that to be a slave is to pay the highest price; to lose not just our choices, not just our lives, but our very souls; and that if we can't afford to lose, we can't lead.

A slave belongs to someone else. His will, his mind, even his life is not his own. A slave is simply obedient, knowing he has nothing but what is given as gift from the master, knowing he loses all in order that his will, his mind, his power may be replaced by that of the master; aware that he must be willing to lose in order to act, willing to lose all that he has in order to become all that he can be.

Jesus taught them with authority, with a privilege of whose consequences he was shockingly aware. Profoundly conscious of the giftedness of life, he confronted them—as he confronts us now—with the reality of one who was so open to the gift of Being that he was wholly filled. With breathless reality this world has seen one whose outward and visible presence reveals an inward experience of totality. The immediacy of his awareness is compelling. He has wrestled with this gift, with both its godly and demonic possibilities; and when he puts it to use, it is a potent consciousness. He teaches and acts with authority, and his every word and deed is gifted with wholeness. His authority, his privilege, his right is complete; and he demonstrates that this privilege is available to you and me as well. He teaches us of a Being who fills us precisely where we are empty, whose strength is made perfect in our weakness, whose Spirit is the power that enables our hidden self to grow strong. For every weakness, there is strength enough to save; for every cowardice, there is courage enough to overcome; for every hostility, there is love enough to endure; for every unbelief, there is faith enough to transcend doubt. He came to proclaim this message of good news, and it is yours and mine to claim.

Compositional Comments

At the center of this narrative complex is the point: "Let us go… that I may proclaim the message…, for that is what I came…to do" (1:38). In other words, the message has precedence over the miracles. And what is that message? It is in part the man himself.

By emphasizing authority in the introductory portion of the homily, I am identifying the teaching with the man, the words with the Word. Implicit in this pericope is the content of his message: repentance. Christlike authority requires repentance of the world's ideas of power. Thus, the *subtext* of this sermon is communicated by its form. The textual movement of the homily presents anew the experience encountered by the first hearers of Jesus' proclamation, through a rhythm of repentance. The homily moves from introductory considerations of authority to anxiety about commonly held views of authority in our own day. Relief from anxiety is offered in the section reflecting on positive desires to fulfill baptismal vows and those traits we find admirable in leadership.

The shock of recognition and reversal comes when we realize Jesus' idea of authority requires the highest price, the loss of life in order to gain it. The despair of that realization gives way to grace with the acknowledgment that if I lose all that I have (the centerpiece of the message of the Gospel according to Mark), then I can become all that God would have me be. The strategy of leaving the completion of the narrative complex to the listener is also the way the content of the sermon ends. However, the assurance that God can effect transformation is stated, with only the choice to accept it left open to the listener.

Mark 2:15—3:6
The Third Narrative Complex

I   JESUS IDENTIFIED WITH TRAITORS (Mk. 2:15–17)

{15} A   And as he sat at dinner in Levi's house,   MIXING WITH SINNERS
          many tax collectors and sinners were also
          sitting with Jesus and his disciples—
          for there were many who followed him.
{16}   B   When the scribes of the Pharisees saw that
               he was eating with sinners and tax collectors,
               they said to his disciples, "Why does he eat   WHY SIT WITH SINNERS?
               with tax collectors and sinners?"
{17}   B' When Jesus heard this, he said to them,   JESUS' PRONOUNCEMENT
               "Those who are well have no need of a physician,   SINNERS NEED SITTING
               but those who are sick;
      A' I have come to call not the righteous but sinners."   COME TO CALL SINNERS

II JESUS BREAKS TRADITION (Mk. 2:18–20)

{18} A   Now John's disciples and the Pharisees were fasting;   FASTING
          and people came and said to him,
           B   "Why do John's disciples and the disciples of the   WHY NO FASTING?
               Pharisees fast,
               but your disciples do not fast?"
{19}   B' Jesus said to them, "The wedding guests cannot fast   JESUS' PRONOUNCEMENT
               while the bridegroom is with them, can they?   FASTING INAPPROPRIATE
      A' As long as they have the bridegroom with them,
          they cannot fast.   FASTING INAPPROPRIATE
{20}   The days will come when the bridegroom is taken away   THEN THEY WILL
          from them, and then they will fast on that day.   FASTING

III THE NEW AND THE OLD: TWO PARABLES (Mk. 2:21–22)

{21} 1   "No one sews a piece of unshrunk cloth on an old cloak;   NO ONE
      2   otherwise, the patch pulls away from it, the new   OTHERWISE
          from the old,
      3   and a worse tear is made.   WORSE
{22} 1' And no one puts new wine into old wineskins;   NO ONE
      2' otherwise, the wine will burst the skins,   OTHERWISE
      3' and the wine is lost, and so are the skins."[1]   RUINED

II' JESUS RATIONALIZES TRADITION-BREAKING (Mk. 2:23–28)

{23} A   One sabbath he was going through the grainfields;   SABBATH
          and as they made their way his disciples began to pluck
          heads of grain.
{24}   B   The Pharisees said to him, "Look,
               why are they doing what is not lawful on the sabbath?" UNLAWFUL?
{25}   B' And he said to them,   PRONOUNCEMENT
               a   "Have you never read what David did
                   when he and his companions were hungry and   COMPANIONS
                   in need of food?
{26}   b   He entered the house of God,
                   when Abiathar was high priest,   HIGH PRIEST
               b' and ate the bread of the Presence,
                   which it is not lawful for any but the priests to eat, HIGH PRIEST
               a' and he gave some to his companions."   COMPANIONS

{27}	A		Then he said to them,		PRONOUNCEMENT
		a	"The sabbath was made		SABBATH
			b for humankind,		HUMANKIND
			b' and not humankind		HUMANKIND
		a'	for the sabbath;		SABBATH

MARCAN *KATACRUSIS*
{28} so the Son of Man is lord even of the sabbath."

I' JESUS IS IDENTIFIED AS A TRAITOR (Mk. 3:1–6)

{3:1}	A	1		Again he entered the synagogue, and a man was there who had a withered hand.	UNUSABLE HAND
{2}		2		They watched him to see whether he would cure him on the sabbath, so that they might accuse him.	ACCUSE?
{3}		B		And he said to the man who had the withered hand, "Come forward."	WITHERED HAND
{4}			C	Then he said to them, "Is it lawful to do good or to do harm on the sabbath, to save life or to kill?"	QUESTION
			C'	But they were silent.	SILENCE AS RESPONSE
{5}		B'		He looked around at them with anger; he was grieved at their hardness of heart	HARDENED HEARTS
	A'			and said to the man,	
		1'		"Stretch out your hand." He stretched it out, and his hand was restored.	HAND RESTORED
{6}		2'		The Pharisees went out and immediately conspired with the Herodians against him, how to destroy him.	CONSPIRE TO DESTROY

The Rhetorical Shape of the Narrative Complex

The first suggestion of conflict with religious leaders was introduced in Episode II' of the previous narrative complex but remained undeveloped because conflict was not the subject of the fictive argument of that collection. The episode concluded by stating that everyone was amazed and praised God concerning what Jesus had said and done (2:12). The discerning reader, who already knew some of the Jesus story, would have been reminded that most of Jesus' interactions with these people did not turn out as well. The episode plants the idea of conflict like a seed ready to sprout in the reader's expectations. Wayne Booth describes this rhetorical technique as the work of an author making his or her subject available to the audience.[2]

The rhetorical shape of Mark's third narrative complex represents one of the most perfectly conceived chiastic arrangements to be found in Mark's Gospel.[3] The symmetry of this narrative complex is such that given the first three stories, the fourth episode could virtually be generated whole cloth from the chiastic pattern Mark imposes on the material:

    I Leaders ask disciples why Jesus breaks eating traditions:
       Pronouncement.
    II Leaders ask Jesus why disciples break eating traditions:
       Pronouncement.
      III Two central parables
    II' Leaders ask Jesus why disciples break Sabbath traditions:
       Pronouncement.

Chiastically, the conclusion to the pattern *Jesus-disciples-disciples-?* is predictably *Jesus*. And with *eating traditions* the focus of Episodes I and II, and *Sabbath traditions* introduced at Episode II', the issue in debate at Episode I' would predictably be *Sabbath traditions*. Thus, according to the pattern, the final episode should be summarized,

    I' Leaders ask disciples why *Jesus* breaks *Sabbath traditions:*
       Pronouncement.

In fact, the only portion of this rhetorically predictable pattern not part of the actual final episode is "asks disciples." Why this drops out will be discussed in the next section. The juxtaposition of the episodes in the third narrative complex can be visualized thus:

    I JESUS IDENTIFIED WITH TRAITORS   Mk. 2:15–17
      II JESUS BREAKS TRADITION   Mk. 2:18–20
        III THE NEW AND THE OLD: TWO PARABLES   Mk. 2:21–22
      II' JESUS RATIONALIZES TRADITION-BREAKING   Mk. 2:23–28
    I' JESUS IS IDENTIFIED AS A TRAITOR   Mk. 3:1–6

The Central Motif

As schematized here, the collection begins when the religious leaders make accusations against Jesus because of his conduct at Levi's party. It concludes in a showdown between the leaders and Jesus in the synagogue. The intervening stories depict the attack against Jesus through the activities of his disciples, but the stage has been set in the framing stories. Jesus is the focus of growing hostility.

The reported alignment of the Pharisees with the Herodians at the conclusion of this chapter is startling. The former represent the religious fundamentalists who stood for the purity of the Israelite faith against the encroachments of Hellenism. The Herodians represented the antithesis of Pharisaic aspirations. They were landed gentry who preferred to find ways to retain peaceably the status quo with Rome. Joining forces with the friends and supporters of Herod would seem a vulgar compromise for these religious purists. And this is precisely the point. Mark portrays the Pharisees as willing to stop at nothing to bring an end to this desecration of their sacred "law," even if it meant consorting with the Hellenizers.

The scribal schools that developed in Israel prior to the time of Jesus had moved in two trajectories: those that accepted some form of the intellectual and cultural assimilation toward Hellenism and a reactionary school that attempted to conserve the old traditions. Pharisaism was a development of this later school. It represented a radicalization of historical Jewish piety and shaped a new face for Judaism. It shifted traditional religious understanding to a more individualistic, future-oriented faith.[4] This shift occurred, in part, because Pharisaic separation of Torah from its own history had brought about a scrupulous fixation on the text. Practical traditions and popular customs were often elevated to a new level of law (halakah), as well as oral "lore" (aggadah).[5] This attempt to preserve customs and traditions in the face of encroaching Hellenism had created a second "law," which became a litmus test of loyalty to the written law. But the method used to derive this "teaching" from the written law was divorced from the situation and history of the former text.[6] From a faith that once had been rooted in the notion of a developing historical revelation, Pharisaism became a fixed system of religious observance. In the name of preserving the ancient traditions, the movement transformed the center of Israelite faith. In his in-depth study of the relationship between Judaism and Hellenism, Hengel finds that "the pious Jew in the Rabbinic tradition was constantly concerned, like the Stoic, 'to live in conformity with the law of the world.' The difference was that he encountered this law not so much as an inner norm but rather in the form of countless individual requirements expressed in minute detail."[7]

The Pharisees may have held many things in common with Jesus and his followers, but at this crucial point Mark graphically contrasts the two. He offers a portrait of Jesus confronting the Pharisaic approach to faith and history and summarizing the problem with their religious worldview, "No one sews a patch of unshrunk cloth on an old garment. If he does, the new piece will pull away from the old making the tear worse. And no one pours new wine into old wineskins. If he does, the wine will burst the skins, and the wineskins will be ruined."

The growing antipathy Mark depicts in the questioning of Jesus and his followers in this narrative complex suggests a reason why no question occurs in the final episode. The Pharisees are depicted as so outraged by Jesus' continued challenging of the law that they simply observe to see if he will defy the Sabbath law in the synagogue. Their question (e.g., as framed in Mt. 12:10) is placed on the lips of Jesus in this Gospel, leaving their infuriated silence giving voice to the real question in this episode. When Jesus does heal the man's withered hand, they leave the synagogue, and in Mark's second surprising move, they join with the Herodians (unmentioned to this point in the text) and begin to plot the death of Jesus. Instead of a pronouncement by Jesus like that in Matthew 12:11–12, the episode concludes with a harbinger of death. The two parables offered at the point-of-turning for the complex become the actual, final pronouncement on the unyielding rigidity of these leaders of the piety party. If this reconstruction of Mark's purpose is correct, it would be wholly inappropriate to interpret the parables of the new and old cloth and the new and old wineskin apart from the context of the four stories that surround these sayings.

Thus, with the deft hand of a rhetorical master, Mark depicts in four marvelously crafted stories precisely how it was that the leading social and political piety activists, first introduced in Mark 2:7, move from troubled praise to outright persecution. Jesus' confrontation with religious particularism was the basis of his rejection of the old and announcement of the new. It was also, according to Mark, the reason that he was executed. Rhetorically, it is placed at this point in the narrative because it clearly parallels narrative complex seventeen, the third from the last collection in the Gospel. In that narrative complex, Mark portrays the Jewish Sanhedrin as condemning Jesus to death because of his refusal to have regard for their authoritative role as interpreters of the Torah tradition. The shocking collusion at the close of this narrative complex makes literary sense when its foreshadowing relationship is established in the overarching parallelism of the meta-narrative arrangement presented in the conclusion to this study.

Mark 3:7—4:1
The Fourth Narrative Complex

I JESUS AND THE CROWDS (Mk. 3:7–10)

{7}	A		Jesus departed with his disciples to the sea,	DISCIPLES BY THE SEA
		B	and a great multitude from Galilee followed him;	MULTITUDE
{8}		B'	hearing all that he was doing, they came to him in great numbers from Judea, Jerusalem, Idumea, beyond the Jordan, and the region around Tyre and Sidon.	MULTITUDE
{9}	A	1	He told his disciples to have a boat ready for him because of the crowd,	DISCIPLES BY THE SEA
		2	so that they would not crush him;	CRUSH HIM
{10}		1'	for he had cured many,	REASON FOR THE BOAT
		2'	so that all who had diseases pressed upon him to touch him.	PRESS UPON HIM

II UNCLEAN SPIRITS IDENTIFY JESUS (Mk. 3:11–12)

{11}	A		Whenever the unclean spirits saw him,	SPIRITS RECOGNIZE HIM
		B	they fell down before him	SPIRITS BOW BEFORE HIM
		B'	and shouted, "You are the Son of God!"	SPIRITS IDENTIFY HIM
{12}	A'		But he sternly ordered them not to make him known.	SPIRITS SILENCED BY HIM

III THE CALL AND COMMISSION OF THE TWELVE (Mk. 3:13–19)

{13}	A		He went up the mountain and called to him those whom he wanted, and they came to him.	THOSE WHOM HE WANTED
{14}		B	And he appointed twelve, whom he also named apostles, to be with him,	APPOINTED TWELVE
			C and to be sent out to proclaim the message,	CENTRAL TASK
{15}			C' and to have authority to cast out demons.	CENTRAL TASK
{16}		B'	So he appointed the twelve:	APPOINTED TWELVE
	A'		Simon (to whom he gave the name Peter);	
{17}			James son of Zebedee and John the brother of James (to whom he gave the name Boanerges, that is, Sons of Thunder);	THOSE WHOM HE PICKED
{18}			and Andrew, and Philip, and Bartholomew, and Matthew, and Thomas, and James son of Alphaeus, and Thaddaeus, and Simon the Cananaean,	
{19}			and Judas Iscariot, who betrayed him.	

II' JESUS IDENTIFIED WITH UNCLEAN SPIRITS (Mk. 3:20–35)

Scene 1 (3:20–21)

{20}	1		Then he went home;	HOME
		2	and the crowd came together again, so that they could not even eat.	ODD BEHAVIOR
{21}	1'		When his family heard it, they went out to restrain him,	FAMILY
		2'	for people were saying, "He has gone out of his mind."	ODD BEHAVIOR

Scene 2 (3:22–30)

{22}	A		And the scribes who came down from Jerusalem said, "He has Beelzebul, and by the ruler of the demons he casts out demons."	HE HAS AN UNCLEAN SPIRIT

{23}	B	And he called them to him, and spoke to them in parables,	
	a	"How can Satan cast out Satan?	SATAN DIVIDED?
{24}	b	If a kingdom is divided against itself,	KINGDOM DIVIDED
		that kingdom cannot stand.	
{25}	b'	And if a house is divided against itself,	HOUSE DIVIDED
		that house will not be able to stand.	
{26}	a'	And if Satan has risen up against himself	SATAN DIVIDED?
		and is divided, he cannot stand, but his end has come.	
{27}	C	But no one can enter a strong man's house	A STRONG MAN
		and plunder his property	PLUNDER HIS PROPERTY
	C'	without first tying up the strong man;	A STRONG MAN
		then indeed the house can be plundered.	PLUNDER HIS HOUSE
{28}	B'	"Truly I tell you,	AMEN (KINGDOM) SAYING
	a	people will be forgiven for their sins	
	b	and whatever blasphemies they utter;	
{29}	b'	but whoever blasphemes against the Holy Spirit	
	a'	can never have forgiveness,	
		but is guilty of an eternal sin"—	
{30}	A'	for they had said, "He has an unclean spirit."	HE HAS AN UNCLEAN SPIRIT

Scene 3 (3:31–35)

{31}	A	Then his mother and his brothers came;	OLD FAMILY CALLS
		and standing outside, they sent to him and called him.	
{32}	B	A crowd was sitting around him;	
		and they said to him, "Your mother	
		and your brothers and sisters are outside, asking for you."	OLD FAMILY IDENTIFIED
{33}	B'	And he replied,	FAMILY IDENTITY
		"Who are my mother and my brothers?"	QUESTIONED
{34}	A'	And looking at those who sat around him, he said,	
		"Here are my mother and my brothers!	NEW FAMILY IDENTIFIED
{35}		Whoever does the will of God	
		is my brother and sister and mother."	

I' JESUS AND THE CROWDS (Mk. 4:1)

{4:1}	1	Again he began to teach beside the sea.	BY SEA
	2	Such a very large crowd gathered around him	LARGE CROWD
	1'	that he got into a boat on the sea and sat there,	ON SEA
	2'	while the whole crowd was beside the sea on the land.	WHOLE CROWD

The Rhetorical Shape of the Narrative Complex

Most critics accept that 3:7–10 is the first episode of this collection, but the same critics would group the short, independent scene in 4:1 with the collection of parabolic teaching that follows. Tradition has associated the brief scene with the latter collection, but once the independence of the scene is acknowledged,[1] its rightful role as the conclusion of the fourth narrative collection becomes possible. When we turn to examine the framing narratives of the fifth narrative collection, it will become equally obvious that the scene stands outside of the complex. As in the first episode of this complex, this last, brief story brings Jesus back to the seashore, back to the press of the crowds, and back into the safety of an off-shore boat. Only this time, instead of escaping the crowds, he teaches them. The introduction of his teaching ministry in this last story becomes yet another example of Mark making a subject available to the audience in one narrative complex that will become the central motif of the next complex.[2]

In the center of the collection is the unparalleled episode of the calling and commissioning of the Twelve, while the framing sections II and II' are concerned with stories of others who were able to or should have been able to recognize who Jesus was. The unclean spirits of Episode II readily name Jesus' true identity and announce it. On the other hand, Episode II' is a multilayered account of all the groups in the physical world who should have been willing to recognize who he was, but could or would not.

In the first scene of Episode II', Jesus' family sets out to bring him home, labeling him crazy after they "heard about this." Although some critics think the vague "this" is a reference to Jesus' inability to eat properly, mentioned in the previous verse, it is more likely that his family is depicted as aghast that, as an unschooled villager, he had gathered to himself a following of disciples like a highly regarded rabbi.

The scene then shifts to Jesus' interaction with the ancient equivalent of a Jerusalem fact-finding commission that had labeled his ministry as demonically inspired. Mark's Jesus responds to the assertion that he is in league with Beelzebul by appropriating the premise of their argument and turning it back on them.[3] He counters their accusation with a stunning denouncement of those who would deny what God does in the power of his spirit, stating that the unwillingness of the religious establishment to authenticate the work of the Spirit of God is both blasphemous and an unforgivable sin.

In an A-B-A' circle, the third scene draws the reader back to the charge made in scene 1. Having arrived to take him home, Jesus' mother and brothers now serve as a narrative foil. The device provides Mark with an opportunity to allow Jesus to make a pronouncement concerning the nature of the true family: his real mothers, brothers, and sisters are those who do God's will.[4]

Like the second narrative complex, this complex begins and ends with stories about Jesus teaching ministry by the Galilean lakeside. The rhetorically observant reader would have recognized that this formulaic setting suggests that the first four narrative complexes have a step-parallel relationship with each other:

```
    I  Mk. 1:1–15      The Beginning: Ministry Credentialed by God
     II  Mk. 1:16—2:14  The Temptation: Responding to Calling and Expectations
    I'  Mk. 2:15—3:6   The Conflict: Ministry Rejected by Religious Leaders
     II' Mk. 3:7—4:1    The Affirmation: Responding to Calling and Confrontation
```

These four narrative collections are organized as a self-contained unit of tradition in the same progression as that found for the final four narrative complexes that make up the passion narrative (14:1—16:8). By developing the first four complexes as a step-progression, a boundary is naturally placed on the portion of the Gospel that comprises this beginnings meta-narrative. However, in the reverse ordering of the overarching meta-narrative of the Gospel, this final narrative of the beginnings meta-narrative parallels the first narrative in the passion meta-narrative. As will become evident later, the themes introduced to this point in the narrative will begin to unravel in reverse order at the outset of the passion meta-narrative.

The juxtaposition of the episodes in the fourth narrative complex can be visualized thus:

```
    I   JESUS AND THE CROWDS                              Mk. 3:7–10
     II   UNCLEAN SPIRITS IDENTIFY JESUS                   Mk. 3:11–12
       III  JESUS CALLS AND COMMISSIONS THE TWELVE     Mk. 3:13–19
     II'  JESUS IDENTIFIED WITH UNCLEAN SPIRITS         Mk. 3:20–35
              Scene 1                                    (vv. 20–21)
              Scene 2                                    (vv. 22–30)
              Scene 3                                    (vv. 31–35)
    I'  JESUS AND THE CROWDS                             Mk. 4:1
```

The Central Motif

In this final narrative complex in the beginnings meta-narrative, the tight organization emphasizes the relationship Jesus has with each significant group that has been introduced in the opening portion of the Gospel:

```
(I and I')    the crowds who respond to his ministry,
(II and II')  the institutional and spiritual forces capable of credentialing him, and
(III)         in contrast to those individuals who respond to his message and do his will.
```

Like the second narrative complex, the focus has returned once again to defining the nature of the disciple's vocation, both in the time of Jesus and in Mark's day as well. It was the bracketing motif in the former collection. In this one it is central.

The Twelve were originally called to "be with him and to be sent out to proclaim the message and to have authority to cast out demons" (vv. 14–15), but "true family" is "whoever does God's will" (v. 35). The implication is that, like their master, followers in Mark's community will likely face the accusation from other family members that they are also "out of their mind" (v. 21). In the conflict with diaspora Judaism that helped give birth to Christianity as a separate community of faith, they may even have found themselves opposed by synagogue leaders who accused them of being misled by unclean spirits (vv. 22 and 30). In all of this, Jesus is depicted as facing the same social and familial expectations disciples would experience. But the picture Mark presents is that a disciple, like Jesus, cannot live by any other set of expectations than to do the will of God. Opposition will come from many quarters, but disciples must bind it and defeat the strong man, just as Jesus silenced both the unclean spirits and those who would demonize him. Proclaiming the message and exercising authority in the name of Jesus is that which identifies those who would not be bound or crippled by opposition or misunderstanding.

Jesus' pronouncement to the religious leaders in his day is also a pronouncement for the commissioned religious leaders of the church in Mark's day. They cannot be a house divided, deterred from the course to which they were commissioned. From the outset of his Gospel, Mark reminds the church and its leaders that it was born to mission and that it should not be deterred either by fear of or by deference to those who would deny that which the Spirit has credentialed.

As indicated earlier, this collection is the fourth and final complex in the beginnings meta-narrative and is also parallel with the first of the final four complexes of the passion meta-narrative (14:1–53). In that complex, Jesus spends time in prayer that he might also be one who does the "will of God" rather than what he would desire to do on his own (Mk. 14:36), Judas Iscariot is named as the one who betrays Jesus (3:19), and the remaining Eleven betray their calling and flee (becoming a de facto "house divided"?). Reference made to an unforgivable sin in the present narrative complex (3:29) sounds surprisingly similar to the "Woe!" pronounced on the one who would betray the Son of man in this balancing complex of the passion narrative ("It would be better for him if he had not been born," Mk. 14:21). Both pronouncements are indictments of those who deny, either by what they say or what they do, that which God is doing.

The stories of conflict between Jesus and Jewish religious leaders undoubtedly was read by Mark's readers in light of the conflict they were experiencing between church and synagogue. Suetonius' report that in A.D. 49 Emperor Claudius expelled Jews from Rome because of their constant riots instigated by "Chrestus" (*Life of*

Claudius 25.4) probably reflects this division. It was a division made all the more acute by the fact that Rome made distinctions between *religiones lictae et illicitae*, with Judaism a legally recognized religion, while a "new" religion of Christianity would have failed the test. Although initially Roman officials dismissed Christians as a sect of Judaism (cf. Acts 16:20; 18:12–17), Jewish synagogue leaders eventually sought to label Christianity as a religion clearly distinguished from themselves.

Just as Luther was not trying to establish "Lutheranism," the oral community of the Twelve did not begin by trying to establish "Christianity" as a separate religion. That sense of separate identity (cf. Acts 11:26; 26:28) came about through turmoil with the synagogue, but it also came about with turmoil within the Christian community as well. As will soon become apparent, the fictive argument of Mark's Gospel embodies that challenge to the leadership represented in the oral tradition of the Twelve, who still wanted to cling to the legitimacy of legal recognition as a sect of Judaism. Complicating this tension is the great Jewish war of 66–73 and the catastrophic loss of the temple in 70. Without the temple and temple worship, Jews throughout the world lost the focus of their religious life and their interpretive self-understanding. While Judaism suffered this crisis of identity, voices like those of Mark presented a radical interpretation of the meaning of these events. As will become increasingly evident, Mark's fictive argument calls on the church to throw off this drive to normalize Christianity as a sect of Judaism and to take up the real mission to which it was first commissioned. This theme, foreshadowed in this collection, will be developed in much greater depth as we move further into this Gospel. However, the argument functions as a subtext of the Jesus story, with a persuasive appeal (felt anew by successive generations of interpreters) to reject accommodation with the normalizing forces of religious institutionalization and choose, instead, to be people who do the will of God.

Room in the Family
A sermon by Stephen Farris

Sermon Text: Mark 3:7—4:1

As far as I can tell, Jesus needed help just about from the beginning of the Gospel story. As soon as he starts preaching, he calls Simon and Andrew and the Zebedee boys, James and John, professional fisherfolk all. "Follow me and I will make you fishers of people," he says. Perhaps he needs help because, almost from the beginning, crowds follow Jesus. They hear of his authority over evil spirits. They hear of his ability to heal the sick. They seek him here, they seek him there, and soon enough they find him. The potential "catch" is very large, and Jesus needs help with the fishing.

As our part of the story begins, the crowd is so great that Jesus even needs his disciples to ply their old trade for a short time and prepare a boat for him to escape the crush of the crowd as they reach out for his healing touch. All seems to be going well. Even the evil spirits recognize, as they always do, the authority of Jesus. "You are the Son of God," they cry out. So Jesus silences them. Then Jesus successfully recruits not just four but twelve helpers, to be with him and to proclaim his message. What the demons may not say, these helpers must say. Eventually, they become apostles entrusted to tell the world who Jesus is.

So everything is going well. If a firm of marketing consultants were to draw a graph of developments in this part of the Gospel of Mark, the line would be heading steeply upward. But, of course, we know that this is not the whole story. There is another line that works its way through the Gospel of Mark. It is a line that begins with suspicion and ends with hatred. It is heading steeply upward too, up toward a hill outside Jerusalem. Those who follow this line have a very different view of Jesus.

What irony there is in this story! The crowds seek Jesus' healing; but Jesus' neighbors, the ones who talk to his family, say "He is out of his mind." The Twelve are ready to spread his word, but his family seeks to shut him away. The evil spirits can see who Jesus is, yet the experts in religion, the scribes, cannot. The demons hail him as Son of God, but the scribes say he is ruled by the devil. He came to his own and his own received him not.

The climax of this part of the story occurs when his own flesh and blood—mother, sisters, brothers—come to see him. Once more, there is a crowd. They are sitting and listening. We do not know what the family intends. Perhaps they want to try yet again to take him away and restrain him, but they can't get at him. They don't "get" Jesus in more ways than one in Mark's Gospel. They are both physically and symbolically separated from Jesus. The crowd is ready to help them, however: "Your family is outside, asking for you," they tell him. And Jesus replies, saying the words that bring this part of the story to a climax, the reason the whole story is told: "Here are my mother and my brothers. Whoever does the will of God is my brother and sister and mother."

Whoever does the will of God! Not just those who are related to Jesus by blood. Not just those who were fortunate enough to hear him in the flesh. Not just the people of Judah and Galilee of A.D. 30. Whoever does the will of God. It might be the Christians of the far-off church in Rome, huddling in the catacombs against the dawn of persecution, the people for whom Mark wrote his Gospel. If they do God's will, they're his family. It might be an early preacher faithfully declaring the word, though the lions await in the Colosseum. It might be a medieval monk squinting as he copies the faded manuscript by the uncertain light of a guttering candle. It might be a woman whose house is a station on the Underground Railroad. It might be Christians at just about any point in the long and sometimes shameful, sometimes glorious, history of the church. It doesn't matter. If they are doing God's will, they're Jesus' family.

It might even be people who attend a rather ordinary church in our community. It might be people who take warm clothing to the refugees in the Kingdom Road motel strip. They're Jesus' brothers. It might be the Sunday school teacher struggling out there in the church hall to teach a gospel lesson to hyperactive preschoolers. She's Jesus' sister. It might be a senior lady who can't get out anymore, but she prays every day for so many. She's Jesus' mother. You meet so many members of Jesus' family around here! Because if we are doing God's will, we are Jesus' family. That's the wonderful thing about the Gospel. It's not just about doing things; it's about belonging. Jesus doesn't just recruit helpers; he adopts into a family.

I think these words were written to comfort those first listeners to Mark's Gospel. I think they were written to comfort us.

But perhaps that's not quite the whole story. It would be very pleasant to see ourselves among the crowd. It would be even more pleasant to take our seat with the Twelve, to have Jesus point at us and say, "These are my sisters and my brothers and my mother!"

But what if we're more like the mother and sisters and brothers who are on the outside of the crowd? What if we're like the neighbors who say he's crazy? What if, and may God forbid that this should be so, what if we're like the scribes? After all, the family, the neighbors, the scribes, these are the people who ought, in theory, to have been most able to recognize Jesus for what he was. The first two groups know Jesus and the last group knows the Bible. They're the ones who ought to know about Jesus. And they just don't seem to be able to recognize him for what he is. And in our world, we too are the people who ought to know who Jesus is.

Perhaps the story is a warning to us. The church doesn't own Jesus. There are people outside the church who do his will while we fail even to recognize him in our world. I suppose there is some truth in that notion. I have no difficulty in believing that Mahatma Gandhi, for example, did God's will better than almost any Christian. And that makes him Jesus' brother. I know of atheists and agnostics who faithfully help serve in the kitchen down at the Scott Mission. May the God they do not know bless them, for they are doing God's will.

But that interpretation doesn't quite sit right. It almost makes it sound as if being part of the Christian church doesn't matter…as long as you do good things for other people. Make no mistake, it is a wonderful and blessed thing that there are those who do God's will without the comfort and encouragement and strength that can be found in the church of Jesus Christ. I believe that those who do such things will find a strange mercy from the God who is mercy. But the gospel was written for the church. It would not willingly slight those who share in its fellowship.

As far as I can tell, the chief characteristic, in this story, of all those who fail to recognize Jesus is this: They think they can render a verdict about Jesus. They think they can look at him in a detached way, in a superior way, they can weigh his words and his actions and come to their own judicious decision about him. "He's crazy." "He needs to be shut away." "He is ruled by the devil." Such people suffer from the delusion that they, not Jesus, are in control. Even scholars in the Jesus seminar drop their little colored marble into bowls to register their verdicts about his words and his actions. And journalists write cover stories for national newsmagazines and offer calm, judicious decisions about Jesus. And they invite us to do the same.

We love the feeling that we are in control,
> that we can make the decisions that matter about our lives,
>> that we are the masters of our own destinies.

Perhaps this wonderful feeling of control is true for us—part of the time. But perhaps it is, in part, nothing more than wishful thinking.

In fact, Jesus is out of my control. Who can predict what he will do. Perhaps he will allow himself to be known, at least a little bit, to those who think they are in control. But that's not what usually happens. In our story it's the people who are in desperate need and can't do anything else to meet their needs who come to Jesus. It's people who are so out of control because of their encounter with Jesus that they drop whatever they are doing in their ordinary life and follow him who become his disciples.

Let me make a guess about you and then a prediction. Here is the guess: There are probably areas of your life in which you do have control. But I imagine that there are other areas of your life that are beyond your control, where you struggle and struggle and struggle some more and still can't seem to achieve what you want to achieve. In those areas you just can't help yourselves. So, silently, voicelessly, you cry to someone, to anyone, for help. The reason I make this guess about you is that there are areas like that in my life. Here's the prediction: It's in those areas that you are most likely to meet Jesus and come to know him.

And that is a wonderful possibility for anyone. For anyone. One of Jesus' brothers was named James. Tradition says, and I think rightly, that he did not believe in Jesus during his ministry. That's entirely understandable. Would you believe that your brother was the Messiah? Yet he too came to accept this as his brother's identity and became the leader of the church in Jerusalem. And Mary, his mother? Well, she was there at the foot of the cross. Anyone can become Jesus' kin, even his own flesh and blood. So there is room for people like us.

There are still crowds and they're still wondering about Jesus. And as far as I can tell, Jesus still needs help. What's more, there is still room in the family. What about you? Would you care to join? Care to help?

Compositional Comments

I like what Bob Reid has done with this section of the Gospel of Mark. His layout of this narrative complex helps us to see the contrasting threads that make up the story as whole. I take the two intertwining threads of this narrative complex to be, on the one hand, the surprising reception of Jesus by those who could not be expected to recognize who he is and, on the other hand, the contrasting failure of those who should have known him best. Once those threads are observed in this narrative complex, it is also possible to see that they have been present earlier in the Gospel as well. I have attempted to let these contrasting threads form the structure of the sermon. The Gospel narrative is shaped by a series of contrasts that reappear in the sermon, both in the treatment of the text and in the treatment of contemporary reality.

I believe it is important to be specific in a homiletical treatment of contemporary reality, so some of the references are, therefore, unapologetically specific to the situation of my family church in the east end of Toronto. As I say in this sermon, I believe this text to have been written as good news and as an encouragement to an early church, to the church in Rome according to a tradition I accept. I did not want to interpret this text in such way that it would demean the value of participation in a church. I also tried to avoid treating "doing the will of God" as only material charity. Worship and teaching are surely also part of the will of God. There is, I think, in this narrative complex also an implicit warning amidst the good news. As I look back on the sermon, I fear that I may have emphasized the warning to the detriment of the good news. But then, it is not only Jesus who is out of our control. Sermons sometimes are as well.

Mark 4:2–34
The Fifth Narrative Complex

I JESUS TAUGHT IN PARABLES (Mk. 4:2)
{2}   He began to teach them many things in parables,   PARABLES

   II FIRST KINGDOM GROWTH PARABLE COLLECTION (Mk. 4:3–20)
   Saying One: The Parable (4:3–9)
{3}   A   and in his teaching he said to them: "Listen!   LISTEN!
       1 A sower went out to sow.
{4}   And as he sowed, some seed fell on the path,   PLACE OF SOWING
         2 and the birds came   SITUATION OF RECEIVING
         3 and ate it up.   RESULT
{5}   1 Other seed fell on rocky ground,   PLACE OF SOWING
         2 where it did not have much soil,   SITUATION OF RECEIVING
            and it sprang up quickly, since it had no depth of soil.
{6}   And when the sun rose, it was scorched;   RESULT
         3 and since it had no root, it withered away.
{7}   1 Other seed fell among thorns,   PLACE OF SOWING
         2 and the thorns grew up and choked it,   SITUATION OF RECEIVING
         3 and it yielded no grain.   RESULT
{8}   1 Other seed fell into good soil   PLACE OF SOWING
         2 and brought forth grain,   SITUATION OF RECEIVING
         3 growing up and increasing and yielding   RESULT
            thirty and sixty and a hundredfold."
{9}   A' And he said, "Let anyone with ears to hear listen!"   LISTEN!

   Saying Two: The Secret of Parables (4:10–13)
{10} A   When he was alone, those who were around him   DESIRE TO UNDERSTAND
       along with the twelve asked him about the parables.
{11}   B   And he said to them, "To you has been given
          the secret of the kingdom of God,   SECRET GIVEN
         C   but for those outside, everything comes
{12}   in parables; in order that 'they may indeed look,   ISAIANIC SAYING OF
            but not perceive, and may indeed listen,   REVERSAL
            but not understand;
         C' so that they may not turn again and be forgiven.'"   ISAIANIC REVERSAL
{13}   B' And he said to them, "Do you
          not understand this parable?   UNDERSTAND SECRET?
     A'   Then how will you understand all the parables?   NEED TO UNDERSTAND

   Saying Three: The Parable Interpreted (4:14–20)
{14} 1   The sower sows the word. These are the ones
{15}   on the path where the word is sown: PLACE OF SOWING
      2 when they hear, Satan immediately comes   SITUATION OF HEARING
      3 and takes away the word that is sown in them.   RESULT
{16} 1   And these are the ones sown on rocky ground: PLACE OF SOWING
      2 when they hear the word, they immediately   SITUATION OF HEARING
        receive it with joy.
        But they have no root, and endure only for a while;
      3 then, when trouble or persecution
{17}   arises on account of the word, immediately   RESULT
        they fall away.
{18} 1   And others are those sown among the thorns: PLACE OF SOWING
      2 these are the ones who hear the word,   SITUATION OF HEARING

		but the cares of the world, and the lure of wealth,	
{19}		and the desire for other things come in and choke the word,	
	3	and it yields nothing.	RESULT
{20}	1	And these are the ones sown on the good soil:	PLACE OF SOWING
	2	they hear the word and accept it	SITUATION OF HEARING
	3	and bear fruit, thirty and sixty and a hundredfold."	RESULT

III THREE PARABLES OF KINGDOM REVERSAL (Mk. 4:21–25)

Saying One: An Eschatological Reversal Parable (4:21–25)

{21}	A	He said to them, "Is a lamp brought in	NOT FOR HIDING
		to be put under the bushel basket, or under the bed,	
	B	and not on the lampstand?	TO BE SEEN
{22}	B'	For there is nothing hidden, except to be disclosed;	TO BE DISCLOSED
	A'	nor is anything secret, except to come to light.	NOT FOR HIDING

Central Saying: An Eschatological Reversal Parable (4:23–24a)

{23}	A	Let anyone with ears to hear	HEAR
	B	listen!"	LISTEN!
{24}	B'	And he said to them, "Pay attention	LISTEN!
	A'	to what you hear;	HEAR

Saying Three: An Eschatological Reversal Parable (4:24b–25)

	A	the measure you give will be the measure you get,	RECIPROCITY
	B	and still more will be given you.	MORE
{25}	B'	For to those who have, more will be given;	MORE
	A'	and from those who have nothing,	REVERSAL
		even what they have will be taken away."	

II' SECOND KINGDOM GROWTH PARABLE COLLECTION (Mk. 4:26–32)

Saying One: Kingdom Parable (4:26–29)

{26}	A	He also said, "The kingdom of God is [thus]:	KINGDOM COME
	B	As if someone would scatter seed on the ground,	
{27}		and would sleep and rise night and day,	
		and the seed would sprout and grow,	
		he does not know how.	GROWTH WORKING
{28}	B'	The earth produces of itself, first the stalk,	GROWTH WORKING
		then the head, then the full grain in the head.	
{29}	A'	But when the grain is ripe,	KINGDOM COME
		at once he goes in with his sickle,	
		because the harvest has come."	

Saying Two: Kingdom Parable (4:30–32)

{30}	A	He also said, "With what can we compare	
		the kingdom of God, or what parable	KINGDOM COME
{31}		will we use for it? It is like a mustard seed,	
	B	which, when sown	SOWN
		upon the ground,	IN GROUND
		is the smallest of all the seeds on earth;	SMALLEST
{32}	B'	yet when it is sown	SOWN
		it grows up	GROWTH WORKING
		and becomes the greatest of all shrubs,	GREATEST
	A'	and puts forth large branches, so that the birds of the air	
		can make nests in its shade."	KINGDOM COME

I' JESUS TAUGHT IN PARABLES (Mk. 4:33–34)

{33}	1	With many such parables he spoke the word to them,	PARABLES
	2	as they were able to hear it;	UNDERSTAND
{34}	1'	he did not speak to them except in parables,	PARABLES
	2'	but he explained everything in private to his disciples.	EXPLAINED

The Rhetorical Shape of the Narrative Complex

Mark begins and ends the fifth narrative complex by asserting that Jesus' teaching was parabolic. With regard to the collection of characteristic parables, Episode II has three separate sections: first, the parable of productivity; second, a section in which Jesus explains the function of parables; and, third, the interpretation by Jesus of the parable of productivity.[1] The corresponding Episode II' develops two more parables about receptive soil and sowing seed. Like the parables in Episode II, these are not parables about growth. They are parables of productivity. For example, the first parable in II' notes that good soil needs only to be tended—it is not up to the farmer to produce ("The earth produces of itself"), while the second parable suggests that productivity, when it occurs, is marvelous to see. From something quite small to something quite large, the contrast is between meager beginnings and vast productivity.

Where the parables in Episodes II and II' draw on the agricultural image of productivity in order to reveal the secret of the kingdom, the central unparalleled episode, III, provides three additional parabolic sayings about eschatological reversal. Their placement in the heart of the matter forces the reader to consider the way in which the kingdom, though spoken of in parables, is a secret revealed for those who are willing to listen. The central set of parables could be rendered individually, with the saying in 4:21–22 paralleled by the saying in 4:24b–25. Either way, the point of turning in the parable is the call to listen, a challenge that will be repeated by the divine voice at the Mount of Transfiguration (Mk. 9:7).

Just as the collection of eschatological parables and teaching of the fifteenth narrative complex stands alone prior to the passion meta-narrative, this collection of kingdom parables and teaching stands alone between the beginnings meta-narrative (1:1—4:1) and the Galilean ministry meta-narrative (4:35—9:29). The juxtaposition of the episodes in the fifth narrative complex can be visualized thus:

```
I JESUS TAUGHT IN PARABLES                              Mk. 4:2
   II FIRST KINGDOM GROWTH PARABLE COLLECTION           Mk. 4:3–20
      Saying One: The Parable                           (vv. 3–9)
      Saying Two: The Secret of Parables                (vv. 10–13)
      Saying Three: The Parable Interpreted             (vv. 14–20)
```

III THREE PARABLES OF KINGDOM REVERSAL	Mk. 4:21–25
Saying One: An Eschatological Reversal Parable	(vv. 21–22)
Central Saying: An Eschatological Reversal Parable	(vv. 23–24a)
Saying Three: An Eschatological Reversal Parable	(vv. 24b–25)
II' SECOND KINGDOM GROWTH PARABLE COLLECTION	Mk. 4:26–32
Saying One: Kingdom Parable	(vv. 26–29)
Saying Two: Kingdom Parable	(vv. 30–32)
I' JESUS TAUGHT IN PARABLE	Mk. 4:33–34

The Central Motif

Drury observes that Jesus' choice to teach in parables classed his argument as aggadah in distinction to the rabbinic halakah instruction. Instead of making argument based on careful scholarship meant to appeal to the elite, Drury colorfully suggests that aggadah was considered the "junk jewelry of the peddler," fine as a way of presenting a moralistic religion to the masses, but unworthy of argument that would serve as legislative precedent.[2] In light of this, we might wonder why the disciples were so puzzled by teaching that was meant for the masses. On the face of it, the disciples do not appear to be good listeners. They, along with everyone else who does not get it, are contrasted with the hard-hearted people to whom Isaiah was called to preach with little hope they would get it either. Mark casts the disciples as those to whom Jesus revealed the secrets of the kingdom. Yet these same disciples seem befuddled about teaching that even the crowds appear to understand. Readers would be forced to wonder why? Drury notes that,

> The stupidity of Mark's disciples is both flattering and instructive to his readers. We understand Jesus better than the people in the text usually do. Their incomprehension assists our comprehension. It signals the dead-end paths—namely, any routes other than the road to the Cross, which the disciples, naturally, do not want to know about…For Mark is after an extraordinary kind of comprehension…Genuine understanding, Mark tells us, is supernatural.[3]

The effect is to create readers "who have the key to this wild parade."[4] These are readers who come to realize that they "get" Jesus (after all, they have already read Mk. 1:1 and know who Jesus really is). In fact, they appear to understand that which confused the original community of the Twelve.

Drury's analysis aptly summarizes what will become a theme throughout the remainder of the Gospel. From this point onward, the disciples, especially the Twelve, are invariably depicted as obtuse. The effect is to plant a seed of doubt concerning whether the remaining leaders of that oral community of the Twelve in Mark's day remain equally obtuse. At the center of this first collection in which the Twelve are shown to lack understanding, Mark adjures those who do understand to act on that which they have received — to respond by allowing the "secret of the kingdom of God" to illuminate rather than to be cloistered—to respond lest (through eschatological reversal) that which they have already received be taken away from them. The central parabolic sayings are all characterized by a sense of boldness. If someone possesses light, it should be placed in such a way as to illuminate—if someone has ears to hear, let that person consider the magnitude of what has been said —if someone responds with boldness, that person will be blessed with more—to responsiveness comes increase, but to lack of productivity comes loss of all.

The central parables appear to be directed to those who might be prone to contain the gospel rather than to release it. Taken together, the parables teach that it is not the work of disciples to create the kingdom; theirs is only to act on what they have been told to do. It is the work of the "Word" to effect the kingdom. Crossan has made this point well, arguing that these parables are not about the growth between planting and harvest. Rather, they are descriptions of the miraculous advent of the kingdom that comes about from the most humble beginnings. The kingdom is like the productivity that occurs when good soil yields bountifully, produces a full harvest, bears with largesse. Disciples do not grow the kingdom; the kingdom is gift.[5]

In this fifth collection, Mark gathers several illustrative stories concerning the nature of productivity and joins them together to underscore the relationship of careful listening to becoming disciples through whom fruitfulness can be multiplied. Traditional exegesis has spotted the agricultural motif and noted that this appears to be a Marcan collection, but it has generally been more concerned with possible problems created by the collection's seams than the central message focused in the demands of the narrative: "Listen!" "Let anyone with ears to hear listen!" "Do you not understand?" "Pay attention to what you hear." "Produce a crop." "More will be given." "The harvest has come." "Becomes the greatest of all shrubs."[6] These verbal pictures speak to a pressing need to attend to the possibilities of the kingdom come. More than a simple collection of the "kind" of parables Jesus taught, Mark has juxtaposed this kingdom teaching and these kingdom sayings of Jesus into a powerful sermon. The miracle of the kingdom is not being good soil. The miracle is what God can do with good soil. God can do the kingdom.

Mark 4:35—5:43
The Sixth Narrative Complex

I JESUS' POWER OVER NATURE (4:35—5:1)

{35}	A		On that day, when evening had come,	
			he said to them, "Let us go across to the other side."	GO ACROSS SEA
{36}			And leaving the crowd behind, they took him	
			with them in the boat, just as he was.	
			Other boats were with him.	
{37}		B	A great windstorm arose, and the waves	WINDSTORM ARISES
			beat into the boat, so that the boat was	
			already being swamped.	
{38}			C But he was in the stern, asleep on the cushion;	UNFEARFUL
			D and they woke him up and said to him,	WOKE HIM
			"Teacher, do you not care that we are perishing?"	THEIR RESPONSE
{39}			D' He woke up and rebuked the wind,	WOKE UP
			and said to the sea, "Peace! Be still!"	HIS RESPONSE
			Then the wind ceased, and there was a dead calm.	
{40}			C' He said to them, "Why are you afraid?	WHY FEARFUL?
			Have you still no faith?"	FAITH
{41}		B'	And they were filled with great awe	
			and said to one another, "Who then is this,	
			that even the wind and the sea obey him?"	WINDSTORM OBEYS
{5:1}	A'		They came to the other side of the sea,	ARRIVE AT OTHER
			to the country of the Gerasenes.	SIDE OF SEA

II JESUS' POWER OVER THE DEMONIC (Mk. 5:2–20)

Scene 1—Possessed Man Begs Jesus (5:2–6)

{2}	A		And when he had stepped out of the boat,	
			immediately a man out of the tombs	
			with an unclean spirit met him.	MAN COMES TO JESUS
{3}		B	He lived among the tombs;	AMONG THE TOMBS
			C and no one could restrain him any more, even with	UNSTOPPABLE
			a chain;	
{4}			D for he had often been restrained	CHAINS RESTRAIN
			with shackles and chains,	
			D' but the chains he wrenched apart,	CHAINS BIND
			and the shackles he broke in pieces;	
			C' and no one had the strength to subdue him.	UNSTOPPABLE
{5}		B'	Night and day among the tombs and on the mountains	AMONG THE TOMBS
			he was always howling and bruising himself with stones.	
{6}	A'		When he saw Jesus from a distance, he ran	MAN COMES TO JESUS
			and bowed down before him;	

Scene 2—Legion Speaks (5:7–10)

{7}	A		[A]nd he shouted at the top of his voice,	
			"What have you to do with me,	
			Jesus, Son of the Most High God?	WHAT THE DEMON SAID
			I adjure you by God, do not torment me."	
{8}		B	For he had said to him,	
			"Come out of the man, you unclean spirit!"	WHAT JESUS SAID
{9}		B'	Then Jesus asked him, "What is your name?"	WHAT JESUS SAID
	A'		He replied, "My name is Legion;	
			for we are many." He begged him earnestly	WHAT THE DEMON(S)
{10}			not to send them out of the country.	SAID

Scene 3—Jesus Permits Pig Possession (5:11–13)

{11} A Now there on the hillside
     a great herd of swine was feeding;   LARGE HERD FEEDING
{12}   B and the unclean spirits begged him,
      "Send us into the swine;   INTO SWINE?
      let us enter them."
{13}   C So he gave them permission.   PERMISSION GRANTED
        C' And the unclean spirits came out   DEMONS COME OUT
   B' and entered the swine;   GO INTO SWINE
 A' and the herd, numbering about two thousand,
     rushed down the steep bank into the sea,   LARGE HERD DROWNED
     and were drowned in the sea.

Scene 2'—Witnesses Speak (5:14–16)

{14} A The swineherds ran off and told it in the city   PIG-TENDERS REPORT
     and in the country.
   B Then people came to see what it was that had happened. PEOPLE CAME TO SEE
{15}   B' They came to Jesus and saw the demoniac   PEOPLE SAW
      sitting there, clothed and in his right mind,
      the very man who had had the legion;
      and they were afraid.
{16} A' Those who had seen what had happened
     to the demoniac and to the swine reported it.   PIG-TENDERS REPORT

Scene 1'—The Freed Man Begs (5:17–20)

{17} A Then they began to beg Jesus to leave their neighborhood. LEAVE
{18}   As he was getting into the boat,
     the man who had been possessed by demons
     begged him that he might be with him.   BE WITH HIM
{19}   B But Jesus refused, and said to him,
      "Go home to your friends,
     B' and tell them how much the Lord has done for you, TELL OTHERS
      and what mercy he has shown you."   TELL OF MERCY
{20} A' And he went away and began to proclaim in the Decapolis WENT AWAY
     how much Jesus had done for him; and everyone was amazed. TOLD OF HIM

III THE MIRACLE OF FAITH (Mk. 5:21–24)

{21} A When Jesus had crossed again in the boat
     to the other side, a great crowd gathered around him;
     and he was by the sea.   LARGE CROWD GATHERS
{22}   B Then one of the leaders of the synagogue
      named Jairus came and,   JAIRUS COMES
      when he saw him, fell at his feet   PHYSICALLY IMPLORES
{23}   B' and begged him repeatedly,   VERBALLY IMPLORES
      "My little daughter is at the point of death.
      Come and lay your hands on her,   COME WITH JAIRUS
      so that she may be made well, and live."
{24} A' So he went with him.
     And a large crowd followed him   LARGE CROWD PRESSES
     and pressed in on him.

II' JESUS' POWER OVER DISEASE (Mk. 5:25–34)

{25} A Now there was a woman who had been suffering   WOMAN SUFFERS
     from hemorrhages for twelve years.
{26}   B She had endured much under many physicians,
      and had spent all that she had; and she was no better,
      but rather grew worse.   FOUND INCURABLE
{27}   C She had heard about Jesus,
        and came up behind him in the crowd

			and touched his cloak,	TOUCHED HIS CLOAK
{28}			for she said, "If I but touch his clothes, I will be made well."	
{29}		D	Immediately her hemorrhage stopped; and she felt in her body that she was healed of her disease.	SHE FELT HEALING
{30}		D'	Immediately aware that power had gone forth from him, Jesus turned about in the crowd and said, "Who touched my clothes?"	HE FELT POWER GO FORTH
{31}	C'		And his disciples said to him, "You see the crowd pressing in on you; how can you say, 'Who touched me?'"	WHO TOUCHED ME?
{32}			He looked all around to see who had done it.	
{33}	B'		But the woman, knowing what had happened to her, came in fear and trembling, fell down before him, and told him the whole truth.	REPORTS CURE
{34}	A'		He said to her, "Daughter, your faith has made you well; go in peace, and be healed of your disease."	FAITH PRONOUNCED HEALED

I' JESUS' POWER OVER DEATH (Mk. 5:35–43)

{35}	A		While he was still speaking, some people came from the leader's house to say, "Your daughter is dead. Why trouble the teacher any further?"	THE CHILD IS DEAD
{36}		B	But overhearing what they said, Jesus said to the leader of the synagogue, "Do not fear, only believe."	CALL FOR BELIEF
{37}			C He allowed no one to follow him except Peter, James, and John, the brother of James.	WITNESSES
{38}			D When they came to the house of the leader of the synagogue, he saw a commotion, people weeping and wailing loudly.	DESPAIR EXPRESSED
{39}			E When he had entered, he said to them, "Why do you make a commotion and weep? E' The child is not dead but sleeping."	DESPAIR QUESTIONED BELIEF EXPRESSED
{40}			D' And they laughed at him. C' Then he put them all outside, and took the child's father and mother and those who were with him, and went in where the child was.	BELIEF MOCKED WITNESSES
{41}		B'	He took her by the hand and said to her, "Talitha cum," which means, "Little girl, get up!"	JESUS' EXPRESSION OF BELIEF
{42}	A'		And immediately the girl got up and began to walk about (she was twelve years of age). At this they were overcome with amazement.	THE CHILD IS ALIVE
{43}			He strictly ordered them that no one should know this, and told them to give her something to eat.	

The Rhetorical Shape of the Narrative Complex

For most critics the contents of this narrative complex are self-evident: It consists of four episodes: the storm on the lake, the Gerasene demoniac, the raising of Jairus' daughter, and the cure of the woman whose bleeding would not stop.[1] If we consider the collection in this way, we might construe the complex as juxtaposing two sets of commensurable kinds of miracles:

```
A   POWER OVER ELEMENTS MIRACLE
  B   POWER OVER THE DEMONIC MIRACLE
  B'  POWER OVER DISEASE MIRACLE
A'  POWER OVER DEATH MIRACLE
```

The only problem with this rather simple juxtaposition of the episodes is the way Mark introduces the story of the final miracle in 5:21–24. He interrupts this miracle with the story of the woman with the constant flow of blood in 5:25–34 and then returns to the story of raising Jairus' daughter from her deathbed in 5:35–43. This two-in-one technique of storytelling has already been used at 3:20–35 in which the family's desire to rescue Jesus brackets the more serious charges of the religious leadership. Rhoades and Mitchie suggest that Mark used the classic framing technique of *inclusio* in order to create suspense.[2] Yet, for our purposes, the scheme complicates what otherwise would be a straightforward chiastic juxtaposition of four miracle stories. In other words, when considered in relation to the whole collection, Mark's way of telling the story of Jairus and his daughter places Jairus' plea for mercy at the heart of the complex.

The juxtaposition of the episodes in the sixth narrative complex can be visualized thus:

```
I   JESUS' POWER OVER NATURE                        Mk. 4:35—5:1
  II  JESUS' POWER OVER THE DEMONIC                 Mk. 5:2–20
        Scene 1—Possessed Man Begs Jesus              (vv. 2–6)
        Scene 2—Legion Speaks                         (vv. 7–10)
        Scene 3—Jesus Permits Pig Possession          (vv. 11–13)
        Scene 2'—Witnesses Speak                      (vv. 14–16)
        Scene 1'—The Freed Man Begs                   (vv. 17–20)
    III THE MIRACLE OF FAITH                        Mk. 5:21–24
  II' JESUS' POWER OVER DISEASE                     Mk. 5:25–34
I'  JESUS' POWER OVER DEATH                         Mk. 5:35–43
```

The Central Motif

Mark uses the noun form of the verb "to believe" only five times in his Gospel: once at 2:5, describing the faith of those who lowered the paralytic through the roof, twice in the twelfth narrative complex (where he commends the faith of blind Bartimaeus at 11:22 and when he commends faith to his disciples at 11:22), and twice in the present narrative collection. In the first of the latter, Mark's Jesus asks of his disciples, "Why are you afraid? Have you still no faith?" (4:40). In the second occurrence in the complex, Mark's Jesus says, "Daughter, your faith has made you well; go in peace and be healed of your disease" (5:34). In addition, Mark uses the verb form of "to believe" when the synagogue ruler's faith suffers a setback at the announcement of his daughter's death: "Don't be afraid. Just believe." And to the Gadarene demoniac Jesus says, "Go,...and tell...how much the Lord has done for you and what *mercy* he has shown you" (5:19). Thus, the merciful response of the Lord to those who would have faith is sustained throughout the complex.

Robert Meye has argued that Mark's structure of this collection is significantly influenced by Psalm 107.[3] I would add that, once Mark's fictive argument is grasped, the collection serves as a kind of Christian midrash on Psalm 107, the theme of God's deliverance amidst distress. The psalm begins with the charge: "O give thanks to the LORD; for he is good / for his steadfast love endures forever. / Let the redeemed of the LORD say so, / those...gathered in from the lands, / from the east and from the west, / from the north and from the south" (107:1–3). This is followed by a description of four kinds of situations the redeemed of the Lord may find themselves in and how the Lord delivers those who in such distressing circumstances call on the mercy of God. The first of these describes how people who wander in deserts, unable to find their way back to inhabited cities and whose lives are ebbing away, call on the Lord and are delivered from their distress and led back to an inhabited town (vv. 4–9). The second describes prisoners shackled in bondage, living in darkness and gloom, who cry out to the Lord in their trouble (vv. 10–16). The third situation describes those who are sick to the point of no longer eating and who, close to death, call on the Lord, who saves them from their distress (vv. 17–22). The fourth situation describes the pleading of seamen whose courage has melted away in the face of God's awesome power to command the storm-tossed seas (vv. 23–32). Critics have long noted the relationship between the fourth distress in Psalm 107 and the crisis the disciples face on the Sea of Galilee. But I would argue that there are enough other allusions to suggest that Mark has crafted this collection as a midrash on the psalm; for example,

> Deliverance from hunger and thirst in the wilderness (Ps.107:4–9) shapes Mark's story of the deliverance of a woman whose life is "ebbing away" back into community (Mk. 5:25–34).
>
> Deliverance of those in darkness and bondage (Ps.107:10–16) shapes Mark's story of the deliverance of the shackled demoniac (Mk. 5:21–20).

Deliverance from death's door (Ps. 107: 17–22) shapes Mark's story of the deliverance from death's door (Mk. 5:35–43).

Deliverance from peril at sea (Ps. 107:23–32 shapes Mark's story of the deliverance from peril at sea (Mk. 4:35—5:1).

By depicting Jesus as the one who fulfills the promise of prayed-for deliverance, the concluding counsel of Psalm 107 becomes Mark's counsel to his own community, as if Mark had written, "Let those who are wise give heed to these things and consider the steadfast love of the Lord." The running refrain of Psalm 107 is that God's people, once made aware how God delivers them from distress, *must* speak out and give thanks to the Lord who expresses such steadfast and enduring love toward them.

Viewed in this way, the story of Jairus' plea for mercy functions as a performative of the psalmist's refrain. It depicts the ideal behavior of the disciple in need: They are to cast themselves on the mercy of the Lord in faith. As the synagogue leader, Jairus is the representative head of the community, the one capable of leading his people in the liturgy of victory:

> Let them thank the LORD for his steadfast love,
>   for his wonderful works to humankind.
>
> Let them extol him in the congregation of the people,
>   and praise him in the assembly of the elders.
>   (Ps. 107:31–32)

At the center of the miracle collection, the arrangement of Mark's narrative art brings to focus the relationship between faith and deliverance—a relationship that has always been proclaimed in the community of those willing to thank the Lord for his steadfast love and kindness.

In discussing the miracles found in the gospels, Raymond Brown describes their function in the narratives as instruments of revelation concerning the kingdom.[4] Mark presents the stories in a way that discerning readers would see them as further evidence of God's redemptive hand in deliverance of God's people. Like the psalmist, he wants his readers to "Have faith!"—faith that Jesus offers deliverance for disciples in captivity—for disciples near death—for disciples in peril—and for disciples ravaged by disease and the evil influence of the spirit world. The purpose of his fictive argument is clear. For discerning readers, Mark presents Jesus' ministry of miracles as the embodiment of the invitation in Psalm 107 to "consider the great love of the Lord." By placing the story of Jairus' plea for mercy as the performative ideal in the heart of the matter, Mark calls readers to affirm that Jesus continues on as the one who, in the words of Colin Brown, "embodies and actualizes God's response to his people's needs."[5]

Hope at the Center
A sermon by Robert S. Reid

Sermon Text: Mark 5:21–24

Several years ago I attended a retreat in which a husband and wife told an inspiring story of receiving their daughter back from the dead. They had moved into their new home in Ellensburg, Washington when their six-year-old son ran inside, announcing that a big boy had taken his little sister from the yard. The next hour was filled with sirens, frantic searching, and telephone calls. Eventually, the police discovered her lifeless body lying face down in the waters of an irrigation ditch. Because of the icy waters she was airlifted to Seattle. Physicians there worked on her for well more than an hour without a heartbeat. Medical personnel joined the family in prayer. Finally the news came. She was alive again! She was all right. Her parents rejoiced. They had claimed the confidence of Psalm 50:15 in their prayers: "Call on me in the day of trouble; I will deliver you, and you shall glorify me." So their question for us at the retreat was, "What resources do you have to prevent, stop, or ride out an emergency?"

A woman in my small group sat stoically until someone asked about her resources. Her feelings tumbled out in a rush. "I'm thankful their daughter is alive. Of course they should rejoice. I'm glad their doctors believed in miracles. But I also 'called on the Lord in the day of trouble' when one of my closest friends had cancer. I begged and pleaded with God for deliverance. I sat in the hospital and by his bedside at home, watching this once vibrant man wither to a shrunken seventy-pound shell, and no deliverance came. How much confidence do I have in my resources? They make it sound as if the fervency of your willingness to surrender the person completely to God brings about the miracle. I don't want people who asked and got the miracle to tell me how to feel. I want people who asked and didn't get the miracle to tell me what honor I should give to God because of God's response to my prayer."

We rejoice with the parents. We despair with the woman. And we feel the dilemma. Most of us have wondered whether to have hope for a miracle, haven't we? What do you make of miracle stories in the gospels? How do you deal with them? Truth is, there's no getting around the fact that miracles are at the center of Jesus' story. More than 200 of the 425 verses in just the first ten chapters of Mark deal directly or at least indirectly with miracles. There's no getting around Jesus' miracles. They're not an appendage to his story. You can't come to him like some people want to and say, "Oh, I think Jesus was a great teacher, but I don't buy all this miracle stuff." This miracle stuff is at the center of his story.

What do you do with stories like this collection of four miracles in Mark's Gospel? In the first story, scared disciples beg Jesus to do something. And he does. He stands up and stops the raging storm. The text says that the winds cease and the sea turns dead calm. Now the disciples' eyes are popping out. They have a pretty reasonable reaction. They get scared. And Jesus looks at them and says, "What are you scared about? Don't you have any faith?" Ouch! Tell me, is faith what you think about when things get that desperate? Before we judge them too harshly, I think we need to give them enough grace just to be scared. I know I would have been. I think you would have been. No wonder they cry out, Who is this guy?

And look at the last story. Jairus was both the religious and the political leader in his community. He was the most respected elder in the town. And while Jesus was waylaid by one of its least respected daughters, some men tell Jairus not to bother. His daughter is dead. Jesus, Jairus, and the handpicked disciples have to fight their way through the gaggle of professional mourners already blocking the doorway of the home of the Right Reverend Doctor, his Honor, Mr. Mayor. And just like the disciples in the boat, Jesus has to turn to the brokenhearted man and say, "Don't get worked up; don't be afraid. Believe!" Now, I suspect I know what you would feel if the doctor pushed through the door and said, "I'm sorry Mr. Jairus, but I have some bad news…" I think we need to give poor Jairus the same grace we would want extended to us. I know if someone told me that news I'd be scared. But Jesus doesn't offer to do any grief work. He just pushes into the house, takes the child's hand, and says, Little girl, its time to wake up. And she does! You want to know what joy is? That's joy. And Jesus says, Now hush up 'bout this. What do you do with a person who *can speak* and the seas are calm, who *can speak* and the dead sit up, who *can speak* and all of creation must listen up? What do you do with him?

"Hope at the Center" 65

But don't stop here. Look at the other two miracle stories about a man possessed by a legion of demons and a woman with an intractable disease. Here's a man who didn't have any hope. He was possessed by so much evil that a herd of pigs are driven to a death frenzy as a result. When we hear the story, most of us tend to think about how it isn't fair to the pigs or to the local Association of Pork Purveyors. But the people who first heard this story didn't worry all that much about pigs or pig property rights. They were simply astounded: *that much evil*! But the hopeless man found hope. Can you feel what the first audience must have felt? "Praise God," they cried out! "No evil, no matter how great, has any power in the presence of faith in Jesus!"

And here's this woman who didn't have any hope. She had suffered a twelve-year sentence of banishment because her unstoppable bleeding was a disease that literally made her a social outcast. When we hear the story, we get caught up in the injustice of social hierarchies and medical barbarism, but the people who first heard this story were simply astounded: *twelve years of disease*! And then her faith turned hopelessness to wholeness! And those first listeners cried out, "Praise God! No disease, no matter how intractable, can persist in the presence of faith in Jesus!"

Mark provides us with four incredible stories about Jesus' power over nature, evil, disease, and death. But wait a minute. There's one more—a little piece of a story left over right in the heart of the matter. It's the first part of the Jairus story all by itself in the middle. Here is Jairus, desperately casting himself at the feet of Jesus. Now, Jairus was the one man who had everything to lose by throwing himself at the feet of Jesus. The religious bureaucracy that Jairus was part of had already labeled Jesus as persona non grata and here was the leading citizen of the community throwing himself at Jesus' feet. Why?

Because without hope does anything else really matter? I'll tell you what really matters:

> "My little daughter is at the point of death.
> Come and lay your hands on her,
> so that she may be made well, and live."

In the essential moments of your life, when you've come to the end of your rope and there are no more strings to pull, what are you going to do? What is hope worth? Will faith matter? Jairus' story is about hope at the center: all these people willing to do anything if they could just have hope, all these stories about miracles. What should we make of them? No matter how immense the evil, no matter how intractable the illness, Mark paints the picture of hope as the beginning of faith by placing the first half of Jairus' story at the heart of the matter.

Gospel stories are so filled with people experiencing miracles of healing and wholeness that, if we're not careful, they can seem like window dressing. Far from it. Miraculous intervention is a sign of the power and love of God's kingdom. It is the promise of the future breaking into our present. Miracles are surprise instances of God's promise healing a broken creation. They represent the hope of kingdom come. They are and have always been meant to be an occasion for all of God's people to proclaim God's glory. Whatever the kind of need, what matters is whether we will face it with hope in the possibilities of a God who delivers.

Imagine being an ancient Israelite who settled into captivity because you had lost hope of ever being delivered and being able to return to the promised land. The fact of the matter was that people who lost hope in that situation stopped being the people of God. They often became so comfortable in their disbelief that when the moment came they were unwilling to risk returning and were eventually assimilated away from God. Hope defined the identity of Israelites as the people of God. *But hope in what*? Truth is, I don't know why a little girl dead for hours can be resuscitated and the forty-five-year-old man still dies of cancer. Do you? I do know hope matters. I do know that however sophisticated we may think we are, if we give up on hope, we give up on God. That's why miracles matter.

No. Miracles are *not* the resource to ride out the storms of life. Faith is the resource. Faith can move us to moments when we see what God can do in our lives or maybe even see what God has been doing all along. And in that moment, when we recognize God at work, in whatever way God works in our lives, just maybe like Jesus' disciples, like the possessed man, like the ailing woman, like the man with everything at stake, we too will pause, dumbfounded, to ask, "Who is this man?" It takes faith to ask that question. It takes faith to answer it. Faith born of hope. The kind of hope that defines our identity with God. What defines your hope?

Compositional Comments

In designing this sermon I decided to take up the whole of Mark's argument strategy concerning Jesus' ministry of miracles rather than focusing on just one miracle. Because I think he presents the stories as a collective challenge to his listeners to "Have faith," my task was to design a sermon that takes up that same concern for listeners today. I wanted to design a sermon that helps listeners push past the initial question of whether miracles are still available to the more fundamental questions about their own sense of hope. In order to provoke the question for my own audience, I initially tell a story that poses two very real, strongly held responses about miracles today. I suspect that most of my listeners will find both the positions voiced too extreme. The intention is to force them to dust off their own lack of resolution about the relationship of faith, hope, and miracles.

By talking listeners through the miracle stories I am able to suggestively indicate ways in which they relate to one another. Listeners will intuitively recognize the interrelatedness of the deliverance from disaster and deliverance from death stories. Similarly, my discussion of the stories of the possessed man and the ailing woman is designed to enhance their commonality. By lifting up the way Mark has isolated the story of Jairus' faith and made it central to the four stories, I am able to separate the issue of hope from a particular act of deliverance.

The real challenge was to connect this refrain of hope to the stories in a way similar to the effect of the continuing refrain of Psalm 107. Unlike Mark, I cannot assume that my audience will make a connection to the psalm as the echo balance of the miracle stories. Connecting those dots would be cumbersome in the sermon, so I use the underlying theme of the psalm's refrain to remind listeners that Israel's faith identity is founded in hope based on the ritual reminder of redemptive history.

Without defining the appropriate position to "hold" on miracles today, the sermon design pushes through the question to suggest that hope in a God of deliverance is central to a life of faith. The initial "mystery" of what to think about miracles yields to the more important question of (re)defining hope.

Mark 6:1–52
The Seventh Narrative Complex

I HARD-HEARTED VILLAGERS (Mk. 6:1–6)

{6:1}	A		He left that place and came to his hometown, and his disciples followed him.	CAME TO HOMETOWN
{2}		B	On the sabbath he began to teach in the synagogue, and many who heard him were astounded.	MANY ASTOUNDED
			C They said, "Where did this man get all this? What is this wisdom that has been given to him? What deeds of power are being done by his hands!	QUESTION SOURCE
{3}			D Is not this the carpenter, the son of Mary and brother of James and Joses and Judas and Simon, and are not his sisters here with us?"	SON OF A WOMAN
			D' And they took offense at him.	TAKE OFFENSE
{4}			C' Then Jesus said to them, "Prophets are not without honor, except in their hometown, and among their own kin, and in their own house."	QUESTION SOURCE
{5}		B'	And he could do no deed of power there, except that he laid his hands on a few sick people and cured them.	
{6}			And he was amazed at their unbelief.	JESUS AMAZED
	A'		Then he went about among the villages teaching.	WENT AMONG VILLAGES

II THE WORK OF THE KINGDOM AND HEROD'S BANQUET (Mk. 6:7–33)

Scene 1: Disciples Commissioned to Ministry (6:7–13)

{7}	A	1		He called the twelve and began to send them out two by two,	HE SENT OUT
		2		and gave them authority over the unclean spirits.	CAST OUT DEMONS
{8}		B		He ordered them to take nothing for their journey except a staff; no bread, no bag, no money in their belts;	INSTRUCTIONS
{9}				but to wear sandals and not to put on two tunics.	
{10}		B'		He said to them, "Wherever you enter a house, stay there until you leave the place.	INSTRUCTIONS
{11}				If any place will not welcome you and they refuse to hear you, as you leave, shake off the dust that is on your feet as a testimony against them."	
{12}	A'	1'		So they went out and proclaimed that all should repent.	THEY WENT OUT
{13}		2'		They cast out many demons, and anointed with oil many who were sick and cured them.	CAST OUT DEMONS

Scene 2: Herod's Response to Jesus' Ministry (6:14–16)

{14}	A		King Herod heard of it, for Jesus' name had become known. Some were saying, "John the baptizer has been raised from the dead; and for this reason these powers are at work in him."	HEROD HEARD OF IT / IT'S JOHN
{15}		B	But others said, "It is Elijah."	ELIJAH
		B'	And others said, "It is a prophet, like one of the prophets of old."	A PROPHET
{16}	A'		But when Herod heard of it, he said, "John, whom I beheaded, has been raised."	HEROD HEARD OF IT / IT'S JOHN

Scene 3: Herod Once Feared John (6:17–20)

{17}	A		For Herod himself had sent men who arrested John, bound him, and put him in prison on account of Herodias, his brother Philip's wife,	PUT IN PRISON

				because Herod had married her.	
{18}		B		For John had been telling Herod, "It is not lawful for you to have your brother's wife."	UNRIGHTEOUSNESS / JOHN'S CHARGE
{19}			C	And Herodias had a grudge against him, and wanted to kill him.	HERODIAS' DESIRE
			C'	But she could not,	HINDERED
{20}		B'		for Herod feared John, knowing that he was a righteous and holy man,	HEROD FEARED JOHN RIGHTEOUS
	A'			and he protected him.	PROTECTED HIM

Scene 2': Herod's Feasting Undoes His Fears (6:21–29)

{21}	A				When he heard him, he was greatly perplexed; and yet he liked to listen to him.	JOHN KEPT ALIVE
		B	1		But an opportunity came when Herod on his birthday gave a banquet for his courtiers and officers and for the leaders of Galilee.	HERODIAS' OPPORTUNITY
{22}			2		When his daughter Herodias came in and danced,	THE TEMPTATION
			3		she pleased Herod and his guests;	HEROD PLEASED
			C		and the king said to the girl, "Ask me for whatever you wish, and I will give it."	HEROD OFFERS
{23}					And he solemnly swore to her, "Whatever you ask me, I will give you, even half of my kingdom."	SWEARS AN OATH / HEROD EXPECTS A CHILD'S EXTRAVAGANCE?
{24}				D	She went out and said to her mother, "What should I ask for?" She replied, "The head of John the baptizer."	JOHN'S DEATH
{25}				D'	Immediately she rushed back to the king and requested, "I want you to give me at once the head of John the Baptist on a platter."	JOHN'S DEATH
{26}			C'		The king was deeply grieved; yet out of regard for his oaths and for the guests, he did not want to refuse her.	FULFILLS OATH
{27}		B'	1		Immediately the king sent a soldier of the guard with orders to bring John's head.	HEROD ORDERS DEATH
{28}			2		He went and beheaded him in the prison, brought his head on a platter, and gave it to the girl.	JOHN IS EXECUTED
			3		Then the girl gave it to her mother.	HERODIAS PLEASED
{29}	A'				When his disciples heard about it, they came and took his body, and laid it in a tomb.	JOHN'S BODY TAKEN

Scene 1': Disciples Regather (6:30–33)

{30}	1		The apostles gathered around Jesus, and told him all that they had done and taught.	APOSTLES RETURN
{31}			He said to them, "Come away to a deserted place all by yourselves and rest a while."	DESERTED PLACE
	2		For many were coming and going, and they had no leisure even to eat.	MANY WERE COMING / NO LEISURE
{32}	1'		And they went away in the boat to a deserted place by themselves.	DESERTED PLACE
{33}	2'		Now many saw them going and recognized them, and they hurried there on foot from all the towns and arrived ahead of them.	MANY SAW THEM GOING

II' THE WORK OF THE KINGDOM AND JESUS' BANQUET (Mk. 6:34–45)

{34}	A	As he went ashore, he saw a great crowd; and he had compassion for them, because they were like sheep without a shepherd; and he began to teach them many things.	COMES ASHORE / GATHERS A CROWD

{35}   B   When it grew late, his disciples came to him
           and said, "This is a deserted place,
           and the hour is now very late;
{36}   send them away so that they may go
           into the surrounding country and villages
           and buy something for themselves to eat."   NOT ENOUGH TO EAT
{37}   C   But he answered them,
             "You give them something to eat."   FEED THEM
             D   They said to him, "Are we to go
                 and buy two hundred denarii worth of bread,
                 and give it to them to eat?"   GIVE IT TO THEM?
{38}   E   And he said to them, "How many loaves   HOW MANY?
                     have you? Go and see."
                     When they had found out, they said, "Five, FIVE AND TWO
                     and two fish."
                     F   Then he ordered them to get all the people
                         to sit down in groups on the green grass. GROUPS
{39}
{40}   F' So they sat down in groups of hundreds GROUPS
                             and of fifties.
{41}   E' Taking the five loaves and the two fish, FIVE AND TWO
                     he looked up to heaven, and blessed
                     and broke the loaves,   BLESSED AND BROKE
                 D' and gave them to his disciples
                     to set before the people;   GIVE IT TO THEM
                     and he divided the two fish among them all.
{42}   C' And all ate and were filled;   ALL ATE
{43}   B' and they took up twelve baskets full   TWELVE BASKET
           of broken pieces and of the fish.   SURPLUS
{44}   those who had eaten the loaves
           numbered five thousand men.
{45} A' Immediately he made his disciples get into the boat DISCIPLES DEPART
          and go on ahead to the other side, to Bethsaida,   BY BOAT
          while he dismissed the crowd.   JESUS DISMISSES CROWD

I' HEART-HARDENED DISCIPLES (Mk. 6:46–52)
{46}   A   After saying farewell to them,
           he went up on the mountain to pray.   PRAYER
{47}   B   When evening came, the boat was out on the sea, BOAT
             and he was alone on the land.
{48}   When he saw that they were straining at the oars
             against an adverse wind, he came towards them   WIND ARISES
             early in the morning, walking on the sea.
               C   He intended to pass them by.[1]   "PASS THEM BY"
{49}   D   But when they saw him walking on the sea, THEY SAW HIM
                     they thought it was a ghost and cried out; TERRIFIED
{50}   D' for they all saw him and were terrified. THEY SAW HIM
                                                               TERRIFIED
               C' But immediately he spoke to them and said,
                   "Take heart, it is I; do not be afraid."   "*EGO EMI*": FEAR NOT
{51}   B' Then he got into the boat with them   BOAT
             and the wind ceased.   WIND CEASES
          A' And they were utterly astounded,   DISCIPLES AMAZED
{52}   for they did not understand about the loaves,   LACK OF UNDERSTANDING
             but their hearts were hardened.

The Rhetorical Shape of the Narrative Complex

Since most critical examinations of this complex have been deeply involved in presenting or defending viewpoints on the nature of the miracle of the feeding of five thousand, it may be fair to say that many have quite missed the point of Mark's fictive argument. Episode II', the feeding of five thousand hungry listeners, functions as a proleptic eucharist-banquet and is offered in comparison to the Herodian banquet of indulgence and death in Episode II. However, by begining and ending the story of Herod's banquet with scenes of Jesus commissioning disciples to engage in ministry and listening to the results, both episodes (II and II') are placed in a context of the mission and ministry of the commissioned disciples. By their actions these disciples demonstrate the ideal of what it means to become the leaders and bearers of faith within the post-resurrection community.

As presented here, the bookends for this narrative complex juxtapose the rejection of the heart-hardened villagers of Jesus' hometown in Episode I and the heart-hardened disciples who refuse to understand the evidence before their own eyes in Episode I'. For the most part, critics have not viewed the material gathered together here as a single, thematically unified collection.[2] However, the framing episodes appear to indicate that Mark has returned to the motif, raised in the fourth narrative complex, presenting those with the most opportunity to understand as people who missed the point. In addition, the focus on the commissioning of the disciples in the heart of the fourth narrative complex is also explored in greater depth in the heart of the present collection. The repetition of these same, thematically interrelated motifs signals the unity of this collection.

The juxtaposition of the episodes in the seventh narrative complex can be visualized thus:

```
I   HARD-HEARTED VILLAGERS                              Mk. 6:1–6
 II  THE WORK OF THE KINGDOM AND HEROD'S BANQUET        Mk. 6:7–33
      Scene 1: Disciples Commissioned to Ministry        (vv. 7–13)
      Scene 2: Herod's Response to Jesus' Ministry       (vv. 14–16)
      Scene 3: Herod Once Feared John                    (vv. 17–20)
      Scene 2': Herod's Feasting Undoes His Fears        (vv. 21–29)
      Scene 1': Disciples Regather                       (vv. 30–33)
 II' THE WORK OF THE KINGDOM AND JESUS' BANQUET         Mk. 6:30–45
I'  HEART-HARDENED DISCIPLES                             Mk. 6:46–52
```

The Central Motif

The story of Herod's fall and the sacrifice of the Baptist dominates this collection, interrupting the story of Jesus' Galilean ministry.[3] It offers one of Mark's rare instances of narrative indirection, in which he tells Jesus' story through another character. But unlike the scenes in which Judas and the chief priests plot Jesus' death

(Mk. 14:10–11) or Peter denies Jesus (14:66–72), only here does our narrator let Jesus almost wholly recede from view and usher another cast of characters to act out their own brief, ill-fated script on center stage. We are so accustomed to reading this story by way of its invariable title, "Death of John the Baptist," we may actually miss the fact that this is really Herod's tale. This Herod is Antipas, the Tetrarch over Galilee and Perea who governed from 4 B.C. to A.D. 39 Mark, alone, calls him "king," an official title that Herod coveted and an ambition that eventually led to his being stripped of all position and banished.

Told in five scenes, this story is narratively bracketed (Scenes 1 and 1') by the depictions of Jesus "sending out" the Twelve. Mark makes the leap out of Jesus' story by suggesting that Herod feared Jesus because of the rumors that Jesus was John come back from the dead (cf. 8:28). As René Girard notes, persecutors often have difficulty believing definitively in the death of their victims. They have been known to unintentionally give birth to belief in a consecrated resurrection of those on whom they have perpetrated their sacrificial violence.[4] Mark does not report these rumors in a way that his readers would seriously consider this notion of a consecrated resurrection or reimbodiment of John, Elijah, or one of the prophets. Yet, readers cannot escape the sense in which the story, told in "flashback," presents John as the prototype scapegoat and sets up the thematic expectation of another who would be sacrificed as "a ransom for many" (10:45). However, the narrative purpose of Scene 2 is to introduce Herod as author of the violent death of the Baptist.

Scene 3 clarifies this narrative tension. On one hand, Herod keeps John alive because he fears him as a prophet. On the other hand, Herodias desires that the Baptist be put to death for his impudent challenge to her marriage. Herod is depicted as torn between his desire to satisfy his own interests and his desire to fulfill godly expectations of being considered a "righteous king" (cf. Jos. *Ant.* 18.5.2). Herodias is depicted as having lost some of her prior influence over Herod because she was unable to get him to put the Baptist to death for her.

Scene 2' brings the story of Herod's competing desires to its tragic climax. Herodias knows well that Herod can be seduced into betraying prior commitments and uses her own daughter to reassert her influence. Part of the scandal of this story is that these banqueting men are depicted as highly "pleased" with seeing Herod's adolescent stepdaughter do the "dance of prostitutes." Regardless of the real

Salome's age, Mark purposefully represents her as a "girl." The Greek word used to describe her is a diminutive form of the word for a young woman. Herod's unrestrained magnanimity is depicted as hyperbole directed to a child who would be expected to ask for a childish reward. The scene unfolds with the inevitable tragedy of Herod's flawed weaknesses and desire to "have it all." Whatever intentions he may have entertained that he "feared" or "listened" to the prophet of righteousness, these are finally betrayed by his own unrighteous desires to play the "king" before the audience of his gathered court.

Mark returns to the primary narrative with Scene 1'. The disciples regather and report the results of their ministry in his name. By framing the Herod story in this way, Mark depicts the "king's" moral failure of leadership in direct contrast with a story of the disciple's first efforts to exercise leadership as ones who were "sent out" by Jesus (6:7). Telling the story this way poses the question for readers, "What does Jesus commissioning of the Twelve as ones who are 'sent out' have to do with the story of Herod's fall and the sacrifice of the Baptist?" Sending his followers without many provisions certainly contrasts with the lavish consumption at Herod's banquet, but the key is found in Mark's *only* use of the words "send out" to describe the mission of the Twelve. The word "apostle" is a transliteration of the Greek "to send out" in this story. In surrounding the story of Herod's fall and the sacrifice of John with the apostolic commission, Mark clarifies what he believes to be the task of the apostolic leaders of the church following the sacrifice of Jesus. Werner Kelber states the matter succinctly: "As John's death coincided with the sending out of the disciples-apostles, so will Jesus' death usher in their mission."[5]

If "apostle" was obviously a word filled with meaning from the vantage point of the church for whom Mark wrote, "shepherd" was equally as meaningful. In the opening segment of the point-of-turning episode of this collection, Mark tells us that Jesus "had compassion for [his listeners], because they were like sheep without a shepherd" (6:34). The Greek word for "shepherd" gets translated elsewhere in the epistles as "pastor" (Eph. 4:11). First Peter makes the implications of this metaphoric usage quite clear by applying this same reference to readers, "For you were going astray like sheep, but now you have returned to the shepherd and guardian of your soul" (1 Pet. 2:25; cf. 1 Pet. 5:2–4; Heb. 13:20).[6] The Greek word translated as "guardian" is literally the "*episkopon* of your soul." The point is that the image of Jesus as the Great Shepherd was developed in the early church with reference to the leadership role of pastor as undershepherd. Mark's use of such language was highly freighted for those who first read this Gospel. In the context of this story, Jesus is being affirmed as the Great Shepherd who sends out the undershepherds to meet the needs of his sheep.[7] The verbal contacts between this passage and the eucharist story in Mark 14:22–26 justify Taylor's observation that Mark has conformed the vocabulary of this story to that of the final passion meal as if this story anticipates the eucharistic ministry of the church.[8]

As fictive argument, this could be called the church in prospect collection. On the other hand, Mark uses the framing episodes functionally to contrast this ideal of church leadership with his own present reality. By juxtaposing the Twelve as hard-hearted followers who did not comprehend who Jesus really was with readers who are able to unlock the secret of the kingdom through allusions to Jesus' sacrificial death and his continued post-resurrection presence as Lord of the church (e.g., "Take heart, it is I [*ego emi*]; do not be afraid."), Mark appears to be addressing a significant gap between the ideal ministry of the Twelve as sent out by Jesus and the expression of that ministry of leadership in his own day. We will discover that this fictive argument is repeated in the parallel collection of the Galilean ministry meta-narrative, 7:31—8:25, and in many of the remaining narrative collections of the Gospel.

Mark 6:53—7:31
The Eighth Narrative Complex

I JEWISH CROWDS HEALED BY JESUS (Mk. 6:53–56)

{53}	1	When they had crossed over, they came to land at Gennasaret and moored the boat.	JESUS TRAVELS
{54}	2	When they got out of the boat, people at once recognized him,	
{55}		and rushed about that whole region and began to bring the sick on mats	PEOPLE BRING THE SICK TO BE HEALED
	3	to wherever they heard he was.	BRING TO LOCATION
{56}	1'	And wherever he went, into villages or cities or farms,	JESUS TRAVELS
	2'	they laid the sick in the marketplaces, and begged him that they might touch even the fringe of his cloak;	PEOPLE BRING THE SICK TO BE HEALED
	3'	and all who touched it were healed.	HEALS THROUGH TOUCH

II PHARISEES CONFRONT JESUS ABOUT UNCLEANNESS (Mk. 7:1–13)

Scene 1 (7:1–5)

{7:1}	A	Now when the Pharisees and some of the scribes who had come from Jerusalem gathered around him,	PHARISEES NOTICE PRACTICE
{2}		they noticed that some of his disciples were eating with defiled hands, that is, without washing them.	
{3}	B	(For the Pharisees, and all the Jews, do not eat unless they thoroughly wash their hands, thus observing the tradition of the elders;	PHARISEE PRACTICE
{4}	B'	and they do not eat anything from the market unless they wash it; and there are also many other traditions that they observe, the washing of cups, pots, and bronze kettles.)	PHARISEE PRACTICE
{5}	A'	So the Pharisees and the scribes asked him, "Why do your disciples not live according to the tradition of the elders, but eat with defiled hands?"	PHARISEES COMMENT ON PRACTICE

Scene 2 (7:6–8)

{6}	A	He said to them, "Isaiah prophesied rightly about you hypocrites, as it is written,	WRITTEN IN PROPHETS
	B	'This people honors me with their lips, but their hearts are far from me;	HONOR
{7}	B'	in vain do they worship me, teaching human precepts as doctrines.'	VAIN
{8}	A'	You abandon the commandment of God and hold to human tradition."	TRADITION OF ELDERS

Scene 3 (7:9–13)

{9}	A	Then he said to them, "You have a fine way of rejecting the commandment of God in order to keep your tradition!	COMMANDMENT OF GOD
{10}	B	For Moses said, 'Honor your father and your mother'; and, 'Whoever speaks evil of father or mother must surely die.'	COMMANDMENT TO HONOR PARENTS
{11}	B'	But you say that if anyone tells father or mother, 'Whatever support you might have had from me is Corban' (that is, an offering to God)—	SUBVERTING THE COMMANDMENT
{12}		then you no longer permit doing anything for a father or mother,	NO HONOR FOR PARENTS

| {13} | A' | thus making void the word of God through your tradition that you have handed on. And you do many things like this." | WORD OF GOD |

II' DISCIPLES ARE CONFUSED ABOUT UNCLEANNESS (Mk. 7:14–23)
Saying 1 (7:14–16)

{14}	A	Then he called the crowd again and said to them, "Listen to me, all of you, and understand:	LISTEN
{15}	B	there is nothing outside a person	EXTERNAL THINGS
		that by going in	GOING IN
		can defile,	DEFILE
	B'	but the things	INTERNAL THINGS
		that come out	COMING OUT
		are what defile."	DEFILE
{16}	A'	[Let anyone with ears to hear listen][1]	LISTEN

Saying 2 (7:17–19)

{17}	A	When he had left the crowd and entered the house, his disciples asked him about the parable.	WAS THIS A PARABLE?
{18}	B	He said to them, "Then do you also fail to understand?	FAIL TO UNDERSTAND?
	B' a	Do you not see that whatever goes into a person from outside	NOTHING FROM OUTSIDE
	b	cannot defile,	DEFILES
{19}	b'	since it enters, not the heart but the stomach,	IT JUST PASSES THROUGH
	a'	and goes out into the sewer?"	
	A'	(Thus he declared all foods clean.)	INTERPRETIVE ADDITION

Saying 3 (7:20–23)

{20}	A	And he said, "It is what comes out of a person that defiles.	WHAT DEFILES
{21}	B	For it is from within, from the human heart, that evil intentions come:	FROM WITHIN
	B'	fornication, theft, murder,	FROM WITHIN
{22}		adultery, avarice, wickedness, deceit, licentiousness, envy, slander, pride, folly.	
{23}	A'	All these evil things come from within, and they defile a person."	WHAT DEFILES

I' A GENTILE WOMAN'S DAUGHTER HEALED BY JESUS (Mk. 7:24–31)

{24}	A	From there he set out and went away to the region of Tyre. He entered a house and did not want anyone to know he was there.	TYRE
	B a	Yet he could not escape notice, but a woman	
{25}		whose little daughter had an unclean spirit immediately heard about him,	UNCLEAN SPIRIT
	b	and she came and bowed down at his feet.	BOWED
{26}	b'	Now the woman was a Gentile, of Syrophoenician origin.	GENTILE
	a'	She begged him to cast the demon out of her daughter.	DEMON
{27}	C	He said to her, "Let the children be fed first, for it is not fair to take the children's food and throw it to the dogs."	DOGS AS SCAVENGERS
{28}	C'	But she answered him, "Sir, even the dogs under the table eat the children's crumbs."	DOGS AS PETS
{29}	B' 1	Then he said to her, "For saying that, you may go—	
	2	the demon has left your daughter."	
{30}	1'	So she went home,	
	2'	found the child lying on the bed, and the demon gone.	HEALED AT HOME
{31}	A'	Then he returned from the region of Tyre, and went by way of Sidon towards the Sea of Galilee, in the region of the Decapolis.	TYRE

The Rhetorical Shape of the Narrative Complex

Virtually all critics agree that Mark 7:1–23 offers a unified collection of topically arranged material clarifying the nature of Jesus' confrontation with Jewish particularism. Rhetorical analysis demonstrates that the collection is framed by two additional episodes at 6:53–56 and 7:24–31. Recognition that the narrative structure places these two episodes parallel with each other makes what otherwise might appear to be minor details in these stories take on greater importance.

The stories of Jesus' confronting Jewish particularism and his own disciples' confusion need to be read in light of the framing stories of people who exercise faith. Note especially that the Gentile woman exercises faith beyond that of the Jewish crowds who bring people to be touched in order to effect a healing. The Gentile woman is depicted as assuming Jesus can heal without being physically present. This idea would not be lost on the post-resurrection community, who also trusted that Jesus could continue to heal even if he is no longer able to be physically present. This contrast between Jewish and Gentile expressions of faith in Sections I and I' reveals the essential contrast in Mark's fictive argument concerning the Gentile mission at the heart of the ninth narrative complex.

The episodes in the interior of this collection fall into two natural divisions: 7:1–13 and 7:14–23. Both are divided into three scenes. Scene 1 of both Episodes II and II' sets the context of the confrontation over defilement as prescribed by the teaching of the elders and then according to Jesus. In Scene 2 of both Episodes II and II', Jesus indicts the religious leadership for having transformed the morality of God into the legality of tradition and then uses a pointed lesson differentiating the biology of the digestive system from the metaphysics of the human heart to demonstrate the contradiction of the human tradition. In Scene 3 of both Episode II and Episode II', Jesus lists the kind of evil God's morality condemns and then offers a vivid example of the way human tradition had turned such behavior into sacred observance.[2]

The juxtaposition of the episodes in the first narrative complex can be visualized thus:

```
 I  JEWISH CROWDS HEALED BY JESUS                    Mk. 6:53–56
   II  PHARISEES CONFRONT JESUS ABOUT UNCLEANNESS    Mk. 7:1–13)
       Scene 1                                       (vv. 1–5)
       Scene 2                                       (vv. 6–8)
       Scene 3                                       (vv. 9–13)
```

II'	DISCIPLES ARE CONFUSED ABOUT UNCLEANNESS	Mk. 7:14–23
	Saying 1	(vv. 14–16)
	Saying 2	(vv. 17–19)
	Saying 3	(vv. 20–23)
I'	A GENTILE WOMAN'S DAUGHTER HEALED BY JESUS	Mk. 7:24–31

The Central Motif

Critics regularly note that Mark wrote his Gospel for Gentile Christians who were familiar with the Hebrew scriptures but unaware of the contemporary traditions and practices of pious Palestinian Jews. The explanations offered in Episode II, Scene 1, as well as his consistent interpretation of Aramaic phrases indicate that Mark assumed that the majority of his audience was unfamiliar with the specific content of these religious observations. His parenthetical asides are one of the two main rhetorical strategies for an author to establish point of view. In the *Rhetoric of Fiction*, Wayne Booth argues that an author may shift the point of view by either dramatizing the point he or she wishes to make or by stepping out of the role of the storyteller to comment directly, but in either contrivance "one eye is always on the reader."[3]

The inclusion of the explanatory material certainly suggests that Mark believed the stories would have a very specific application in the life of the congregation for whom he composed this Gospel. Clearly some form of Jewish particularism was still a formulative factor in the church to which he speaks. Long after the first Christian Pentecost, issues of Jewish particularism—concerning what one could and could not eat, do, or have association with—plagued the early church at Jerusalem as witnessed in the story recounted by Paul in Galatians 2:11–16. It was representatives of the Jerusalem church who came down to Antioch to oppose Peter's custom of eating with Gentiles (cf. Mk. 3:22–30). Paul confronted Peter when he withdrew from the "defiling behavior" by charging, "If you, though a Jew, live like a Gentile and not like a Jew, how can you compel the Gentiles to live like Jews?" (Gal. 2:14). Paul labels this activity as not "acting consistently with the truth of the gospel." Yet, pressure from the Jerusalem church was such that Peter did withdraw from the practice of eating with the Gentiles, effectively labeling them as second-class Christians.[4] By drawing on this example in the letter to the Galatians, Paul makes it obvious that the matter of Jewish particularism in the church was still as pressing a problem as it was when he first confronted Peter with the hypocrisy years earlier.

Only the most radical voices in the early church argued for the complete dissociation of Christianity from Judaistic practice and

Mark's was among them. He depicts Jesus as irrevocably indicting the oral tradition of the elders that lay at the heart of Jewish particularism. In spite of the circumlocutions of our translations, Mark's Jesus could not be more blunt in his analysis of Judaism's religious teachings. References to digestive organs and sewer systems in the present narrative obscure the forcefulness of Jesus' explanation. We might paraphrase, "It is not what you eat and defecate that makes you unclean. No, it is the evil actions and vices excreted from your hearts that defile." And even here I am supplying once-removed, clinical language that may obscure the bluntness of Jesus' words. The point is, however crude or descriptively euphemistic Jesus' words may have been, Mark tells the story in a way that his first-century readers could hardly keep from supplying the shocking language themselves. Matthew makes use of this tradition and adds the report that "the Pharisees took offense when they heard" this (Mt. 15:12), but for Jesus to have described the most sacred teachings of a religion in this manner would certainly justify a far more vitriolic response. Such a vulgar way to summarize and dismiss the totality of Jewish sacred observance would have been unforgivable for any who heard it. With this assessment on Jesus' lips, Mark has Jesus irrevocably severed any Christian relationship with Jewish observance. If this were not sufficiently explicit, Mark spells out the implications in an aside for his own readers: "Thus he declared all foods clean."

We need to keep in mind that Mark's readers would have been stunned to hear that Jesus had said such things, not because they would have been embarrassed about interfaith relationships. Rather, they would have wondered why, if Jesus had really said such things, the leaders of the oral tradition in the church, the community of the Twelve, were still clinging to such outmoded observances. It would have been a shocking indictment of the "Apostolic" desire to accommodate this kind of Jewish particularism in the Jerusalem church. Mark has none of Luke's patience in such matters (cf. Acts 10:1—11:18). To cling to outmoded Jewish particularism is "a denial of the gospel."

Any doubts that Mark argues in favor of an expedited Gentile mission are dispelled by the way the framing stories add to the overall motif of the complex. In the first story, which takes place in Gennesaret, Jewish crowds beg for Jesus' touch in order to be healed. In the parallel story the Gentile woman in the region of Tyre comes to Jesus with a request of healing for her child who is still at home. The contrast is inevitable. Mark has demonstrated his impatience with the racist implications of the Jerusalem church's practice (and inaction) by depicting the faith of the Gentile woman as greater than that of her Jewish counterparts. Mark has laid his cards on the table in this climactic collection. He has no patience with a leadership incapable of deciding between being a sect of Judaism or the necessity to assume the urgent task of the Gentile mission.

Mark is the John Hancock of the early church. On March 5, 1770, four British regiments killed several citizens of Boston in their efforts to quell an unruly mob. Even though most of the blame lay with the mob, the historian Ronald Reid notes that Bostonian colonists felt "unencumbered by anything as trivial as the truth," and declared the event a "massacre."[5] On March 5, Hancock used a speech commemorating "The Boston Massacre" to inspire a rebellion of affiliation, from allegiance to the laws of Parliament to a rule of law to be determined by elected deputies to a new Continental Congress. His speech was heard by several thousand Bostonians and went through five pamphlets. Its incendiary rhetoric inflamed the sensibilities of colonists and became a significant factor in fomenting the revolt against Parliamentary rule in the colonies.[6] Like Hancock, Mark has little patience for those who cannot see the need to declare a new allegiance. In this climactic collection of the Galilean ministry metanarrative, he demands that his readers see ("Do you not see…" 7:18), telling his story of Jesus in a way that makes the necessity of declaring a new allegiance abundantly clear. Whatever doubts could yet remain concerning the real mission of the church are taken up and addressed in the next narrative collection.[7]

Mark 7:32—8:27
The Ninth Narrative Complex

I THE FIRST SPIT STORY (Mk. 7:32–37)

{32}	A	They brought to him a deaf man who had an impediment in his speech; and they begged him to lay his hand on him.	DEAF MAN REQUEST
{33}	B	He took him aside in private, away from the crowd, and put his fingers into his ears,	TOOK ASIDE
	C	and he spat and touched his tongue.	SPIT/TOUCHED TONGUE
{34}	D	Then looking up to heaven, he sighed and said to him, "Ephphatha," that is, "Be opened."	OPEN EARS?
{35}	D'	And immediately his ears were opened,	EARS OPENED
	C'	his tongue was released, and he spoke plainly.	TONGUE RELEASED
{36}	B'	Then Jesus ordered them to tell no one; but the more he ordered them, the more zealously they proclaimed it.	THE PROBLEM OF CROWDS / THE PROBLEM OF APPROBATION
{37}	A'	They were astounded beyond measure, saying, "He has done everything well; he even makes the deaf to hear and the mute to speak."	THE DEAF HEAR

II THE SECOND FEEDING MIRACLE (IN DECAPOLIS?) (Mk. 8:1–9)

{8:1}	A	a	In those days when there was again a great crowd without anything to eat,	NOTHING TO EAT
{2}		b	he called his disciples and said to them, "I have compassion for the crowd, because they have been with me now for three days and have nothing to eat.	COMPASSION
{3}		b'	If I send them away hungry to their homes, they will faint on the way— and some of them have come from a great distance."	SEND THEM AWAY? / THEY WILL FAINT
{4}		a'	His disciples replied, "How can one feed these people with bread here in the desert?"	NOTHING TO EAT
{5–6}	B		He asked them, "How many loaves do you have?" They said, "Seven."	SEVEN
	C	1	Then he ordered the crowd to sit down on the ground; and he took the seven loaves,	TOOK LOAVES
		2	and after giving thanks he broke them and gave them to his disciples to distribute;	BLESSED
		3	and they distributed them to the crowd.	GAVE TO CROWD
{7}	C'	1'	They had also a few small fish;	TOOK FISH
		2'	and after blessing them, he ordered that these too should be distributed.	BLESSED
{8}		3'	They ate and were filled;	CROWD FILLED
	B'		and they took up the broken pieces left over, seven baskets full.	SEVEN
{9}	A'		Now there were about four thousand people. And he sent them away.	SENT THEM AWAY

III INTERPRETING THE SIGN (Mk. 8:10–21)

Scene 1: The Pharisees Don't Get It (8:10–13)

{10}	A	And immediately he got into the boat with his disciples and went to the district of Dalmanutha.	BOAT TRIP JEWISH SIDE
{11}	B	The Pharisees came and began to argue with him, asking him for a sign from heaven, to test him.	ASKING FOR A SIGN
{12}	B'	And he sighed deeply in his spirit and said, "Why does this generation ask for a sign? Truly I tell you, no sign will be given to this generation."	NO SIGN
{13}	A'	And he left them, and getting into the boat again, he went across to the other side.	BOAT TRIP BACK TO GENTILE SIDE

Scene 2: The Disciples Don't Get It (8:14–16)

{14}	A	Now the disciples had forgotten to bring any bread; and they had only one loaf with them in the boat.	FORGOTTEN TO BRING BREAD
{15}	B	And he cautioned them, saying, "Watch out!	WATCH OUT!
	B'	beware of the yeast of the Pharisees and the yeast of Herod."	BEWARE!
{16}	A'	They said to one another, "It is because we have no bread."	CONFERRED HAVE NO BREAD

Scene 3: Does Anyone Get It? (8:17–21)

{17}	A	And becoming aware of it, Jesus said to them, "Why are you talking about having no bread? Do you still not perceive or understand? Are your hearts hardened?	DO YOU NOT UNDERSTAND?
{18}		Do you have eyes, and fail to see? Do you have ears, and fail to hear? And do you not remember?	
{19}	B	When I broke the five loaves for the five thousand, how many baskets full of broken pieces did you collect?" They said to him, "Twelve."	DO THE NUMBERS
{20}	B'	"And the seven for the four thousand, how many baskets full of broken pieces did you collect?" And they said to him, "Seven."	DO THE NUMBERS
{21}	A'	Then he said to them, "Do you not yet understand?"	DO YOU NOT UNDERSTAND?

I' THE SECOND SPIT STORY (Mk. 8:22–27a)

{22}	A	They came to Bethsaida. Some people brought a blind man to him and begged him to touch him.	BETHSAIDA
{23}	B	He took the blind man by the hand and led him out of the village;	AWAY FROM VILLAGE
	C	and when he had put saliva on his eyes and laid his hands on him,	LAID HANDS ON EYES
	D	he asked him, "Can you see anything?"	"CAN YOU SEE?"
{24}	D'	And the man looked up and said, "I can see people, but they look like trees, walking."	"I CAN SEE…BUT…"
{25}	C'	Then Jesus laid his hands on his eyes again; and he looked intently and his sight was restored, and he saw everything clearly.	LAID HANDS ON EYES AGAIN
{26}	B'	Then he sent him away to his home, saying, "Do not even go into the village."	NOT GO BACK TO VILLAGE
{27a}	A'	Jesus went on with his disciples to the villages of Caesarea Philippi;	CAESAREA PHILIPPI

The Rhetorical Shape of the Narrative Complex

The current complex follows the point-of-turning collection of the Galilean ministry meta-narrative (4:35—9:29):

6th	4:35—5:43	I	The Miracle Collection: focusing on call to have faith
7th	6:1–52	II	The Church in Prospect Collection includes the feeding of the five thousand narrative framed by episodes of doubt and misunderstanding
8th	6:53—7:30	III	Public Confrontation Collection: Jesus' repudiation of the tradition of the elders.
9th	7:31—8:25	II'	The Gentile Mission in Prospect Collection includes the feeding of the four thousand narrative punctuated by incomprehension and misunderstanding
10th	8:26—9:29	I'	The Central Climactic Narrative—A Radical Call to Listen and Live, including the miracle of the transfiguration and the miracle of healing the epileptic.

These five collections are arranged as an inversion covering the period of Jesus' teaching ministry while journeying back and forth across the Sea of Galilee.[1] The first and last complexes (sixth and tenth) raise the questions "Who then is this?"/"Who do people say that I am?" and call for faith in Jesus as the one to whom people "cry out to the Lord" in their trouble. The climactic center (the eighth complex) depicts Jesus as willing to engage in battle over the essence of how one is to express faith in God. In the subordinate position on either side of the central narrative are two widely recognized parallel complexes concerned with the ministry of the church in prospect and the Gentile mission in prospect. Identifying these discrete collections and their relationship to one another is an essential element in grasping the fictive argument Mark conducts in the way he structures the overarching meta-narrative of the Gospel.

For the current narrative, the framing stories about the cure of the deaf-mute and the blind man, Episodes I and I', form striking parallels. Note that both cures are performed in semiprivacy, by means of spit and the laying on of hands, and include a charge to maintain secrecy. In each story Jesus avoids the crowds or crowded places and attempts to discourage attention from the nearby villagers. Taylor finds that "the agreements are so many, so close, and so striking that it is not surprising that several critics regard the narratives as duplicate accounts of the same incident."[2] The stories also complement one another: The opening story demonstrates Jesus' power to heal defective human hearing, and the closing story demonstrates Jesus' power to heal defective human seeing. The healing stories function metaphorically, depicting the inability to understand of both the Pharisees and the Twelve. The latter story, which is without parallel in the other gospels, offers a proleptic word of faith to suggest that all is not lost for the dense disciples. Just as the blind man moves from obscure sight to clarity, so it will be (needs to be?) with the disciples.[3]

The second feeding miracle ostensibly occurs in the Gentile territory of the Decapolis (7:31). Jesus does not return to Galilee until after the miracle when he travels by boat to the district of Dalmanutha (8:10). Mark makes redundant use of the verb "to serve" in order to highlight, once again, the role of the disciples. They were the ones who enacted this grace by taking meager portions out in order to feed the racially mixed group of listeners. Provision comes as they step out in faith.

In the central point-of-turning story, Episode II', Mark takes up the implications of the feeding miracle in three scenes. First, Jesus encounters the Pharisees in the district of Dalmanutha, but rather than further debate, we are told merely that the leaders of the piety party were seeking a sign—a request that discourages Jesus. In the second scene Jesus uses the opportunity of a discussion over bread to warn the disciples of the "yeast" of the Pharisees and of Herod, but the disciples "don't get it." So in the third scene Mark's Jesus enigmatically *enumerates* the meaning of the feeding miracles and their relationship to the essential thing he wants them to understand. Of course, the real question Mark poses for readers is "Why are the disciples so dense?" Mark's Jesus is stunned and wonders aloud whether the hearts of the Twelve are so hardened that they will never "get it."[4]

The juxtaposition of the episodes in the ninth narrative complex can be visualized thus:

```
I   THE FIRST SPIT STORY                              Mk. 7:32–37
II  THE SECOND FEEDING MIRACLE (IN DECAPOLIS?)        Mk. 8:1–9
II' INTERPRETING THE SIGN                             Mk. 8:10–21
        Scene 1: The Pharisees Don't Get It               (vv. 10–13)
        Scene 2: The Disciples Don't Get It               (vv. 14–16)
        Scene 3: Does Anyone Get It?                      (vv. 17–21)
I'  THE SECOND SPIT STORY                             Mk. 8:22–27a
```

The Central Motif

The key that unlocks the secret to this collection is Jesus' metaphysical mathematics. He asks, "When I broke the five loaves for the five thousand, how many baskets full of broken pieces did you collect?" They said to him, "Twelve." "And the seven for the four thousand, how many baskets full of broken pieces did you collect?" And they said to him, "Seven." "Don't you get it, yet?" Of course, the question is whether anyone "gets it." This time even the reader strains with the disciples to interpret the numbers. No one wants to be an uncomprehending dunderhead.

Numerous proposals have been made by critics who have attempted to calculate the meaning of these numbers. One of the most satisfying is that advanced by John Drury. Drury approaches the text as if it is a narrative puzzle in which Mark has already alluded to all the clues necessary to solve the riddle.[5] The idea of a certain number of loaves has already been referred to once in the Gospel at 2:25–26 in which Mark has Jesus recount the story of David and the showbread from 1 Samuel 21. The regulations concerning the necessity of maintaining twelve loaves of showbread on the altar are detailed in Leviticus 24. In the Old Testament story, David took five of these loaves, and in the feeding of the five thousand, Jesus is described as also taking five loaves. Jesus multiplies five loaves to meet the need of all his Jewish audience. In the present narrative complex, Jesus takes seven loaves (the number remaining from the Samuel story) and breaks them for the racially mixed audience. There were twelve basketfuls remaining for the twelve tribes of Israel after the first feeding, but there are seven basketfuls left over in the current story. The number seven in biblical numerology is the sacred number of fulfillment. Seven loaves and seven baskets is more resolved than five loaves and twelve basketfuls. The story of the feeding of the four thousand brings the promise of the unresolved numbers of showbread on the altar to a cabalistic resolution. Drury writes, "This is polemical arithmetic in a story about the relation of the new Kingdom of Christ to the old Kingdom of David, [and] the continuity and the discontinuity between them."[6]

If Drury's arithmetic is correct, the solution to the puzzle represents another challenge to engage in the Gentile mission: The sacred numbers will not be fulfilled until all the Gentiles who belong to God are also brought into the sphere of the kingdom. The implication for the church in Mark's day is that trying either to have it all like Herod or to wait for vindication like the Pharisees misses the point. When visualized in this manner the uncomprehending Pharisees are seen to be a foil for the uncomprehending disciples. However, it is the inability of the *latter* group to understand Jesus that is the heart of this narrative complex.

The framing stories in the present complex are clearly enacted parables, placing their emphasis on the final, or ultimate, clarity of sight given the blind man, and in the ability of the man with no voice to finally speak. Set in contrast to this is the central reality that Jesus' works were understood neither by religious leaders nor his own followers. The crowds (nameless, faceless) believed that he did all things well. The crowds were willing to give him due praise as the Holy representative who comes from God. The crowds accepted him at face value. However, the crowds go no deeper than face value and eventually reject him at face value.

When viewing the two feeding miracles, talk of "doublets" in the pre-Marcan tradition misses the narrative point. Mark purposefully casts these two stories to depict an "inclusive Jesus" who impatiently waits on his followers to get with his program. Jesus is greater than "the son of David" (cf. Mk. 12:35–37). David fed his army on five loaves (an implied miracle?) and Jesus did the same. But he went beyond this to feed the remaining loaves in the Samuel story to the rest of the world—to the Gentiles.

Once grasped, Mark's fictive argument presents a frustration that teems off the written page. If Jesus broke bread with Gentiles and took the gospel to Gentile shores, why do the representatives of the Jerusalem church still sit and wait for some sign or miracle (like the Pharisees of old). Mark presents the issue as already settled. The oral community of the Twelve appears to be waiting for a sign that has already happened. Jesus already explained this. If they will not act, then Mark's story implies that they will be surpassed by a generation of Christians who listen, who understand, and who are willing to take up the vital task set before them by Jesus. Once the rhetoric of Mark's design is realized, it becomes clear that his fictive argument challenges the church of his day to turn away from accommodating Jewish particularism in order to embrace the urgency of the Gentile mission. Mark has lost patience with those who practice wait-and-see Christianity.

Mark 8:27—9:29
The Tenth Narrative Complex

I WHO IS THE SON OF MAN? (Mk. 8:27b–33)
   Scene 1 (vv. 27b–29)
{27}   1   On the way he asked his disciples,
           "Who do people say that I am?"   WHO?
{28}   2   And they answered him, "John the Baptist;
               and others, Elijah; still others, one of the prophets."   PROPOSALS
{29}   1' He asked them, "But who do you say that I am?"   WHO?
       2' Peter answered him, "You are the Messiah."   MESSIAH

   Scene 2 (vv. 30–32a)
{30}   A   And he sternly ordered them not to tell anyone about him.   ORDERS SILENCE
{31}   B   Then he began to teach them that the Son of Man
               must undergo great suffering, and be rejected
               by the elders, the chief priests, and the scribes,   PASSION PREDICTED
               and be killed,
           B' and after three days rise again.   RISING PREDICTED
{32}   A' He said all this quite openly.   SPEAKS OPENLY

   Scene 1' (vv. 32b–33)
       A   And Peter took him aside and began to rebuke him.   PETER REBUKES
{33}   B   But turning and looking at his disciples,   JESUS REBUKES
               he rebuked Peter
           B' and said, "Get behind me, Satan!   JESUS' REBUKE
           A' For you are setting your mind not on divine things   DIVINE MATTERS
               but on human things."   VS. HUMAN

II FAITH DEMANDS ALLEGIANCE (Mk. 8:34—9:1)
{34}   *ANACRUSIS:* He called the crowd with his disciples,
       and said to them,
       A   *Saying One (v. 34)*
           a   "If any want to become my followers,   FOLLOWER
               b   let them deny themselves   DENIAL
               b' and take up their cross   CROSS-BEARING
           a' and follow me.   FOLLOWER
{35}   B   *Saying Two (v. 35)*
           a   For those who want to save their life   SAVE
               b   will lose it, LOSE
               b' and those who lose their life for my sake,   LOSE
                   and for the sake of the gospel,
           a' will save it.   SAVE
{36}   C   *Saying Three (vv. 36–37)*
           1   For what will it profit them
               to gain the whole world   GAIN
               2   and forfeit their life?   FORFEIT?
{37}   1' [For what indeed] can they give   GIVE
               2' in return for their life?   EXCHANGE?
{38}   B' *Saying Four (v. 38)*
           1   Those who are ashamed of me and of my words   ASHAMED
               2   in this adulterous and sinful generation,   SINFUL
           1' of them the Son of Man will also be ashamed   ASHAMED
               2' when he comes in the glory of his Father   HOLY
                   with the holy angels."

{9:1} A' Saying Five (9:1)
       a   And he said to them, "Truly I tell you,   TWO AMENS= MAKE IT SO, LORD
       b   there are some standing here   SOME WHO ARE ALIVE
       b'   who will not taste death until they see   WILL NOT DIE BEFORE
       a'   that the kingdom of God has come with power."   KINGDOM COME

I' HE IS THE SON OF GOD (Mk. 9:2–13)
       Scene 1: Honoring Moses and Elijah (9:2–6)
{2} A   Six days later, Jesus took with him Peter
         and James and John,
         and led them up a high mountain apart,
         by themselves. And he was transfigured before them,   TRANSFIGURATION
{3}   and his clothes became dazzling white,   IS DAZZLINGLY
         such as no one on earth could bleach them.   AWESOME
{4} B   And there appeared to them Elijah with Moses,
         who were talking with Jesus.   JESUS/MOSES/ELIJAH
{5} B' Then Peter said to Jesus, "Rabbi, it is good for us to be here;
         let us make three dwellings, one for you,   JESUS/MOSES/ELIJAH
         one for Moses, and one for Elijah."
{6} A' He did not know what to say, for they were terrified.   TERRIFIED BABBLING

       Scene 2: Son of God Transfigured (9:7–8)
{7} A   Then a cloud overshadowed them,   CLOUD PRESENT
     B   and from the cloud there came a voice,   VOICE
     B' "This is my Son, the Beloved; listen to him!"   SON OF GOD
{8} A' Suddenly when they looked around,
         they saw no one with them any more, but only Jesus.   ONLY JESUS PRESENT

       Scene 2': Son of Man to Rise from the Dead (9:9–10)
{9} 1   As they were coming down the mountain,
         he ordered them to tell no one about
         what they had seen,   ORDERS SILENCE
     2   until after the Son of Man
         had risen from the dead.   RISING PREDICTED
{10} 1' So they kept the matter to themselves,   SILENCE MAINTAINED
     2' questioning what this
         rising from the dead could mean.   RISING QUESTIONED

       Scene 1': Dishonoring Elijah (9:11–13)
{11} A   Then they asked him, "Why do the scribes   SCRIBES INTERPRET
         say that Elijah must come first?"   WRITINGS
{12} B   He said to them, "Elijah is indeed coming first   ELIJAH COMES?
         to restore all things.
     C   How then is it written about the Son of Man,
         that he is to go through many sufferings   PASSION PREDICTED
     C' and be treated with contempt?   CONTEMPT PREDICTED
{13} B' But I tell you that Elijah has come,   ELIJAH HAS COME
         and they did to him whatever they pleased,
     A' as it is written about him."   AS IS WRITTEN

II' FAITH DEMANDS ALLEGIANCE (Mk. 9:14–29)
       Scene 1: Disciples Found Fussing (9:14–16)
{14} A   When they came to the disciples,
         they saw a great crowd around them,   DISCIPLES
         and some scribes arguing with them.   ARGUING
{15} B   When the whole crowd saw him,
         they were immediately overcome with awe,   CROWD'S AWE
     B' and they ran forward to greet him.   CROWD GREETS
{16} A' He asked them, "What are you
         arguing about with them?"   ARGUING

Scene 2: The Need for Faithful Belief (9:17–24)

{17} 1 Someone from the crowd answered him,
   "Teacher, I brought you my son;   BROUGHT SON
{18}   2 he has a spirit that makes him unable to speak;
     and whenever it seizes him, it dashes him down;
     and he foams and grinds his teeth   CONVULSES BOY
     and becomes rigid;
       3 and I asked your disciples to cast it out,   DISCIPLES UNABLE
         but they could not do so."   TO HELP
{19}   4 He answered them, "You faithless generation,   FAITHLESS
           how much longer must I be among you?   GENERATION
           How much longer must I put up with you?   JUDGMENT
{20} 1' Bring him to me." And they brought the boy to him. BROUGHT BOY
     2' When the spirit saw him,
        immediately it convulsed the boy,   CONVULSES BOY
        and he fell on the ground and rolled about,
        foaming at the mouth.
{21}   3' Jesus asked the father, "How long
          has this been happening to him?"
          And he said, "From childhood.
{22}   It has often cast him into the fire
          and into the water, to destroy him;
            4' a but if you are able to do anything,   CAN YOU HELP?
                 have pity on us and help us."
{23}   b Jesus said to him, "If you are able!—   JUDGMENT?
                 All things can be done for the one who   ARE YOU FAITHLESS?
                 believes."   BELIEF REQUISITE
{24}   b' Immediately the father of the child cried out, BELIEF AFFIRMED
                 "I believe;
               a' help my unbelief!"   CAN YOU HELP?

Scene 2': Belief Rewarded (9:25–27)

{25} A When Jesus saw that a crowd came running together,
       he rebuked the unclean spirit, saying to it,
       "You spirit that keeps this boy from speaking and hearing, DEMON CAST OUT
       I command you, come out of him, and never enter him again!"
{26} B After crying out and convulsing him terribly,
       it came out, and the boy was like a corpse,   CORPSE
     B' so that most of them said, "He is dead."   DEAD
{27} A' But Jesus took him by the hand and lifted him up,   BOY RESTORED
       and he was able to stand.

Scene 1': Disciples' Need for Prayer (9:28–29)

{28} 1 When he had entered the house,
       his disciples asked him privately,   DISCIPLES ASK
     2 "Why could we not cast it out?"   WHY UNABLE?
{29} 1' He said to them,   JESUS ANSWERS
     2' "This kind can come out only through prayer."   PRAYER REQUISITE

The Rhetorical Shape of the Narrative Complex

Just when the reader has become accustomed to inversion as the predictable rhetorical structure controlling the arrangment of collections, Mark surprises his readers by structuring a complex with step-parallelism. This structure is already familiar at the level of the individual episode and the meta-narrative level (1:1—4:1), but this is

Mark's first use of the technique to structure a whole complex. Taylor posits one of his "small literary complexes" covering this same material.[1] Others have tried to include the story of the two-staged healing from the last collection.[2] Although some of these arguments are well-reasoned when viewed independently, the rhetorical shape of this complex and those surrounding it demand that the complex be considered in terms of step-parallelism.

Mark signals this change in pattern with overt parallels. The first episode poses the question "Who do people/you say that I am?" The step-parallel episode answers the question with the testimony of the heavenly voice, "This is my Son, the Beloved; listen to him!" The second episode of the complex brings together five sayings on the nature of descipleship, while the last episode develops the theme of action in the name of faith as the appropriate response even in the face of doubt. If readers failed to grasp the shift in design, Mark provides graphic clues. For example, the general statement "this sinful and adulterous generation" in Episode II would naturally be paralleled by Jesus' indictment "O unbelieving generation" in Episode II'. The latter was directed against the portion of the Twelve who preferred squabbling to action during his absence. Like building a puzzle by first piecing together the straight-edged borders, when all is said and done, we know that these two phrases must end up in balancing episodes of the complex.

Veiled references to John the Baptist as Elijah already "come among them" and the occurrence of a second announcement from the heavens clearly signal the similarities between this narrative complex and the first narrative complex. The dramatic change in the organizational invention of this collection also alerts the reader to the fact that this complex is the climactic center of the Gospel. The plot will continue from this point, resolving the complications that have been established in the preceding narrative and concluding with the crucifixion and the announcement at the empty tomb. However, readers accustomed to this kind of narrative rhetoric would expect the thematic concerns of the Gospel to be indicated in this collection rather than in the final collection. That expectation is rewarded.

The juxtaposition of the episodes in the tenth narrative complex can be visualized thus:

I WHO IS THE SON OF MAN?   Mk. 8:27b–33
    Scene 1   *(vv. 27b–29)*
    Scene 2   *(vv. 30–32a)*
    Scene 3'   *(vv. 32b–33)*

II **FAITH DEMANDS ALLEGIANCE**	Mk. 8:34—9:1
A Saying One	(v. 34)
B Saying Two	(v. 35)
C Saying Three	(vv. 36–37)
B' Saying Four	(v. 38)
A' Saying Five	(9:1)
I' **HE IS THE SON OF GOD**	Mk. 9:2–13
Scene 1: Honoring Moses and Elijah	(vv. 2–6)
Scene 2: Son of God Transfigured	(vv. 7–8)
Scene 2': Son of Man to Rise from the Dead	(vv. 9–10)
Scene 1': Dishonoring Elijah	(vv. 11–13)
II' **FAITH DEMANDS ALLEGIANCE**	Mk. 8:34—9:1
Scene 1: Disciples Found Fussing	(vv. 14–16)
Scene 2: The Need for Faithful Belief	(vv. 17–24)
Scene 2': Belief Rewarded	(vv. 25–27)
Scene 1': Disciples' Need for Prayer	(vv. 28–29)

The Central Motif

The question is posed at the outset of this central narrative complex, "Who is Jesus?" Peter suggests that he is the Christ but also makes it clear that his conception of what a christ is has little to do with Jesus' talk of impending death. The announcement by Peter that Jesus is "the Christ" does not occur in the climactic center of the episode as one might expect. The heart of that episode contains Jesus' first of three formulaic announcements of his coming rejection and death. Perhaps, to the reader's surprise, the supposed insight that Jesus is "the Christ" is paralleled by Jesus rebuking Peter as having in mind the "things of men" instead of the "things of God." Rather than accepting the diversely defined title of "Christ," the parallel episode of the collection offers the real answer to the question. Jesus is God's beloved "Son." The divine voice exhorts the leaders among the Twelve to "Listen to him!" The charge is the final occurrence in the Gospel challenging disciples to be people who have ears to hear (cf. 4:9, 23; 7:16).

This story of the transfiguration and the subsequent story of faith are both characterized by allusions to the theophany of Exodus 24—32. In that story Moses set out with his aid Joshua to ascend the mountain of God where, *after six days* of cloud-enshrouded waiting, "the glory of the LORD settled on Mount Sinai." The "glory" appeared to the Israelites below as a consuming fire (Dan. 12:3 also employs the same word to describe those who in the resurrection "will shine *like the brightness of heaven*"). God speaks to Moses out of the cloud as well. Similar allusions abound, but the point is made: The transfiguration narrative is decisively tempered by the elements of Exodus 24:13–18.

The force of this collection's fictive argument does not allow readers to ponder the profound implications of the confrontation concerning Jesus' identity, the radical claims of discipleship, or the transfiguration that depicts Jesus as if he were already resurrected. Where we might prefer to linger in the episodes, a step progression builds to a climactic conclusion, placing the emphasis first on Episode II and then on II'. Episode II at 8:34—9:1 contains five sayings that are condensed formulations of instruction on the necessity of persistence, sacrifice, and decisiveness if one chooses to follow Jesus. In their concision, they represent the most radical demands of discipleship to be found in the gospels.[3] Only the fifth saying is a pronouncement rather than instruction. It is the third instance of thirteen occurrences of the formulaic "Amen, I tell you."[4] As with this reference to the kingdom-come, "Amen" sayings are usually self-contained pronouncements often emphasizing a realized eschatology (cf. Mt. 6:10).[5]

Images and allusions from the Exodus 24 story pervade Episode II' as well. When Moses returns from the mountain (Ex. 32) the people have begun to worship other gods. God had accused them of being a "stiff-necked generation" who never learn. So Moses demands, "Who is on the LORD's side? Come to me" and forces those who do follow to make radical decisions setting them apart from sons, brothers, and neighbors. Finally Moses sets his face to journey back up the mountain to God to "make atonement" for their great sin. The appearance of Moses and Elijah at the transfiguration would have suggested to readers that Jesus was meeting with individuals who had never died. According to popular belief these two men ascended to heaven to be received in glory.[6]

As Jesus descends the mountain, he encounters a situation in which his disciples appear to have been incapable of performing the kind of healings they have previously accomplished in his absence (6:12–13). Aggravated, he rails against them as the "unbelieving generation" (9:19). Mark's volatile characterization and language in 9:14–29 was quite probably intended to provide cues to remind the reading audience of the story of the golden calf in Exodus 32. If so, then Mark the preacher has depicted a situation in which contemporary church leaders either have or, in his opinion, are in danger of leading the people of God into apostasy while the return of the master is awaited. Rather than debating why, for example, miracles are not happening in the master's absence, Mark appears to be challenging the leadership to listen to what Jesus told them, to be in prayer, but above all, to act even if all the questions are yet unsettled. Jesus' word is that "Everything is possible for those who believe." And to the father yet willing to act by crying out fledgling faith, Jesus responds by healing the child. Even faltering faith is enough. What the times do not call for is calculating debate among leaders similar to the apparent response of the circumcision-faction of the Jerusalem council that Paul recounts in Galations 2:11–14. The fictive argument makes the point clear that the present moment calls for a zealous response of committing *nothing less than everything* to the cause of following Jesus. It is Mark's call for disciples to act that is meant to define them, not their failure to understand.

In his day, Jesus criticized the Pharisees and other religious leaders for their recourse to rules and precedent rather than responding to persons in immediate need. As Dunn notes, we cannot escape the *charismatic* character that is integral to this kind of challenge.[7] We may want to balance its force with the tempered language of later church experience, but Mark's *argument* looks askance at discipleship conducted "decently and in order." This Gospel does not suggest a faith of tightly structured arguments and detailed planning. Openness to the needs of the moment is openness to the Spirit. Intractable problems are matters of prayer not planning. The immanence of the kingdom calls for a discipleship stripped to bare essentials and ready to act. To an era that was already learning to accommodate reasonable caution in the face of delayed immanence, Mark reminds listeners of the stark charismatic simplicity of the original challenge, "Follow me."

Who Is He—And So What If He Is?
A sermon by James E. Mead

Sermon Text: Mark 9:2–10

Mark has put this wonderful story right at the heart of his Gospel so we will know for certain he considers it a crucial, defining story for people called to follow Jesus. In many ways the Jesus we meet in the transfiguration story may be the Jesus we've always been hoping for: glorious, unambiguous, and divine as all get-out. You just know this Jesus will love us, fix up whatever's wrong with us, defeat our enemies, and give us success. He'll do away with suffering and poverty. He'll save our souls and take us to heaven when we die. Here is a Messiah that *is* a Messiah! But if we read the transfiguration story that way, we'll miss what Mark is trying to tell us.

Mark did not intend for us to read this story out of context from other stories—what's at the center of his Gospel is really four stories, not one, and this is the third in the series of them. Mark begins this series of stories on the road to a place called Caesarea Philippi.

So far no one gets it about Jesus: not the religious leaders, not his family, and not his disciples. And so, going to Caesarea Philippi, Jesus asks his followers, "Who do people say that I am?" "Well, Lord, some say you're Elijah, the great prophet, some say you're John the Baptist back from the dead, and others say you're one of the other prophets." "That's about what I figured," Jesus replies. "And what about *you*, dear followers, who do you say I am?" Peter says, "You are the Messiah."

Now, don't we expect Jesus to say, "At last! Now you get it!"? But that's not what Jesus says in Mark's Gospel. Our translation says Jesus "sternly ordered" the disciples not to tell anyone about him, which seems strange enough, but actually it doesn't even come close to doing justice to what Jesus really said. The Greek word translated by this phrase is exactly the same word used in verse 31 in which Jesus "rebukes" Peter, telling him he is Satan.

Why in the world would Jesus rebuke his followers after Peter calls him Messiah? The answer is related to another scripture passage—Jesus knows that even though the title "Messiah" is right, Peter and the disciples still don't actually get it about him. There were lots of expectations of what a Messiah would be and do. Our scholar-in-residence Bob Reid's description of them is very useful.

> The *Pharisees* believed the Messiah was going to be the promised one, who would come and reward them for doing such a great job as the keepers of the religious flame, for being so good. The *zealots* believed the Messiah was going to be a king like the great king David—he would come and kick the Romans out of Palestine and set up a new kingdom in Jerusalem. The *common people* expected a Messiah who would be like a new Moses—a miracle worker who would provide manna in the wilderness and lead his people to a promised land of good times, prosperity, safety and comfort. Then there were the *Sadducees* who were the ones who knew how to get along with the world. They considered the whole Messiah *bit* a buzzword for a dangerous myth.[1]

So when Peter says, "You are the Messiah," Jesus says, "This is a case of *mistaken identity*. I won't let you define me. I am not, and will not be, the savior of your expectations." That's the first, and shocking, story Mark tells in this series of stories at the heart of his Gospel. Mark means to confront us—to confront those who bear the name of Jesus—and put this question to us: Who defines Jesus for you? In fine American fashion, we tend to feel lots of freedom to define Jesus for ourselves, don't we? If Jesus heard our definitions of him, would he rebuke us: "This is a case of mistaken identity!"?

In the next story, Jesus himself begins to define who he is. Listen. "The Son of man," he says, "must undergo great suffering, and be rejected by the elders, the chief priests, and the scribes, and must be killed, and after three days rise again." Notice all the "musts": must suffer, must be rejected, and must be killed and rise again.

What does Peter do when he hears Jesus' definition of himself as Messiah? He takes Jesus aside and begins to rebuke him, the way you take a small child aside who's done something embarrassing in front of the guests—like sneezing on the buffet, or asking where babies come from. "No, Jesus," Peter says, "that's not what the Messiah is like at all! The Messiah is powerful, glorious, triumphant!"

Everything is at stake for Jesus and his followers. They still don't get it. Jesus looks at all his followers, not just at Peter, but at all of them. Looking at *them*, he rebukes Peter: "Get behind me, Satan! You are not on God's side—your mind is full of human things."

Then Jesus gathers a crowd around with his followers and lays it on the line: "If you want to follow me, you'll have to take up your cross—take up your electric chair—daily. You'll have to do some dying to follow me! If all you want to do is to save your life, you're going to lose it. But those who lose their lives for me and for the message I preach will save their lives!" That's the second shocking story, with it's unpleasant news about a suffering savior and costly discipleship.

Six days later Jesus took three of his closest followers up a mountain. There he was transfigured, changed, and presented in glory before them. His clothing shown whiter that any white we've ever seen. There a shining cloud descended—the *shekinah*, the cloud of the glory of the presence of God, the s*hekinah*-cloud that descended on the mountain when God gave Moses the law. There Moses and Elijah make an appearance—Moses, giver of the law; Elijah, greatest of the prophets in the Old Testament. And in the presence of the whole of the Old Testament tradition, in the presence of disciples who presume to instruct Jesus about Messiahhood, the voice of God comes out of the cloud of glory saying the same words we heard from God way back at Jesus' baptism: "This is my Son. The beloved." God is telling the disciples who Jesus is. He is not a prophet, he's the Son. He isn't the world's most spiritually sensitive soul, he's the Son. He isn't the Messiah of our imaginings or the Savior of our designing, he is the Son.

Okay, he's the Son. Now we know who he is, but so what if he is? God does not leave us in doubt: "This is my Son, the Beloved; *listen to him*." If Jesus says the Messiah must suffer, listen to him, even if that isn't the savior you wanted. If this Shining One tells you that following him is going to involve dying to yourself, listen to him. Stop listening to yourselves about the things of God! Start listening to my Son the Beloved.

To whom are we listening? Who calls the shots for us? When it comes time to disappoint someone, who do we let down and who do we make sure we don't disappoint? God says, "Don't disappoint Jesus. Listen to him."

In the last of the four stories, the scene shifts from the mountain of glory back down to the valley where the other nine disciples are waiting. What are they doing down there while Jesus is shining in glory? No doubt they've been praying for those up on the mountain. No doubt they've been asking God to heal their blind eyes and deaf ears so they can finally get it about Jesus. No, they are locked in an argument with the religious leaders about why they can't heal a boy possessed with a demon.

When Jesus gets the details of their failure, he rebukes his followers again, and it must have stung: "You faithless generation…how much longer must I put up with you?" Jesus has defined the source of powerlessness in his followers: They lack faith, they lack belief. Because they lack faith in him, they are unable to do what God wants them to do and are unable to present him rightly to the crowds and to his religious opponents. They can argue, but they can't do his will. Jesus demands that the boy be brought to him, and the father says, "If you can do anything, have pity on us and help us." Reid says, "Jesus' word is that 'Everything is possible for those who believe.' And to the father yet willing to act by crying out fledgling faith, Jesus responds by healing the child. Even faltering faith is enough." Then Jesus withdraws to a house where he can get down to business with his followers. It's time for them to listen up. It's time for the church in every age to listen up. Jesus has already identified the cause of their powerlessness—their unbelief in him as he defines himself. Now he's going to tell them the cure for powerlessness. The cure is prayer. "This kind can come out only through prayer," Jesus says. You are powerless because you are prayerless. The cure is not to jack up our flagging faith. It's not to put our faith in faith. The cure for powerlessness in a church, in a life, in a home, in a community, is prayerfulness.

To tell the truth, I don't like simple answers. But here is a simple answer from Jesus: "You are powerless as my followers because you don't pray." I wouldn't listen to such a simple answer except for one thing: It is the beloved Son of God who is speaking.

What keeps us from praying? I don't know all your reasons, but I'll tell you one out of my own life. As much as anything else, I don't take the time I know I should for prayer because I'm busy. I start most days early and end them late. Committees, choirs, Sunday school teachers, hands-on helpers, mission leaders—all of us are busy at this church, often with godly business. Too busy to pray, to take time before, during, and after business to talk things out with God, to listen to Jesus in prayer. The consequence, says Jesus, is powerlessness. I believe Jesus is calling me, and you, as leaders and members in the church, to pray. For a lot of us that will mean *learning* to pray—including learning to pray together in groups, classes, committees, and servant situations.

If we don't get something else done because we prayed, that would probably be a good experience for us for a while. We are not a business, we are the body of Christ, the church. The business we handle is important—whether in staff, a committee meeting, or a choir practice. But none of our meetings are more about business and performance than they are about being Jesus' followers, Jesus' community.

Jesus invites us to bet our lives individually, and our life together, on him and his word. Do disciples fail in doing this? Oh yes. But as Reid says, their failures (their lack of faith, their powerlessness and prayerlessness) don't define them. Jesus' call defines them. Jesus' call defines us, not our failures as his people. Since we have that assurance, since we live in the grace that says we don't have to get it right, let's take the risk of faith. Let's believe in Jesus and listen to him. And let's make time in our lives and in our church work for real prayer. The Lord is with us.

Compositional Comments

Mark has placed four stories at the climactic center of the chiastic framework of his Gospel. They echo God's word from chapter 1 ("You are my Son, whom I love") and pre-present the risen, exalted Christ who, though he never actually appears in the last chapter, was known to Mark's readers from the preaching of the church. To get the point of these stories is to finally "get it" about who Jesus is and what it means for us to be his disciples. The broader context for the passage is in Reid's observation that in Mark the disciples never quite get it about Jesus nor about what they are called to do as his followers, and in the passage itself Jesus expresses energetic exasperation with them ("You faithless generation…how much longer must I put up with you?").

The sermon begins with a kind of parody of views of Jesus as Savior in order to foreshadow what's to come and to bridge from the scripture reading (Mark 9:2–13, the transfiguration) to the broader context of the transfiguration story. The sermon is designed to follow the same movements I understood the stories to be making (with brief applications along the way), forcefully moving to an application about prayer that is not only the punchline of this four-story step-parallel presentation, but also painfully relevant to me and the congregation I serve. The four movements are: (1) exposing human definitions of the person and work of Jesus; (2) Jesus' own definition of himself as a suffering Savior along with what it means to be his disciple (if he suffers and dies, what might those who follow him and bear his name expect?); (3) the presentation, in advance, of the exalted Christ who is to be listened to preeminently, even in the presence of the Old Testament tradition, and despite the convictions of disciples who prefer their own definitions of him; and (4) the identification of the cause of powerlessness among Jesus' followers (their lack of belief in him as he, God's beloved Son, defines himself) and Jesus' prescription of a cure for their powerlessness (prayer).

Mark 9:30—10:45
The Eleventh Narrative Complex

I JESUS TEACHES ON THE NATURE OF GREATNESS (Mk. 9:30–35)
Scene 1: Passion Prediction (9:30–33a)

{30}	A		They went on from there and passed through Galilee.	LOCATION
		B	He did not want anyone to know it;	
{31}			for he was teaching his disciples, saying to them,	
			C "The Son of Man is to be betrayed into human hands, and they will kill him,	KILL
			C' and three days after being killed,	KILL
			he will rise again."	RISE AGAIN
{32}		B'	But they did not understand what he was saying and were afraid to ask him.	AFRAID
{33}	A'		Then they came to Capernaum;	LOCATION

Scene 2: Instruction in Following Jesus (9:33b–35)

	1	and when he was in the house he asked them, "What were you arguing about on the way?"	
{34}	2	But they were silent, for on the way they had argued with one another who was the greatest.	FIRST OF ALL
{35}	1'	He sat down, called the twelve, and said to them,	
	2'	"Whoever wants to be first must be last of all and servant of all."	SERVANT OF ALL

II THE COUNTERCULTURE KINGDOM (Mk. 9:36–50)
A Sayings Collection: On Unhindered Reception (9:36–42)

{36}	A		Then he took a little child and put it among them; and taking it in his arms, he said to them,	CHILD
{37}		a	"Whoever welcomes one such child in my name	
		b	welcomes me,	
		b'	and whoever welcomes me	
	a'		welcomes not me but the one who sent me."	
{38}	B		John said to him, "Teacher, we saw someone casting out demons in your name, and we tried to stop him, because he was not following us."	NOT OF US
{39}		C	But Jesus said, "Do not stop him;	DO NOT HINDER
		C'	for no one who does a deed of power in my name will be able soon afterward to speak evil of me.	
{40}	B'		Whoever is not against us is for us.	STILL FOR US
{41}	A'	1	For truly I tell you, whoever gives you a cup of water to drink because you bear the name of Christ	
		2	will by no means lose the reward.	REWARD
{42}		1'	"If any of you put a stumbling block before one of these little ones who believe in me,	LITTLE ONES
		2'	it would be better for you if a great millstone were hung around your neck and you were thrown into the sea.	PUNISHMENT

A Catchword Collection of Instruction for Following Jesus (9:43–50)

{43}	A	If your hand causes you to stumble, cut it off;	
		B it is better for you to enter life maimed	
		B' than to have two hands	
{44}	A'	and to go to hell, to the unquenchable fire.	FIRE
{45}	A	And if your foot causes you to stumble, cut it off;	
		B it is better for you to enter life lame	

Mark 9:30—10:45

{46}	A'	B' than to have two feet and to be thrown into hell.	HELL
{47}	A	And if your eye causes you to stumble, tear it out; B it is better for you to enter the kingdom of God with one eye B' than to have two eyes	
	A'	and to be thrown into hell,	HELL
{48}		where their worm never dies, and the fire is never quenched.	FIRE
{49}	A	"For everyone will be salted with fire.	FIRE/SALT
{50}		B Salt is good;	SALT
		C but if salt has lost its saltiness,	SALTINESS
		C' how can you season it?	SEASONING
		B' Have salt in yourselves,	SALT
	A'	and be at peace with one another."	SALT AS REFINER

III COUNTERCULTURE SERVANTHOOD EXEMPLIFIED (Mk. 10:1–12)

Scene A: Jesus Teaches (10:1)

{10:1}	1	He left that place and went to the region of Judea and beyond the Jordan.	LOCATION
	2	And crowds again gathered around him;	CROWD
	3	and, as was his custom, he again taught them.	JESUS TEACHES

Scene B: Divorce Teaching (10:2–9)

{2}	A	Some Pharisees came, and to test him they asked, "Is it lawful for a man to divorce his wife?"	DIVORCE
{3}	B	He answered them, "What did Moses command you?"	
{4}		They said, "Moses allowed a man to write a certificate of dismissal and to divorce her."	POSSIBILITY OF DIVORCE
{5}	C	But Jesus said to them, "Because of your hardness of heart he wrote this commandment for you.	MOSAIC LAW
{6}	C'	But from the beginning of creation, 'God made them male and female.'	CREATION LAW
{7}	B'	'For this reason a man shall leave his father and mother and be joined to his wife,	
{8}		and the two shall become one flesh.' So they are no longer two, but one flesh.	PERMANENCE OF UNION
{9}	A'	Therefore what God has joined together, let no one separate."	DIVORCE

Scene A': Jesus Teaches (10:10–11)

{10}	1	Then in the house	LOCATION
	2	the disciples asked him again about this matter.	DISCIPLES
{11}	3	He said to them,	JESUS EXPLAINS

Scene B': Divorce Teaching (10:11–12)

	1	"Whoever divorces his wife	DIVORCES
	2	and marries another	MARRIES AGAIN
	3	commits adultery against her;	COMMITS ADULTERY
{12}	1'	and if she divorces her husband	DIVORCES
	2'	and marries another,	MARRIES AGAIN
	3'	she commits adultery."	COMMITS ADULTERY

II' THE COUNTERCULTURE KINGDOM (Mk. 10:13–31)

Scene 1: Another Sayings Collection on Unhindered Reception (10:13–16)

{13}	A	People were bringing little children to him in order that he might touch them;	TOUCH THEM
	B	and the disciples spoke sternly to them.	DISCIPLES SAY NO
{14}	C	But when Jesus saw this, he was indignant and said to them, "Let the little children come to me;	

			do not stop them; for it is to such as these	
			that the kingdom of God belongs.	KINGDOM OF GOD
{15}		C'	Truly I tell you, whoever does not receive	
			the kingdom of God as a little child will never enter it."	KINGDOM OF GOD
{16}		B'	And he took them up in his arms,	JESUS SAYS YES
	A'		laid his hands on them, and blessed them.	LAY HANDS ON THEM

Scene 2: A Narrative on Receiving Eternal Life (10:17–22)

{17}	A		As he was setting out on a journey,	MAN KNEELS BEFORE
			a man ran up and knelt before him, and asked him,	JESUS
		B	"Good Teacher, what must I do to inherit eternal life?"	WHAT MUST I DO?
{18}		C	Jesus said to him, "Why do you call me good?	
			No one is good but God alone.	GOD
{19}			D You know the commandments:	
			'You shall not murder;	COMMANDMENTS
			You shall not commit adultery; You shall not steal;	
			You shall not bear false witness; You shall not defraud;	
			Honor your father and mother.'"	
{20}			E He said to him, "Teacher, I have kept all these	
			since my youth."	EFFORT EXPENDED
{21}			E' Jesus, looking at him, loved him	LOVED HIM
			D' and said, "You lack one thing;	LACK COMMAND
		C'	go, sell what you own, and give the money to the poor,	
			and you will have treasure in heaven;	HEAVEN
		B'	then come, follow me."	
{22}	A'		When he heard this, he was shocked	MAN LEAVES JESUS
			and went away grieving, for he had many possessions.	GRIEVING

Scene 1': A Third Sayings Collection on Unhindered Reception (10:23–27)

{23}	A		Then Jesus looked around and said to his disciples,	
			"How hard it will be for those who have wealth	HOW HARD
			to enter the kingdom of God!"	TO ENTER KINGDOM OF GOD
{24}		B	And the disciples were perplexed at these words.	PERPLEXED
		C	But Jesus said to them again, "Children, how	
			hard it is to enter the kingdom of God!	TO ENTER KINGDOM OF GOD
{25}		C'	It is easier for a camel to go through	
			the eye of a needle than for someone who is rich	
			to enter the kingdom of God."	TO ENTER KINGDOM OF GOD
{26}		B'	They were greatly astounded and said to one another,	ASTOUNDED
			"Then who can be saved?"	
{27}	A'		Jesus looked at them and said,	
			"For mortals	FOR MORTALS
			it is impossible,	IMPOSSIBLE
			but not for God;	FOR GOD
			for God all things are possible."	POSSIBLE!

Scene 2': On Receiving Eternal Life (10:28–31)

{28}	A		Peter began to say to him, "Look,	
			we have left everything and followed you."	WE FOLLOW
{29}		B	Jesus said, "Truly I tell you, there is no one	
			who has left house or brothers or sisters	
			or mother or father or children or fields,	
			for my sake and for the sake of the good news,	GOOD NEWS
{30}		B'	who will not receive a hundredfold now	
			in this age—houses, brothers and sisters,	LIFE NOW
			mothers and children, and fields with persecutions—	
			and in the age to come eternal life.	LIFE TO COME
{31}	A'		But many who are first will be last, and the last will be first."	FOLLOWING ORDER

I' JESUS TEACHES ON THE NATURE OF GREATNESS (Mk. 10:32–45)
Scene 1: Passion Prediction (10:32–41)

{32} A a They were on the road, going up to Jerusalem, and Jesus was walking ahead of them;
        b they were amazed,
        b' and those who followed were afraid.
      a' He took the twelve aside again   ASIDE TO THE TWELVE
        and began to tell them what was to happen to him, saying,

{33}   B 1 "See, we are going up to Jerusalem,
          and the Son of Man will be handed over
          to the chief priests and the scribes,   JESUS'
        2 and they will condemn him to death;   PASSION
        1' then they will hand him over to the Gentiles; PREDICTION

{34}   2' they will mock him, and spit upon him, and flog him, and kill him; and after three days he will rise again."

{35}   C James and John, the sons of Zebedee, came forward to him and said to him, "Teacher, we want you to do for us whatever we ask of you."   ASK?

{36}   D And he said to them,
        "What is it you want me to do for you?"   REQUEST

{37}   D' And they said to him, "Grant us to sit,   GRANT US
        one at your right hand and one at your left,
        in your glory."   POWER POSITIONS

{38}   C' But Jesus said to them,
        "You do not know what you are asking.   ASK?
  B' 1 Are you able to drink the cup that I drink,
        2 or be baptized with the baptism that I am baptized with?"   DISCIPLES'
          PASSION

{39}   3 They replied, "We are able."   PREDICTION
    1' Then Jesus said to them,
        "The cup that I drink you will drink;
      2' and with the baptism with which I am baptized, you will be baptized;

{40}   3' but to sit at my right hand or at my left is not mine to grant, but it is for those for whom it has been prepared."

{41} A' When the ten heard this,
    they began to be angry with James and John.   THE TEN GRUMBLE

Scene 2: Instruction in Following Jesus (10:42–45)

{42} 1 So Jesus called them and said to them,
    "You know that among the Gentiles
    those whom they recognize as
    their rulers lord it over them,   LORD IT OVER
    2 and their great ones are tyrants over them.   TYRANTS OVER

{43}   3 But it is not so among you;   BUT NOT FOR YOU
  1' but whoever wishes to become great among you

{44}   must be your servant,   SERVANTS
    2' and whoever wishes to be first among you must be slave of all.   SLAVE OF ALL

{45}   3' For the Son of Man came   JESUS REVERSES
      not to be served   THE HIERARCHY
      but to serve, and
      to give his life a ransom for many."   SACRIFICIALLY

The Rhetorical Shape of the Narrative Complex

The most sophisticated of Mark's narrative collections, this complex also embodies the clearest statement of his theology. Episodes I and I' are both composed of two scenes, with each scene clearly developed in relationship to its counterpart in the frame. In Scene 1 of both Episodes I and I' the pronouncement of the betrayal, death, and resurrection structures the narratives. This is followed by a second scene in which jockeying for positions of leadership brings about the pronouncement that leadership in the kingdom will be exercised as servanthood. In these framing episodes, Jesus' impending martyrdom is projected as the archetype of servanthood in the kingdom by pairing passion predictions with efforts by the disciples to mount a hierarchy within kingdom relationships.

More than any other collection, this complex combines stories, teaching, and instruction in following Jesus from condensed "whoever" or "if anyone" pronouncements. Many of them are connected to one another by catchwords, bringing otherwise disparate ideas into new theological juxtapositions. One example must suffice. The series of "if anyone" statements about causing one to sin in 9:42–48 raises the image of hellfire. Notice how the refining quality of both salt and fire are then brought together, with the fire of verses 42–48 introducing a final catchword chiasmus in verses 49–50.

a	"For everyone will be salted with fire.		SALT AS REFINER
	b	Salt is good;	SALT AS SUBSTANCE
		c but if salt has lost its saltiness,	SALTINESS AS SEASONING
		c' how can you season it?	SALTINESS AS SEASONING
	b'	Have salt in yourselves,	SALT AS SUBSTANCE
a'	and be at peace with one another."		SALT AS REFINER

Although one could argue that these are instructions on the nature of discipleship,[1] the ethical dimensions of conduct distinguish this set of instructions from those found at 8:34—9:1. In this example, salt becomes a metaphor for the singular quality of Christian virtue that governs "the good" in Christian ethics (cf. Mt. 5:13 and Lk. 14:34f). The final call to "be at peace with one another," whether a reference to the rivalries between competing Christian communities in Mark's day (vv. 38–39) or the debate about prestige within the community in the former episode (vv. 33–35), is a call to dismantle social hierarchies in the kingdom community. In this collection, worldly hierarchy is overturned because the eschatological reversal of the day of the Lord is now reality.

Similar themes could be explored as the ethical dimensions of many of the saying and stories in this collection. Not to be missed, however, is the famous story in 10:17–22 of the wealthy man who seeks to live the "good life" worthy of eternal reward. Mark has Jesus challenge both the Greco-Roman notions of the "good life" and the Hebraic belief that material wealth was the sign of God's blessing. He turns both notions on their head by arguing for an ethic of a life expended sacrificially on behalf of others for the sake of Jesus and the sake of the gospel. By any ancient ethical standard of the "good life," this was a shockingly subversive message.[2] It plainly says that one need not have cultural status or prestige to live the "good life." Rather, the "good life" only comes if one freely chooses to adopt the ethic of a slave: servanthood before self.

The juxtaposition of the episodes in the eleventh narrative complex can be visualized thus:

I JESUS TEACHES ON THE NATURE OF GREATNESS	Mk. 9:30–35
Scene 1: Passion Prediction	(vv. 30–32)
Scene 2: Instruction in Following Jesus	(vv. 33–35)
II THE COUNTERCULTURE KINGDOM	Mk. 9:36–50
A Sayings Collection: On Unhindered Reception	(vv. 36–42)
A Catchword Collection on Entering the Kingdom	(vv. 43–50)
III COUNTERCULTURE SERVANTHOOD EXEMPLIFIED	Mk.10:1–12
Scene A: Jesus Teaches	(10:1)
Scene B: Divorce Teaching	(vv. 2–9)
Scene A': Jesus Teaches	(vv. 10–11a)
Scene B': Divorce Teaching	(vv. 11b–12)
II' THE COUNTERCULTURE KINGDOM	Mk. 10:13–31
Scene 1: Another Sayings Collection on Unhindered Reception	(vv. 13–16)
Scene 2: A Narrative on Receiving Eternal Life	(vv. 17–22)
Scene 1': A Third Sayings Collection on Unhindered Reception	(vv. 23–27)
Scene 2': On Receiving Eternal Life	(vv. 28–31)
I' JESUS TEACHES ON THE NATURE OF GREATNESS	Mk. 10:32–45
Scene 1: Passion Prediction	(vv. 32–41)
Scene 2: Instruction in Following Jesus	(vv. 42–45)

The Central Motif

At the center of the narrative complex is Jesus' teaching on divorce. It functions as the paradigmatic conception of the Marcan ethics, of the brokenness that occurs when people act with hierarchical self-interest rather than making choices that build community with one another. The ideal is not brokered or qualified in this passage as in the other gospels. Mark's Jesus places the same responsibility for mutual servanthood in the relationship on both husband and wife. The saying allows no recourse for the divorcing partner because it is directed toward that individual, whether male or female, who has placed his or her own needs above those of the spouse and/or those of the community. The entire complex is shaped as moral aggadah, a call to the highest ethical ideal. To those who struggle with the unyielding nature of this statement on divorce, the question to be asked is whether one would expect exception clauses in a paradigmatic example of the highest ethical ideal? Surely not. All of the stories and teaching in the surrounding scenes and sayings point to this climactic demand to live servant-centered rather than self-centered lives. In effect, Mark's Jesus ethically calls his followers to *nothing less than everything* in directing their lives after the pattern of his own willingness to journey toward betrayal and death on behalf of others.

The fictive argument of this collection offers a Marcan ethics of the kingdom. Where ancient theories of civic virtue focused on the qualities of character that provided for the "good life," Mark preaches a *sermon on the servant*. He makes no argument for *civitas* as an ideal, supplies no list of household rules, offers no handbook on appropriate morals. Instead, he draws together the starkly condensed "whoever" and "if anyone" formulations to create an ethic of "the two ways."

Critics generally refer to the "paucity" of ethical material in the Gospel of Mark and that what ethical material one does find is not present because of any ethical interests on Mark's part.[3] In one sense this notion holds up. Obviously, Mark has no interest in taking up an abstract consideration of "the good" per se. But like many moral philosophers' of his era, he is intent on identifying the objective, or aim, of human life that controls and orders behavior, the knowledge of which is essential in proposing any code of ethics. Identifying that aim is Aristotle's goal in his *Nicomachean Ethics,* and Mark has the same goal in this narrative collection.

In the *Nicomachean Ethics*, Aristotle identifies *happiness* as the final supreme human "good" on grounds that no one aims at happiness as a means of achieving something else, but that many ends are sought as a means of achieving happiness. According to Aristotle, this happiness, or *eudaimonía,* is realized in the *enérgeia*, or activity of the most divine part of individuals.[4] These aspects of the "soul," and the virtues that Aristotle surveys that pertain to it, do not occur naturally but are developed by consistent right action. Consequently, Aristotle defines virtue as "a deliberately chosen permanent state, representing the mean between two extremes in regard to ourselves and which is ascertained by calculation, and in a manner in which a man of good sense would determine it" (1106b 36–1107a 2).[5]

As discussed in book 10, chapter 7 of the *Nicomachean Ethics*, the highest virtue is *contemplation* and the highest pursuit for an individual is identified as the life of contemplation. As formulated in the fictive argument of this collection, Mark identifies the highest virtue as servanthood and the highest pursuit for an individual as the life of following the model of the Son of man, who "came not to be served but to serve, and to give his life a ransom for many" (10:45). The philosopher Epicurus roundly declared that,

```
a    [I]t is not possible to live pleasantly,                        PLEASANT
  b    without living prudently and honorably and justly,            VIRTUES
  b'   nor again, to live a life of prudence, honor,                 VIRTUES
       and justice
a'   without living pleasantly.                                      PLEASANT
a    For the virtues are by nature bound up                          VIRTUES
  b    with the pleasant life,                                       PLEASANT
  b'   and the pleasant life                                         PLEASANT
a'   is inseparable from them.[6]                                    VIRTUES
```

Mark's ethics subversively overturns cultural and religious hierarchies of this kind, whether they are in the aristocratic assumptions that underlie Greek philosophical conceptions of "happiness" and "the pleasant life" or in the aristocratic assumptions that underlie the Hebrew notion of wealth as the sign of "the blessed life." Not so with followers of Jesus. They have been called to dismount and dismantle the hierarchies by living according to the ethic of the kingdom-come.[7]

In the complex that spans the material between the transfiguration and the triumphal entry, Mark offers a collection of topically organized material juxtaposing the call to servanthood as the model for Christian conduct and quality of character for those individuals who would inherit the kingdom of God. Where the prior narrative complex defined the nature and demands of discipleship, this narrative collection sets the standard for kingdom ethics and what counts as the "good" in the practice of one's faith in Jesus as Lord.

The State of Our Spiritual Pantry
A sermon by Paul Scott Wilson

Sermon Text: Mark 10:13–31

I never knew what a pantry was as a child until I went to the big old home of Mrs. Thorne, one of the stalwart members of the congregation. Her pantry was a small room off the kitchen that had a tiny window looking out on the backyard, and everything else was white wood slat cupboards from the floor to the ceiling. She opened the doors and they were filled with bottles of her homemade raspberry jam, pickled peaches—each half pierced by a clove, cans of soup and vegetables, boxes of crackers, and bags of flour and sugar, and all of the staple items for cooking and baking needs. By the way my parents talked about her and her good deeds, I thought she must be a saint. When she died, I imagined that her spiritual pantry was as full of virtue as her material pantry had been full of foodstuffs.

We do not all have a pantry off our kitchens, but we all have a spiritual pantry adjacent to our lives. In it is stored all of the goods of our life—and the bads too. Every deed we have done or not done, everything that was done to us or by us, its all there, preserved for posterity. The salty deeds are kept alongside the saltine crackers and the salt cod; the kind things with the sugar and jams; the sour deeds are pickled; the stingy deeds are dried out and kept near the prunes—there is a place for everything. Some people get up in the morning and rush right down to the pantry, throw open their pantry cupboard doors, and are quite satisfied that their lives have been exemplary. And then there are the rest of us who avoid the pantry as much as possible, reluctant to do an accurate inventory, and are concerned that when we get to the big pantry inspection in the sky, our grade will be a failing one.

The last thing that Jesus did before going to Jerusalem, to die there on the cross—the last thing that he did was an inspection of the spiritual pantries of his people. For nearly two chapters in the Gospel of Mark, from the middle of chapter 9 through chapter 10, he walks through the region around the Sea of Galilee. Everywhere he goes he preaches. And of course, as he preaches on the hillsides and beaches, the crowds are very attentive, yet at some point, nearly every person quietly slips away in their mind and checks their own pantry of personal deeds to see how they measure up to what Jesus teaches. They cannot remain indifferent to his radical pronouncements. A group of families were gathered on the beach at the seaside. To the adults he said, "If you do anything to prevent these children from believing in me, you are better off out there in the sea with a millstone around your neck." Anyone with a discerning eye could see those adults mentally retreat to their spiritual pantries. Everyone could think of times when they had not shared their faith with a child. On another occasion Jesus spoke to people at a fitness club. "If you sin with your hand, cut it off. If your foot takes you where you should not go, cut it off. If your eye causes you to sin, pluck it out, so you do not end up in hell." These words reminded them of their spiritual pantry shelves, for in fact some had sinned with their hands in taking what belonged to another, some with their feet in going down the wrong paths, some with their eyes coveting things that were not theirs, and some had sinned with their entire bodies. At a summer picnic for a family reunion, where many people present had remarried, Jesus said, "Any divorced person who remarries commits adultery." To a proud woman leaving church, Jesus said, "Whoever does not receive the kingdom of God as a little child will never enter it." Wherever Jesus went, the pantry doors flew open.

And now, as Jesus is gathering his things to move on to Jerusalem, a man comes forward through the crowd. He sticks out from the others in their drab brown and gray clothes. He wears a tailored purple gown of silk embroidered with fine gold thread. His fingers sport rings inlaid with jade and emerald. He has waited until he could speak to Jesus more or less alone. This rich man and those watching expected Jesus simply to bless him, for in that culture, anyone who was rich was already considered blessed by God. "Good Teacher," he says, kneeling before Jesus, "what must I do to inherit eternal life?" Isn't that a question to which we all want the answer? The rich man does not even wait for Jesus to discern what is in his personal pantry of good deeds; he takes him to it and flings open the cupboard doors, giving him a guided tour. "Since my youth I have kept all the commandments: I have not murdered, I have not committed adultery, stolen, lied, or cheated, and I have honored my father and mother. What must I do to inherit eternal life?" Jesus does something surprising. He looks at him and he loves him. And he says words that the rich man does not expect, for he thought that his pantry shelves were in excellent order. Jesus says, "You lack one thing; go, sell what you own, and give the money to the poor, and you will have treasure in heaven; then come, follow me." The man is shocked and goes away grieving, for he has many possessions.

We end up looking in the wrong place when Jesus preaches. We watch the rich man retreat in sadness, when we should see the sadness on Jesus' own face. Who wants always to be understood as merely critical? Who likes to play the role of the critical parent? I heard recently the difference between prophetic preaching and haranguing—if the preacher likes it, its haranguing. When Jesus comes to us and our own pantry doors are open, there is plenty to criticize and condemn. Most of us are not as good as the rich man. Who of us can say, "I have kept the commandments since my youth"? Some of us might not know even the Ten Commandments. Have no other gods. Worship no graven images. Do not take God's name in vain. Remember the Sabbath to keep it holy. Honor your father and your mother. You shall not kill, or commit adultery, or steal, or bear false witness, or covet your neighbor's possessions. Others of us may think that keeping eight out of ten, or six, or five out of ten is okay. So we decide to be an 80 percent Christian, or 60 or 50. Some of us strive for higher marks at school or work than we strive for before God. Each night one out of five children in United States and Canada goes to the fridge, discovers it is empty, and goes to bed with a hungry stomach. Parents are unemployed or denied opportunities. As long as such conditions exist, none of us can feel good about our pantries.

When Jesus comes looking at our pantry shelves, we can so easily think that getting them in order is all up to us. A young woman who formerly lived on the street for several months has finally managed, with help from a couple in the church, to begin straightening out her life. She has gone back and finished high school. Recently she landed a good job in a record store. She has reason to feel good about herself. In her wallet she keeps a picture of her cat, Snowflake, and pictures of her friends. But there are no pictures of her family, and she looks away when asked about them. She says, "No matter what I do, no matter how hard I try, I still feel bad." She is in counseling now, and she is learning to love herself. And that is exactly what Jesus wants her to do—to learn to love herself. We make a mistake, however, of thinking that Jesus came to condemn us for our pantry shelves. Jesus said, "God did not send his Son into the world to condemn the world, but to save the world" (John 3:17). The Christian faith encourages us to get our lives together and to live them as God intended, but that is not the heart of our faith. The heart of our faith is that we cannot get our pantry shelves in order on our own. No amount of our rearranging or reordering our shelves will change the contents. We need God to get our shelves in order.

    God can do it. Only God is good enough, for God is perfect. We cannot save ourselves. "Who then can be saved?" the disciples ask in disbelief when the good rich man is turned away. Jesus responds, "For mortals it is impossible." He could have said, "Everyone's pantry is lacking." A long silence reigns as Jesus watches the rich man disappear from view. Jesus had looked on that man and had loved him. Jesus continues, "For mortals it is impossible but not for God; for God all things are possible." Jesus ends his preaching tour not by condemning all people, but by taking our condemnation on himself. He turns south to Jerusalem, walks to the cross, dies for our sakes, accomplishes for us the perfection we cannot accomplish for ourselves. He does not go just 50 percent of the way to the cross and say, There, that is the general direction, keep heading toward the cross and you will find salvation. He goes all the way to the cross for us. He is not taking 60 percent of our sin with him, he is taking it all, claims it as his own and dies with it. He does not die for 70 percent of all people, but for everyone. It is a good thing there are no compromises. He is not content with us having 80 percent of meaning in life. In Christ we have 100 percent of life. In Christ our faith is made whole. In Christ we receive the Holy Spirit, who enables us to live Christ's perfect ethic; in Christ all people may know God's justice; in Christ the world moves to God's perfect will; in Christ our pathetic pantry of personal deeds is blessed.

    God needs us to do our part. It is like the old saying, Do the best you can and leave the rest with God. In faith God counts our imperfect actions as perfect. It is not too hard to live Christ's perfect ethic. As Jesus says, whoever offers a cup of water will receive salvation (Mk. 9:41).

    My brother-in-law and his brother were on a cycling trip this summer on a wilderness cycling trail that follows an abandoned railway through the interior mountains of British Columbia. The day had started off beautiful, but the clouds rolled in and then it started to rain. They stopped for what shelter they could find under a railway trestle during the worst of it and rode on when they could, but gradually the wetness soaked through. Even with pedaling hard they could not keep warm and they became chilled. They had miscalculated the distance to civilization, and soon they realized that they were in real danger of hypothermia. When they finally reached a campsite near the main highway, it was mostly deserted. A house trailer was parked at one of the sites and they went up to it, almost desperate for warmth and dryness. They knocked on the door. "Hello, is anyone there. We need help." There were so many good reasons for the elderly couple inside to say no. Two unkempt men in the middle of a rainstorm. "Come in, come in," they said, and gave them a place to change their clothing and heated some mushroom soup. Such are the actions that we are empowered to do by God. More than this, such are the actions of God toward us.

So what happened to the rich man? Is it story finished, book closed, game over, door slammed, lights out, for the rich man? We do not know. Only God knows—except that we know Jesus loved him and he is one of the people for whom Jesus died. We do not know his story, but we do know the story of Michigan billionaire Thomas Monaghan. He is the founder of Domino's Pizza, one of the most successful chains in the United States. In the late 1980s, when he was 54, he was at his place on Lake Huron during a gale and reading C. S. Lewis' *Mere Christianity*. Perhaps the reading struck fond boyhood memories of being raised for a short time in a Roman Catholic home for boys. Perhaps he remembered what had originally driven him to enroll in seminary for a brief time before being expelled for pillow fighting and whispering in chapel. Something happened to him while reading C.S. Lewis. The next day he began his renunciation of wealth by raiding his own pantry. First he sold his Sikorsky S-76 helicopter, then the corporate jet, the Bentley Turbo, the Rolls-Royce, the 190-foot sloop, the collection of Frank Lloyd Wright furniture and artifacts, eventually his 240 classic cars, and recently he sold his pizza business for an estimated $1 billion. He is ploughing his wealth into good causes, like his church.

Finally, in this moment, you and I take our turn and go to Jesus and kneel before him as the rich man did, and ask, "What must I do to inherit eternal life?" And Jesus looks down at us and he loves us. He looks into our pantry cupboards and sees the good deeds we have done and the bad and the things that are missing. He does not say, "You get 35 percent, or 60 percent, or 70 percent," as we might expect. He simply says, with remarkable grace and love, "By your faith in me, you lack nothing. Rise up and share what you have."

Compositional Comments

Normally I preach a pericope or small unit of scripture. I do not try to preach a large section, simply because it becomes too unwieldy. A sermon, we are taught, should have simplicity at its heart. The preacher should be able to state clearly the one thought around which the sermon is composed. By the end of the sermon, a listener ideally will be able to identify that thought as a short sentence because it has been repeated, perhaps in several variations, throughout the sermon. The meaning of the sermon as discerned by the listener may well be the meaning that the preacher intended to communicate, but equally the meaning may be a related meaning that the listener derived in silent conversation with the preacher, allowing that the Holy Spirit might speak in different ways to different people through the same sermon. In any case, the most effective communication allows the listener the least doubt about the preacher's own understanding.

To consider preaching most of Mark 9—10 as a unit proved to be a useful departure from my normal preaching approach. The entire section deals with ethics. The clever parallelism of compositional structure that Robert Reid has identified amongst the various pericopes of this section, the accumulation of similar instances of tough ethical import, and the sense of a finished narrative reinforce the sense that this material belongs together as a large unit. Even as Jesus is constructing arguments, so, too, the preacher Mark is constructing arguments in ordering Jesus' material as he does. One can preach from either perspective. Taking the former, a preacher is more likely to preach just one pericope, thus the context of the passage likely will be determined most by the stories and sayings immediately adjacent to the one chosen. In the latter approach, however, allowing Mark's compositional strategy to shape my understanding, I find a significance that I might otherwise have overlooked: Jesus' hard teachings on ethics immediately precede his going to the cross. In other words, an important link exists between the impossibility of living up to God's high ethical standard and what Christ accomplishes on the cross. Here I sensed that I was arriving at something close to the heart of Mark's "sermon" and that I wanted to be at the heart of my sermon: By his death and resurrection, Christ enables us to live his perfect ethic.

I wanted my understanding to be clearly communicated. Thus, I did not want to overwhelm my hearers with all of the material from this ethical section of Mark. I chose one pericope that closely represented the larger picture—the story of the rich young man. However, I also wanted the sectional material to be communicated effectively. I first devised the idea that Jesus was on a preaching tour on the subject of ethics, and chose to "film" some of the places he preached with some excerpts of his sermons, prior to this scene with the rich man. Still, my sermon was too cumbersome, heavy, and complicated. No wonder this was the result with the various heavy sayings reassembled together in condensed form! In order to further simplify and clarify, I sought a unifying image. When it occurred to me that Jesus was doing a loving inspection of his people, I thought of several kinds of inspection and the image of a pantry came to mind. I then followed a theological method I usually follow in sermon composition: In roughly equal sections or "pages," I move from trouble in the biblical text to similar trouble in our world, to God's gracious action in or behind the biblical text, to God's similar gracious action in our world. This movement echoes Mark's larger structure, which moves in these chapters from Jesus' condemnation of those to whom he speaks to the salvation he accomplishes on the cross.

Mark 10:46—11:25
The Twelfth Narrative Complex

I ON FAITH (Mk. 10:46–52)

{46}	A		They came to Jericho. As he and his disciples and a large crowd were leaving Jericho, Bartimaeus son of Timaeus, a blind beggar, was sitting by the roadside.	SIGHTLESS AND SITTING
{47}		B	When he heard that it was Jesus of Nazareth, he began to shout out and say, "Jesus, Son of David, have mercy on me!"	PLEADING FOR MERCY
{48}			C Many sternly ordered him to be quiet, but he cried out even more loudly, "Son of David, have mercy on me!"	PERSISTENT REQUEST
{49}			D Jesus stood still and said, "Call him here."	JESUS SPEAKS
			E And they called the blind man, saying to him, "Take heart; get up, he is calling you."	CALLED
{50}			E' So throwing off his cloak, he sprang up and came to Jesus.	RESPONDS
{51}			D' Then Jesus said to him, "What do you want me to do for you?"	JESUS SPEAKS
			C' The blind man said to him, "My teacher, let me see again."	PERSISTENT REQUEST
{52}		B'	Jesus said to him, "Go; your faith has made you well."	FAITH HEALS
	A'		Immediately he regained his sight and followed him on the way.	SEEING AND FOLLOWING

II THE FIRST TEMPLE VISIT (Mk. 11:1–11)

{11:1}	A		When they were approaching Jerusalem, at Bethphage and Bethany, near the Mount of Olives, he sent two of his disciples	JERUSALEM AND BETHANY
{2}		B 1	and said to them, "Go into the village ahead of you,	"GO…"
		2	and immediately as you enter it, you will find tied there a colt that has never been ridden; untie it and bring it.	BRING COLT
{3}		3	If anyone says to you, 'Why are you doing this?' just say this, 'The Lord needs it and will send it back here immediately.'"	HOW TO ANSWER
{4}		1'	They went away	"WENT…"
		2'	and found a colt tied near a door, outside in the street. As they were untying it,	FIND COLT
{5}		3'	some of the bystanders said to them, "What are you doing, untying the colt?"	
{6}			They told them what Jesus had said; and they allowed them to take it.	HOW TO ANSWER
{7}		B' a	Then they brought the colt to Jesus and threw their cloaks on it; and he sat on it.	JESUS ACTS THE ROLE OF HAILED KING
{8}		b	Many people spread their cloaks on the road, and others spread leafy branches that they had cut in the fields.	PEOPLE GIVE KINGLY HOMAGE
{9}		b'	Then those who went ahead and those who followed were shouting, "Hosanna! Blessed is the one who comes in the name of the Lord!	PEOPLE SHOUT KINGLY HOMAGE
{10}		a'	Blessed is the coming kingdom of our ancestor David! Hosanna in the highest heaven!"	JESUS ASSERTED TO BE THE KING
{11}	A'		Then he entered Jerusalem and went into the temple;	JERUSALEM

		and when he had looked around at everything,	AND
		as it was already late, he went out to Bethany with the twelve.	BETHANY

III THE FRUITLESS FIG TREE AS ENACTED PARABLE (Mk. 11:12–15)

{12}	A	On the following day,	
		when they came from Bethany, he was hungry.	BETHANY
{13}	B	Seeing in the distance a fig tree in leaf,	TREE IN LEAF
		he went to see whether perhaps	
		he would find anything on it.	FRUIT-BEARING?
		C When he came to it, he found nothing but leaves,	ONLY LEAVES
		C' for it was not the season for figs.	WRONG SEASON
{14}		B' He said to it,	
		"May no one ever eat fruit from you again."	NO LONGER
		And his disciples heard it.	FRUIT-BEARING
{15}	A'	Then they came to Jerusalem.	JERUSALEM

II' THE SECOND VISIT TO THE TEMPLE (Mk. 11:15–19)

	A	And he entered the temple and began to drive out	ENTERS
		those who were selling and those who were buying in the temple,	
	B	and he overturned the tables of the money changers	OVERTURNS
		and the seats of those who sold doves;	TEMPLE OUTRAGES
{16}		and he would not allow anyone to carry anything	REFUSES "THINGS"
		through the temple.	
{17}		C He was teaching and saying, "Is it not written,	
		'My house shall be called a house of prayer	HOUSE OF PRAYER
		for all the nations'?	
		C' But you have made it a den of robbers."	DEN OF ROBBERS
{18}		B' And when the chief priests and the scribes heard it,	
		they kept looking for a way to kill him;	BECOMES TEMPLE
		for they were afraid of him, because the whole crowd	TEMPLE OUTRAGE
		was spellbound by his teaching.	OFFERS "WORDS"
{19}	A'	And when evening came, Jesus and his disciples	DEPARTS
		went out of the city.	

I' ON FAITH (Mk. 11:20–25)

{20}	A	In the morning as they passed by,	
		they saw the fig tree withered away to its roots.	
{21}		Then Peter remembered and said to him,	WHAT YOU SAID
		"Rabbi, look! The fig tree that you cursed has withered."	HAPPENED
{22}	B	Jesus answered them, "Have faith in God.	HAVE FAITH
{23}		B' 1 Truly I tell you, if you say to this mountain,	
		'Be taken up and thrown into the sea,'	WHATEVER YOU ASK
		2 and if you do not doubt in your heart, but believe	BELIEVE IT WILL BE DONE
		that what you say will come to pass,	AND IT WILL
		3 it will be done for you.	
{24}		1' So I tell you, whatever you ask for in prayer,	WHATEVER YOU ASK
		2' believe that you have received it,	BELIEVE IT WILL BE DONE
		3' and it will be yours.	AND IT WILL
{25}	A'	"Whenever you stand praying, forgive,	
		if you have anything against anyone;	
		so that your Father in heaven	FORGIVE, SO THAT IT ALSO
		may also forgive you your trespasses."	MAY HAPPEN FOR YOU

The Rhetorical Shape of the Narrative Complex

As indicated in the discussion at the sixth narrative complex, Mark uses the noun form of the verb "to believe" only five times. The first instance was an isolated use in the story of the paralyzed man lowered through the ceiling before Jesus (Mk. 2:5). The second and third instances are integral to the fictive argument of the sixth narrative complex in which the disciples are encouraged to have more faith and the expression of a woman's faith brings healing (Mk. 4:40 and 5:34). The fourth and the last uses of the noun form of "faith" identify the framing stories of the present collection. Jesus affirms that the expression of a man's faith has brought healing (Mk. 10:52) and encourages his disciples to have more faith (Mk. 11:22). The repetition of this motif correlates strongly to the sixth narrative collection in the overarching meta-narrative of the Gospel.

With the departure from Jericho, Mark moves his audience into the first of a cycle of tradition played out over three days. The first day begins with the healing of Bartimaeus and concludes with Jesus entering the temple precincts at dusk (10:46—11:11). The second day details the cursing of the fig tree and the "cleansing" of the temple (11:12–19). The third day begins with the disciples drawing attention to the withered fig tree and includes Jesus' teaching concerning the nature of faith (11:20–26). Thematically, the structure of this individual collection is similar to the structure of the entire Galilean ministry meta-narrative. An unparalleled, central story of judgment on the temple-cult (cf. the judgment of Jewish particularism) is flanked by two stories of Jesus visiting the temple (cf. two feeding miracle stories). These stories, in turn, are bracketed by two episodes on the subject of "having faith" and the importance of prayer.

The juxtaposition of the episodes in the twelfth narrative complex can be visualized thus:

```
 I   ON FAITH                                          Mk. 10:46–52
   II   THE FIRST TEMPLE VISIT                         Mk. 11:1–11
     III   THE FRUITLESS FIG TREE AS ENACTED PARABLE   Mk. 11:12–15a
   II'  THE SECOND VISIT TO THE TEMPLE                 Mk. 11:15b–19
 I'  ON FAITH                                          Mk. 11:20–25
```

The Central Motif

Early in the ministry, Mark depicts disciples gasping in wonder and fear in the face of Jesus' remarkable acts of faith. In the calm after the storm, the question rings in the ears of disciples and readers, alike, "Why are you so afraid? Do you still have no faith?" (Mk. 4:40). A woman of great "faith" believes that she will be healed if only she can touch his garment. She risks the condemnation of the community in her desperate need to believe and act (Mk. 5:24–34). Mark's Jesus responds, "Daughter, your faith has made you well." In the present complex, a blind man begs beside the highway, and in the face of continued discouragement from those around him, persistently cries out in utterly helpless "faith" for the healing touch of Jesus; "Go, your faith has made you whole" is the response. Will the disciples fail to understand? Mark left them at risk throughout his Galilean ministry meta-narrative. Now, as Jesus arrives in the Holy City, he adjures them again, "Have faith in God!"

The setting for the triumphal entry story finds its interpretive horizon in both Zechariah 9:9 and Psalm 118. Matthew makes the dependence explicit (Mt. 21:5), but Mark used the promise of these texts to shape the image that Jesus' entry was the fulfillment of the longed-for Davidic kingdom (2 Sam. 7:16). The culmination builds to a climax at the point-of-turning in the story when the promise of Psalm 118:25–26 is given voice by the crowd. But the story concludes anticlimactically, with Jesus' "looking around at everything" and then just leaving. The resolution to his enigmatic departure awaits its denouement in the balancing episode of the second visit to the temple in 11:15–19.

In the two-stage story of Jesus' arrival at the temple, Mark shapes the stories as fulfillment of Isaiah 56:7 and Jeremiah 7:11. Aside from these cited references, he also appears to have drawn on Malachi 3:1 (which promises that the Lord will one day arrive in the temple and judge it), Zechariah 14:21 (which indicates that the merchants will be the focus of this judgment), and Hosea 9:15 (which describes the Lord as driving out of the temple those who have compromised it). Again, texts such as these, together with Jeremiah 8, provide both a horizon of interpretation and the cloth out of which the stories have been shaped. By structuring a story in light of these references, Mark draws attention to the severity of judgment upon the temple-cult of Jesus' day. In depicting Jesus as ousting the vendors from the court of the Gentiles, he also has furthered the dramatic action of the story, since the religious leaders of Jerusalem were the ones who collected the revenues from merchants renting space within the temple walls.

At the heart of the complex, an enacted parable depicts God's judgment on activity that has become faithless. The framing stories depict and call for a tenacious faith. Doubt and lack of faith are not cast as a failure of nerve (a perspective one might adopt if the definition of faith is limited to Jesus' discussion of it in 11:20–25). With the whole complex in view faith is depicted as that which must be acted upon (11:25). It must be persistent in the face of continued discouragements (10:48). Faith must risk at a fundamental level (5:34) and must be willing to respond to the demonstration of God's power.

The one who stumbles in the face of a display of the power of God (4:40) will never possess the faith to believe he or she can truly move a mountain (11:23).

In this respect, Mark depicts the temple-cult as the epitome of a bureaucratized faith no longer willing to risk discovering what God was saying and doing in their midst. Episode II provides the elements for the opportunity to "Have faith," but instead of a final response of faith, Mark's Jesus is confronted with a massive distortion of the purpose of the temple and the temple-cult when he looked around. In his break with the temple-cult as depicted in the second temple episode, Mark offers elements not found in the other synoptics. Jesus not only cast out the vendors, but overturned the tables filled with sacrificial animals and prohibited those attempting to carry sacrificial implements through the corridors from doing so. The act of driving the vendors from the temple evokes the classic image of prophetic dissatisfaction with the way in which sacrifices had displaced faith in the name of worship (Jer. 6:20; 7:21–23; 18:15–17).[1]

Westerners often fail to appreciate the enacted parable of withering the fig tree because they anthropomorphize feelings of injustice on behalf of the tree or the owner of the orchard. Although there are any number of Old Testament references to the lack of fruit from Israel through the symbolism of the fig tree, the word of the Lord in Jeremiah 8 is probably the controlling image. In the latter text the charge is made that the "false pen of the scribes" has made the law of the Lord into a lie. Judgment on this "abomination" is cited by the prophet, for "When I wanted to gather them, says the LORD, / there are no grapes on the vine, / nor figs on the fig tree; / even the leaves are withered, and what I gave them has passed away from them" (Jer. 8:8–13). The text is rich with images that shape the entire Jerusalem debate meta-narrative (Mk. 10:46—13:44) through the fifteenth narrative complex (Mk. 13:1–36).

Although allusions to Jeremiah 8 and Psalm 118 clearly shape this complex and those to follow, the point is not to suggest that any one or two texts provides the final key to what may be a Marcan midrash. Rather, the point is that judgment and reversal was a pervasive prophetic theme in providing a horizon of interpretation. This was no obscure opinion that requires a cabalistic reading of the ancient texts. Mark appears to have much to say about God's judgment on the temple-cult in Jerusalem and finds ample warrant for his conclusions from the judgment of God on a previous generation's lack of faithfulness. For Mark and Mark's Jesus, the ideal of Israelite faith was certainly not the institution of the temple regardless of how marvelous its "one stone on another" edifice may have appeared. The ideal response is that of Bartimaeus, who, by faith, followed Jesus along the way and provides a model for the otherwise confused disciples who need to be adjured to "Have faith!" The most striking aspect of this complex is not that we can find rich meaning in Old Testament citations and allusions. It is that the disciples, unlike readers, don't see what appears to be obvious in Mark's telling.

The form forces the reader to consider what situation would call forth Jesus' lesson (11:20–25) on the importance of courage and forgiveness? Mark's use of the tradition at this point appears to suggest that too much timidity on the part of leadership (cf., "If you do not doubt...") and too little grace or trust in others (cf., "Forgive if you have anything against anyone...") makes for a ministry "withered away at its roots." Such faith is little better than the faith of the temple leadership in Jesus' day? The question posed in the fictive argument is whether the post-Pentecost community of the Twelve had finally become the very thing Jesus opposed throughout most of his ministry? Had it also become a leadership no longer willing to risk discovering what God was saying and doing in their midst?

Once, Jesus came to the most glorious shrine to prayer in his day, looking for a "house of prayer for all nations." When he arrived, he found its sworn protectors had packaged faith, merchandised it, and controlled the concession on hawking its insidious displacements. At its core, the triumphal entry story is really about judgment more than faith, but judgment is only a threat to those whose actions, however pious they may appear, fail to produce the fruit of faith. And what produces fruit that would keep the axe from being laid to the root of the withered tree? The answer lies with blind Bartimaeus, who persisted in the face of all the naysayers in his will to see. When the moment came, he cast aside the cloak that embodied his former identity as a beggar. Jesus identified this man's persistence in the face of the naysayers as faith, his willingness, at the necessary moment to resist the comforting claim of returning to his beggar's cloak, his willingness to believe that the "mountain" that seemed immovable in his life could be moved, and his willingness to proclaim that it was the Son of David to whom he looked for this deliverance.

Mark 11:27—12:12
The Thirteenth Narrative Complex

I JESUS UNSTOPPABLE "FOR FEAR OF THE CROWD" (Mk. 11:27–33)

{27} A   Again they came to Jerusalem.
      As he was walking in the temple, the chief priests,
      the scribes, and the elders came to him
{28}   and said, "By what authority are you doing these things?
      Who gave you this authority to do them?"   BY WHAT AUTHORITY
{29}   B   Jesus said to them, "I will ask you one question; answer   QUESTION
      me, and I will tell you by what authority I do these things.
{30}   C   Did the baptism of John come from heaven,   HEAVEN
        or was it of human origin? Answer me."   HUMAN ORIGIN
{31}   C' 1   They argued with one another, "If we say,
        'From heaven,'   HEAVEN?
        2   he will say, 'Why then did you not believe him?'   BELIEVE IN JOHN?
{32}   1'   But shall we say, 'Of human origin'?   HUMAN ORIGIN?
          2'   —they were afraid of the crowd,
            for all regarded John as truly a prophet.   BELIEVE IN JOHN
{33}   B'   So they answered Jesus, "We do not know."   EQUIVOCATION
   A'   And Jesus said to them, "Neither will I tell you
      by what authority I am doing these things."   BY WHAT AUTHORITY

II THE PARABLE OF THE VINEYARD (Mk. 12:1–11)

{12:1} A   Then he began to speak to them in parables.
      1   "A man planted a vineyard,   THE OWNER INITIATES
        2   put a fence around it, dug a pit for the wine press,
          and built a watchtower;
   B   1'   then he leased it to tenants
      2'   and went to another country.
{2}   1   When the season came, he sent a slave
      to the tenants to collect from them his share   SENT
      of the produce of the vineyard.
{3}   2   But they seized him, and beat him,   RESPONSE
      and sent him away empty-handed.
{4}   1   And again he sent another slave to them;   SENT
      2   this one they beat over the head and insulted.   RESPONSE
{5}   1   Then he sent another,   SENT
      2   and that one they killed.   RESPONSE
     1   And so it was with many others;   SENT
      2   some they beat, and others they killed.   RESPONSE
{6}   B' 1   He had still one other, a beloved son.   SON IDENTIFIED
     2   Finally he sent him to them,
      saying, 'They will respect my son.'   RESPECT SON?
{7}   1'   But those tenants said to one another,
      'This is the heir; come, let us kill him,   SON IDENTIFIED
      and the inheritance will be ours.'
{8}   2'   So they seized him, killed him,   KILL SON
      and threw him out of the vineyard.
{9}   A' 1   What then will the owner of the vineyard do?   WHAT OWNER WILL DO
     2   He will come and destroy the tenants
      and give the vineyard to others.   REVERSAL
{10}   1'   Have you not read this scripture:
      'The stone that the builders rejected
      has become the cornerstone;   WHAT THE LORD IS DOING

| {11} | | 2' this was the Lord's doing, and it is amazing in our eyes'?" | REVERSAL |

I' JESUS UNSTOPPABLE "FOR FEAR OF THE CROWD" (Mk. 12:12)
{12}	1	When they realized that he had told this parable against them,	THEY REALIZED IMPORT
	2	they wanted to arrest him,	WHAT THEY WANTED
	1'	but they feared the crowd.	THEY FEARED THE CROWD
	2'	So they left him and went away.	WHAT THEY DID

The Rhetorical Shape of the Narrative Complex

Structuring an entire narrative complex with only three episodes is surprising.[1] Yet the brief reference to the "fear of the crowd" at 12:12 obviously brings readers back to the mention of the "fear of the crowd" at the heart of the first episode (11:27–33). Between these two episodes is one extended parable that in its very isolation draws attention to its significance.

The parable of the vineyard obviously is a recasting and updating of the Septuagint version of Isaiah 5:1–5 and its depiction of salvation history. That history is summarized in the repetition of the parable's simple step progression of a sending-1/response-1, sending-2/response-2, and so forth, formula in segment B. Balanced against the traditional story of rejection of prophetic counsel comes another story of the rejection of the son in B'. The original judgment on the rejection of the prophets was, "Therefore my people go into exile without knowledge" (Isa. 5:13), but Mark has Jesus supplant a judgment of exile with the judgment of vindication drawn from Psalm 118. Rejection in this "kingship psalm" is overturned by victory. The promise implied in the psalm is that the work of the longed-for king, who unites his troops and wins an otherwise impossible victory, is actually the work of the Lord. The king who can serve as catalyst for this kind of unity is likened to the most important stone in the architecture of a building, and the authority of such a king is that of the Lord.[2] And only those who will serve this vindicated king are permitted to enjoy his rule and reign.

Drury contends that this parable and the parable of the sower, the two largest parables in Mark's Gospel, are the central parabolic visions of the work. For Drury, the parable of the sower becomes a metaphor for what Jesus is attempting to do in his ministry, and the allegory of the vineyard describes what Mark believes God plans to do in salvation history.[3] He finds that Mark's combination of the citation from Psalm 118 with the parable of judgment cannot be disentangled from the subsequent execution of Jesus and birth of the Gentile mission. In Mark's Gospel, the Gentile mission is an integral aspect of Jesus' teaching.[4] Of course, some scholars attempt to rework the parable, finding a core that could have been credible in the life of Jesus.[5] But for Mark's readers, nothing is veiled in the way the account of salvation history is presented here. As Mack observes, "attempts to redeem the parable as an aesthetic object simply wilt in the light of the transparent purposes of the author. Mark did not have Jesus tell the parable to the temple authorities to instruct them in the Gospel, but to provoke the fruition of the plot of the parable which was at the same time the plot of the Gospel."[6] We need constantly to remind ourselves that, unlike those of us who are children of the literate revolution, Mark's audience members were not concerned with the effort to recover the actual words of Jesus. They were only concerned to hear Jesus' word for them in their time and their place, engaged as they were in a battle of identity with Judaism and with the legitimacy of their continued existence in the empire.

The juxtaposition of the episodes in the thirteenth narrative complex can be visualized thus:

```
 I  JESUS UNSTOPPABLE "FOR FEAR OF THE PEOPLE"    Mk. 11:27–33
 II THE PARABLE OF THE VINEYARD                   Mk. 12:1–11
 I' JESUS UNSTOPPABLE "FOR FEAR OF THE PEOPLE"    Mk. 12:12
```

The Central Motif

The inevitable conflict between priest and prophet in the first episode of this collection offers a classic example of Max Weber's famous distinction between institutional and charismatic authority. On one hand, the chief priests are the embodiment of institutional authority with all its ties to the monarchy, to the temple, to the temple cult and priestly bureaucracy and with all its interpretive responsibilities as the final arbiter of interpretation, its command of the scribes, and its command of the written Torah, which possessed the authority of law. On the other hand, charismatic authority is individualistic and ad hoc. According to Weber, "[I]t is sharply opposed to rational and particularly bureaucratic, authority, and to traditional authority, whether in its patriarchal, patrimonial, or estate variants, all of which are everyday forms of domination."[7] Weber's distinction is predicated on nineteenth-century Romanticism and antinomian theories that privileged the role of prophet over that of priest, as in Wellhausen's highly influential *Prolegomena to the History of Israel*. We have many contemporary organizational theorists who would argue that power is more complicated than this. However, they would say this as those who have stood on Weber's shoulders to gain their perspective. In the present text, Mark's fictive argument represents an excellent example of Weber's theory. The chief priests who confront Jesus for the first time in these episodes are depicted as bureaucrats deeply angered by this upstart who would challenge their authority. Far from word games, the issue here is power and who has the right to wield it. The first episode makes this point in a Marcan interpretive aside that occurs at the climactic moment of a step progression in the point-of-turning in the episode. The story pits codified institutional authority against charismatic authority. The aim of the questions "By what authority…Who gave you authority…" was to expose the lack of priestly or rabbinic sanction of Jesus' teachings and actions. In reply Mark has Jesus set a sharp antithesis between authority from "heaven" and authority from "human origin." The authority of an institutional response is sharply juxtaposed to a kind of charismatic authority—the very authority that usually authorized the institution in the first place.

This is the story of power. Movements are founded by the centralizing charisma of a visionary or a group of visionaries. Eventually this expression of charisma becomes codified, institutionalized, and an organization is born that, generally, threatens the continued exercise of the very kind of power that once gave it life. The confrontation between these two authorities at this point presages the reason why the Gospel narrative must end in a death. Either the leaders of the temple-cult or Jesus must be defeated. The death of one or the other becomes a narrative necessity. We know this conflict in the life of Jesus. Its contours have been explored in a variety of ways. The more intriguing question is, Who or what is the institutionalizing force that is trying to silence the authority of charisma in Mark's church? Against whom is the fictive argument of this collection addressed?

Mark's Gospel has already provided ample evidence that depicts Jesus as having judged the temple-cult in Jerusalem. In repudiating the misuse of the court of the Gentiles in the previous complex, Mark had already established that Jesus confronted the temple leadership over their abuse of Yahweh's outreach to Gentiles. Now, in this complex, he has Jesus unilaterally declare the Gentile mission as the task of the church rather than any further efforts to constitute Christianity as a sect of Judaism. Just as Mark used the seventh narrative complex to depict the ideal role of leaders within the church, this complex provides a definitive mission statement for the church.

The Jerusalem church, according to Acts, conceded the possibility of an outreach that could include Gentiles in "the way" (cf. Acts

15). Yet this story, told by Luke, still envisions Jerusalem Christianity and the effort to convert other Jews as the primary vision of the Jerusalem church. Mark has no patience for this version of Christianity, which effectively soft-pedals Jesus as Messiah without acknowledging the implications of his "sonship." Mark's Jesus will have none of this. He pronounces, in advance of his martyrdom, the judgment of God on those who would kill the Son. The judgment amounts to a quitclaim deed of the kingdom. All future interests in salvation history and the kingdom-come are hereby granted to the "others" (12:9) who comprise the Gentile mission.

This shocking pronouncement must be placed in context. If these words seem intolerant, they are born of a period of increasing religious intolerance as the Roman edict against any new religions increased hostilities between the church and the synagogue. As such, the pronouncement is yet another example of Mark's radical rhetoric. However, if the argument put forward here is accepted, charging Mark with anti-Semitism would be not only anachronistic but also naive. For Mark's readers, antipathy between synagogue and church was already a given. The *news* for these readers would have been the clarity of vision for the Gentile mission Mark attributed to Jesus. In this parable, the purpose and person become one. The *news* would have been the not-so-veiled indictment of the community of the Twelve for its bureaucratic inaction arising from a failed policy of clinging to a Jewish identity.

Mark 12:13–44
The Fourteenth Narrative Complex

I DEBATE OVER WHAT TO RENDER TO GOD (Mk. 12:13–17)

{13} A   Then they sent to him some Pharisees and
some Herodians to trap him in what he said.   SENT TO TRAP
{14}   B a And they came and said to him,
"Teacher, we know that you are sincere,
        b and show deference to no one;   ABOUT DUE
        b' for you do not regard people with partiality,   DEFERENCE
      a' but teach the way of God in accordance with truth.
     C Is it lawful to pay taxes to the emperor, or not?   EMPEROR
{15}   Should we pay them, or should we not?"
      D But knowing their hypocrisy, he said to them,
"Why are you putting me to the test?
Bring me a denarius and let me see it."   BRING ME THE TEST
{16}   D' And they brought one.   THEY BROUGHT IT
     C' Then he said to them, "Whose head is this, and whose
title?" They answered, "The emperor's."   EMPEROR
{17}   B' Jesus said to them, "Give to the emperor
the things that are the emperor's,   ABOUT DUE
and to God the things that are God's."   DEFERENCE
  A' And they were utterly amazed at him.   AMAZED AT HIM

II DEBATE OVER KNOWING SCRIPTURE (Mk. 12:18–27)

{18} A Some Sadducees, who say there is no resurrection,   NO RESURRECTION
came to him and asked him a question, saying,
{19}   B "Teacher, Moses wrote for us that   WHAT MOSES WROTE
'if a man's brother dies, leaving a wife
but no child, the man shall marry the widow
and raise up children for his brother.'
{20}   C There were seven brothers; the first married and,   EARTHLY MARRIAGES
when he died, left no children;
{21}   and the second married her and died,
leaving no children; and the third likewise;
{22}   none of the seven left children.
Last of all the woman herself died.
{23}   D In the resurrection whose wife will she be?   QUIBBLING QUESTION
For the seven had married her."
{24}   D' Jesus said to them, "Is not this the reason
you are wrong, that you know neither   QUESTION OF POWER
the scriptures nor the power of God?
{25}   C' For when they rise from the dead,   HEAVENLY
they neither marry nor are given in marriage,   RELATIONSHIPS
but are like angels in heaven.
{26}   B' And as for the dead being raised, have you not read
in the book of Moses, in the story about the bush,   WHAT MOSES WROTE
how God said to him, 'I am the God of Abraham,
the God of Isaac, and the God of Jacob'?
{27} A' He is God not of the dead,
but of the living; you are quite wrong."   RESURRECTION

III KNOWING WHAT IS MOST IMPORTANT (Mk. 12:28–34)

{28} A One of the scribes came near and heard them
disputing with one another,   DISPUTING
  B and seeing that he answered them well, he asked him,   ANSWERED WELL
    C 1 "Which commandment is the first of all?"   WHICH?

{29}			2 Jesus answered, "The first is, 'Hear, O Israel: the Lord our God, the Lord is one;	GOD IS ONE
{30}			3 you shall love the Lord your God with all your heart, and with all your soul, and with all your mind, and with all your strength.'	LOVE GOD
{31}			4 The second is this, 'You shall love your neighbor as yourself.'	LOVE NEIGHBOR
			5 There is no other commandment greater than these."	NOTHING GREATER
{32}		C' 1'	Then the scribe said to him, "You are right, Teacher;	CORRECT CHOICE
			2' you have truly said that 'he is one, and besides him there is no other';	GOD IS ONE
{33}			3' and 'to love him with all the heart, and with all the understanding, and with all the strength,'	LOVE GOD
			4' and 'to love one's neighbor as oneself,'	LOVE NEIGHBOR
			5' —this is much more important than all whole burnt offerings and sacrifices."	NOTHING GREATER
{34}		B'	When Jesus saw that he answered wisely, he said to him, "You are not far from the kingdom of God."	ANSWERED WISELY
	A'		After that no one dared to ask him any question.	NO MORE DISPUTING

III' JUDGMENT ON THE ABUSE OF KNOWLEDGE (Mk. 12:35–37)

{35}	A		While Jesus was teaching in the temple, he said,	JESUS TAUGHT
	B		"How can the scribes say that the Messiah is the son of David?	HOW CAN HE BE SON?
{36}		C	David himself, by the Holy Spirit, declared, 'The Lord said to my Lord,	DAVID'S LORD
			"Sit at my right hand, until I put your enemies under your feet."'	
{37}		C'	David himself calls him Lord;	DAVID'S LORD
	B'		so how can he be his son?"	HOW CAN HE BE SON?
	A'		And the large crowd was listening to him with delight.	CROWD LISTENED

II' CONDEMNATION FOR POWER ABUSED (Mk. 12:38–40)

{38}	A		As he taught, he said, "Beware of the scribes,	BEWARE SCRIBES
	B		who like to walk around in long robes, and to be greeted with respect in the marketplaces,	SEEK RESPECT
{39}			and to have the best seats in the synagogues and places of honor at banquets!	SEEK HONOR / SEEK HONOR
{40}	B'		They devour widows' houses and for the sake of appearance say long prayers.	SEEK RESPECT
	A'		They will receive the greater condemnation."	CONDEMNATION

I' WHAT TO RENDER TO GOD (Mk. 12:41–44)

{41}	1		He sat down opposite the treasury, and watched the crowd putting money into the treasury.	PUT MONEY IN
	2		Many rich people put in large sums.	RICH IN ABUNDANCE
{42}		3	A poor widow came and put in two small copper coins, which are worth a penny.	POOR BY POVERTY
{43}	1'		Then he called his disciples and said to them, "Truly I tell you, this poor widow has put in more than all those who are contributing to the treasury.	PUT MONEY IN
{44}		2'	For all of them have contributed out of their abundance;	RICH IN ABUNDANCE
		3'	but she out of her poverty has put in everything she had, all she had to live on."	POOR BY POVERTY

The Rhetorical Shape of the Narrative Complex

Both framing stories in this collection use the issue of money to lift up the question about what is to be rendered to God. In the first episode the religious leadership come to Jesus with a question calculated to force him either to commit sedition or to compromise himself with the people and their hope to throw off the yoke of Roman taxation. The last episode recounts the story of a simple peasant woman who comes to the court of women and deposits all she has in the temple treasury. If the first story explains how one is to "give to Caesar what is Caesar's," the last story depicts one person giving unto "God what is God's." The material that falls between these two episodes has much to do with the difference between giving God what is rightfully God's and the confusion that can come about when professional religious leaders lose sight of who and what they serve.

In Episode II the Sadducees present Jesus with a interpretive conundrum of a childless widow who marries, one by one, each of the brothers of one family in hopes of presenting the original descendent with an heir. In forcing an illustration through the sieve of the letter of the Levitical law, these contentious legalists hoped to catch Jesus in a riddle that they confidently believed repudiated the possibility of a resurrection. For the Sadducees, the woman in their puzzle was merely a cipher, empty of meaning except to raise the riddle's question, "Whose wife will she be?" Sexist to the core, they meet in Mark's Jesus one who turns both their sexism and their skepticism upside down. Mark reminds his readers in the balancing Episode II' that it is precisely individuals like these who "devour widow's houses," all the while seeking the seats of honor and offering lengthy public prayers. In fact, he declares, it is they who neither know the scriptures nor the power of God. They are the empty ciphers! And the result is, "They will receive the greater condemnation."

Episode III introduces the question at the heart of interpretive tradition: "What should be rendered to God?" Representatives of each of the mainstream influence groups have already confronted Jesus' authority, each in turn. Now a scribe asks the fundamental question that connects the work of interpreting the canon to the reality of daily living. In essence he asks, "What does our tradition teach as the center of faith practice?" In response, Jesus affirms the centrality of Torah. First, he cites Deuteronomy 6:4, the closest approximation the Hebrew tradition has to a confession of faith. Then he applies the confession to the practice of piety by way of Leviticus 19:18, saying that the latter is like the former precept. Mann notes that this particular combination is unique in the written tradition, but this is not to say that in oral rabbinic discussion the relationship between love of neighbor and love of God was not discussed.[1] In fact, the response of the scribe, "You are right, teacher," lends credence to the latter. And with Jesus' commendation of the scribe's response, the reader is able to see that Jesus did not view his authority as discontinuous from that of Torah and its interpretive tradition. He may have understood his charismatic-prophetic authority to come directly from Yahweh, but it was not interpretation meant to overthrow the tradition itself. Rather it challenges the interpreters of the tradition to remain true to its spirit.

In the point-of-turning episode (III'), Jesus responds to the attack waged in the first half of the collection concerning his right to authoritatively interpret scripture. He raises a question of genuine interest to his listening audience, and this time he is the one who offers the conundrum. Jesus notes that it is the interpretive position of the scribal authorities that the Messiah will be "the son of David." In scribal interpretation, the Messiah was to be a son of David, making David hierarchically the more revered of the two in the lineal equation. "So how," Jesus asks, "can an inspired David have referred to this son as *my lord*?" Former notions of social hierarchies do not apply. The crowds listen with delight as Jesus *scores* his point in this verbal joust precisely at the issue in debate—who can best interpret the meaning of Messiah? Jesus challenged his adversaries to account for a messianic expectation that transcends their hermeneutic categories. If the leaders refused to admit that one greater than David would come, then they would be judged the very enemies put under the feet of the Lord in this allusion.[2] Jesus turned the tables on his adversaries in a most outrageous manner, and the crowd listened to him with delight.

The juxtaposition of the episodes in the fourteenth narrative complex can be visualized thus:

```
     I   DEBATE OVER WHAT TO RENDER TO GOD         Mk. 12:13–17
     II  DEBATE OVER KNOWING SCRIPTURE             Mk. 12:18–27
     III  KNOWING WHAT IS MOST IMPORTANT           Mk. 12:28–34
     III' JUDGMENT ON THE ABUSE OF KNOWLEDGE       Mk. 12:35–37
     II' CONDEMNATION FOR POWER ABUSED             Mk. 12:38–40
     I'  WHAT TO RENDER TO GOD                     Mk. 12:41–44
```

The Central Motif

Mark's Jesus bluntly charges the scribes with being interpreters of the faith who supposedly agree that to love God and to love one's neighbors is the essence of true piety but actually interpret the tradition of teaching in ways that inscribe a social hierarchy in which they can have places of honor. So rather than finding in favor of their hypothetically vulnerable widow whom successive brothers have no desire to marry, they actually foreclose on the houses of such widows and regularly oust them into the streets. There are no ciphers in Jesus' charge. Everyone would have known widows who had been treated in this way. Furthermore, these bureaucrats are equally as hypocritical as the Pharisees and Herodians of Episode I. They have allowed their middling social-climbing status to obscure their ability to hear what scripture says or to act as scripture would call them. In their efforts to climb the social hierarchy, Jesus declares them morally bankrupt. In a word of judgment that would undoubtedly shock these masters of casuistry, Jesus says that the individuals who have mastered the craft of going along in order to get along—where getting along is always up the hierarchy—such people are the functionaries of what Weber would eventually call the "everyday forms of domination."[3] Even though such people probably view themselves only as "cogs in the wheel," these are the ones who will receive the greater condemnation. They are quite far from the kingdom of God!

In addition to this final judgment on the scribes, Mark also depicts the strange political collusion of the Pharisees and the Herodians again (cf. Mk. 3:6). The reader was meant to ask "What are these two groups doing conspiring together?" The former party represent the religious purists who pride themselves in their separatism. The latter group represent the cultural compromisers. Only the temple held the power to draw these diverse parties into an antagonistic unity of purpose. Herod built the temple, but the Pharisees revered it as the center of their hope. So together they come with a question that clearly divided them and place it before Jesus. Mark depicts Jesus as listening and knowing "their hypocrisy." The fact that both groups would conspire to take the very question that fiercely divided them and use it to try to trap him demonstrated their ethical hypocrisy. His enigmatic answer, that one should render back to Caesar whatever Caesar has provided and to God what God provides should be understood against the backdrop of his observations concerning the woman who offered her "tax" to God. She gave not one but both coins. She rendered everything she had to God. Money was not an intrinsically significant commodity to Jesus. Motives were. He refused to be co-opted into the debate about taxes by people whose vested interest was materialism. If he had said only "Render to Caesar

Caesar's due," his answer would have been clever but unsatisfying. By adding "and to God God's due" to the aphorism, Jesus places the question in the larger and more forceful context of God's claims upon the world.[4] He responded to their question by shifting the venue. Mark's juxtaposition of this episode with that of the widow's offering suggests that issues of money are significant in a kingdom ethic only as they reveal motives and allegiances.

While Mark advances the theme of conflict between Jewish leaders and Jesus, he raises several other issues as well. He portrays the conflict between the worldview that inordinately reveres the Caesarean power and the worldview that fully reveres and trusts the power of God. He portrays the conflict between prophecy and canon, echoing the words of Jeremiah, "How can you say, 'We are wise, / and the law [Torah] of the Lord is with us,' / when, in fact, the false pen of the scribes has made it into a lie? / The wise shall be put to shame, / they shall be dismayed and taken; / since they have rejected the word of the Lord, what wisdom is in them?" (Jer. 8:8–9).[5]

The prophet depicts a world of two consciousnesses.[6] One is the way of blessing; the other, regardless of its sleekness at any given moment, is the way of cursing. Brueggemann finds that the prophet saw a significant difference between what he saw as the *Davidic-royal* consciousness and a *Mosaic-covenantal* consciousness.[7] The former is concerned with order, peace, prosperity, and the establishment of societal riches, wisdom, and might. The latter, from the prophet's point of view, is occupied with recovering covenantal concern for righteousness, justice, and kindness. The issue is trust. Those who preach trust in the *Davidic-royal* consciousness place their confidence in the institutions designed to create and maintain order, in the institutional support of social and financial hierarchies, in a belief that these are necessary structures to weather the "droughts" of uncertain times. On the other hand, the Mosaic-covenantal consciousness views God as the great intruder and the function of a prophet is to continually challenge the establishment-consciousness to trust in God. The prophetic task is to make plain the oppressive reality of the Davidic-royal consciousness by giving voice to the charge that riches, might, and the wisdom that supports this institutional consciousness inevitably will practice oppression (Jer. 9:6). Their trust inevitably destroys the possibility of knowing the blessing of covenantal solidarity.

As with Jeremiah, Jesus does not betray the tradition of Torah; in his eyes, he attacks only its detractors, who happen to serve in the capacity as regents of the Davidic-royal consciousness. The cleansing of the temple initiates the crisis with the temple-cult, and for a brief moment Jesus puts an end to the "detestable things" in the house that bears the name of the Lord (Jer. 7:11). Obedience had always meant more than all the burnt offerings and sacrifices (cf. Jer. 7:21ff). He was forcing the religious community to face anew the meaning of Israel's destiny as the people of God and the necessity to reclaim the promise of the Mosaic-covenantal consciousness.

In the public debate collection, Mark depicts the religious leadership losing face at every turn. This man humiliates them time and again because he will not compromise. They are concerned with questions of authority. He is consumed with turning positions into practice, in forcing the question of "In the name of God, what will you render to God?" This motif structures the public debate collection and, in many ways, lies behind the entire ethic of servanthood narrative complex. Mark makes it clear that the Jerusalem religious leaders finally had Jesus put to death because he dared confront their power in the heart of their temple. They rightly sensed in Jesus' activities that he was proclaiming the abrogation of the temple religion. His repudiation of everything that appeared to them to be sacred in the tradition could not be tolerated. For Mark, the kingdom of God can no longer be reconciled with the temple or the temple-cult and its leaders. For their part, it was clear that these people no longer could reconcile themselves to Jesus, either.[8]

Only one person receives Jesus' unqualified commendation. The character is not a highly placed male, but a poor widow, a woman who conveys the essence of the kingdom by her actions. Instead of admiring the socially ostentatious and other such social climbers, Jesus draws his disciples' attention to a socially sidelined individual who clings to God as her hope. She, like Bartimaeus in the first story of the Jerusalem debate collection, is a model of faithfulness. Only she, among this litany of the would-be protectors of the Torah tradition, actually characterizes the qualities to be found in those who would lead the way for others: She acts with absolute belief and renders all she has to God. Her actions demonstrate that she is the one who in sacrificial practice lives out a faithful understanding of the greatest commandment.[9]

Mark 13:1–37
The Fifteenth Narrative Complex

I THE *TIME* AND THE *SIGN* (Mk. 13:1–6)

{13:1} *Scene 1: How Will We Know When? (13:1–4)*
       1 As he came out of the temple, one of his disciples
          said to him, "Look, Teacher,
          what large stones and what large buildings!"   TEMPLE BUILDINGS
{2}   2 Then Jesus asked him, "Do you see   JUDGMENT
          these great buildings? Not one stone   PREDICTION
          will be left here upon another;
       3 all will be thrown down."   FINALITY
{3}   1' When he was sitting on the Mount of Olives
          opposite the temple, Peter, James, John,   OPPOSITE TEMPLE
          and Andrew asked him privately,
{4}   2' "Tell us, when will this be,   TIME?
       3' and what will be the sign that all these things   WHAT SIGNS?
          are about to be accomplished?"

Scene 2: And What Will Be the Sign? (13:5–6)
{5}   A Then Jesus began to say to them,
         "Beware that no one leads you astray.   ASTRAY
{6}   B Many will come in my name   IMPOSTORS
     B' and say, 'I am he!'   IMPOSTORS
     A' and they will lead many astray.   ASTRAY

II HOW WILL WE KNOW WHEN? (Mk. 13:7–13)

{7}   A When you hear of wars and rumors of wars,   WHEN
         do not be alarmed; this must take place,
         but the end is still to come.   END YET TO COME
{8}   B For nation will rise against nation,
           and kingdom against kingdom;
           there will be earthquakes in various places;   NATURE INDICATORS
           there will be famines.
           This is but the beginning of the birthpangs.
{9}   C As for yourselves, beware; for they will
             hand you over to councils; and you will be   BROUGHT TO TRIAL
             beaten in synagogues; and you will stand
             before governors and kings because of me,   GOOD NEWS
{10}   as a testimony to them. And the good news   PROCLAIMED
             must first be proclaimed to all nations.
{11}   C' 1 When they bring you to trial   WHEN
               and hand you over, do not worry beforehand
               about what you are to say;   WHAT YOU SAY
                 2 but say whatever is given you at that time,   SPEAK WHAT IS GIVEN
             1' for it is not you who speak,   NOT YOU SPEAKING
                 2' but the Holy Spirit.   THE HOLY SPIRIT SPEAKS
{12}   B' Brother will betray brother to death,
            and a father his child, and children will rise   INTERPERSONAL
            against parents and have them put to death;   INDICATORS
{13}   and you will be hated by all because of my name.
    A' But the one who endures to the end will be saved. ENDURE TO THE END

III AND WHAT WILL BE THE SIGN? (Mk. 13:14–18)

{14}   A But when you see the desolating sacrilege   THE WHEN OF
         set up where it ought not to be   THE SIGN

			(let the reader understand), then those in Judea	
			must flee to the mountains;	
{15}	B		the one on the housetop must not go down	BE UNDIVIDED
			or enter the house to take anything away;	
{16}	B'		the one in the field must not turn back to get a coat.	BE UNDIVIDED
{17}	A'		Woe to those who are pregnant and to those who	
			are nursing infants in those days!	PRAY ABOUT WHEN
{18}			Pray that it may not be in winter.	THE SIGN HAPPENS

III' WHAT ELSE WILL BE THE *SIGN*? (Mk. 13:19–27)

{19}	A	a	For in those days there will be suffering,	IN THOSE DAYS
		b	such as has not been from the beginning	SUFFERING
			of the creation	CREATION
		b'	that God created until now,	CREATED
		a'	no, and never will be.	SUFFERING
{20}	B	a	And if the Lord had not cut short those days,	CUT SHORT
		b	no one would be saved;	SAVED
		b'	but for the sake of the elect, whom he chose,	ELECT
		a'	he has cut short those days.	CUT SHORT
{21}	B'	1	And if anyone says to you at that time, 'Look!	
			Here is the Messiah!' or 'Look! There he is!'	HERE IS MESSIAH!
		2	—do not believe it.	DO NOT BELIEVE
{22}		1'	False messiahs and false prophets will appear	FALSE MESSIAHS
			and produce signs and omens,	APPEAR
			to lead astray, if possible, the elect.	
{23}		2'	But be alert; I have already told you everything.	BE ALERT!
{24}	A'	1	But in those days, after that suffering, the sun will be darkened,	IN THOSE DAYS
			and the moon will not give its light,	COSMIC SIGNS
{25}		2	and the stars will be falling from heaven,	STARS FALL
		3	and the powers in the heavens will be shaken.	HEAVENS SHAKEN
{26}		1'	Then they will see 'the Son of Man coming	SON OF MAN
			in clouds' with great power and glory.	APPEARS
{27}		2'	Then he will send out the angels,	ANGELS SENT
			and gather his elect from the four winds,	
		3'	from the ends of the earth to the ends of heaven.	ALL POWERS

II' AND HOW ELSE WILL WE KNOW WHEN? (Mk. 13:28–29)

{28}	1		From the fig tree learn its lesson:	
	2		as soon as its branch becomes tender	WHEN YOU SEE
			and puts forth its leaves,	
	3		you know that summer is near.	THEN YOU KNOW
{29}	1'		So also,	
	2'		when you see these things taking place,	WHEN YOU SEE
	3'		you know that he is near, at the very gates.	THEN YOU KNOW

I' WHAT WILL BE THE *SIGN* AND THE *TIME*? (Mk. 13:30–37)

Scene 1': Final Word on the True Sign (13:30–32)

{30}	A		Truly I tell you,	AMEN AMEN
	B		this generation will not pass away	
			until all these things have taken place.	PASS AWAY
{31}	B'		Heaven and earth will pass away,	
			but my words will not pass away.	PASS AWAY
{32}	A'		But about that day or hour no one knows,	
			neither the angels in heaven, nor the Son,	IN HEAVEN
			but only the Father.	ONLY GOD

Scene 2': Final Word on How to Know When (13:33–37)

{33}	1		Beware, keep alert;	KEEP ALERT
			for you do not know when the time will come.	WHEN

{34}	2	It is like a man going on a journey, when he leaves home and puts his slaves in charge, each with his work,	DIVISION OF WORK
	3	and commands the doorkeeper to be on the watch.	ALERT AT WATCH
{35}	4	Therefore, keep awake—	KEEP AWAKE
	1'	for you do not know when the master of the house will come,	WHEN
	2'	in the evening, or at midnight, or at cockcrow, or at dawn,	DIVISION OF TIME
{36}	3'	or else he may find you asleep when he comes suddenly.	ASLEEP AT WATCH
{37}	4'	And what I say to you I say to all: Keep awake."	KEEP AWAKE

The Rhetorical Shape of the Narrative Complex

From public debate, Mark moves to private teaching. There is little disagreement about the boundaries of this collection generally known as the Little Apocalypse.[1] Together with Mark 4, Mark 13 represents the second major collection of *logia* in this Gospel. Whole theologies of Mark have been developed from this collection of teaching. These theories generally depend on the thesis that, with minor editorial adaptation, Mark has melded a preexisting Jewish (or a Jewish-Christian) Apocalypse into the Jesus tradition.[2]

My schematization takes the two questions in 13:1–4 as the touchstone of the arrangement: "Tell us, when will *this* be, and what will be the sign that *all these things* are about to be accomplished?"(13:4). The first *"this"* refers to the destruction of the temple still under construction in this setting. The second *"all these things"* assumes that with the destruction of the temple the events of the end must surely be set in motion. Thus, the question of *"When?"* implies a general desire to know about the events surrounding the destruction of the temple. The question of *"What?"* indicates the desire to know the *sign* or signs that would precipitate the final cataclysm in which all things are consumed. With the questions introduced, Mark organizes Jesus' response in the following manner:

I The *When* and *What*
   1 *When* and *What* questions are posed. (vv. 1–4)
     2 *What* matters declared: watch out for the sign of impostors. (vv. 5–6)
  II *When* material: the end is yet to come when these things occur (vv. 7–13)
      III *What* is described further: immediate sign of the desolating sacrilege (vv. 14–18)
      III' *What* is described further: signs of the consummation and cosmic end (vv. 19–27)
  II' *When* material: a parable about knowing when (vv. 28–29)
I' Final words on *When* and *What*
   1' *When* and *what* matters delimited: the day or hour will not be told (*when*), but Jesus' words (*what*) "will never pass away." (vv. 30–32)
     2' *When* matters finally delimited: watchfulness is required. (vv. 33–37)

This proposal has weaknesses. For example, *when* questions can not be fully disentangled from the use of temporal language concerning the final *what* sign; e.g., in verse 14, *when* is used to introduce a discussion that indicates the *what* sign of the desolating sacrilege. The strength of the proposal is that it presents the organizational invention of Mark 13 as consonant with the inventional arrangement of all the preceding narrative complexes in the Gospel.

The juxtaposition of the episodes in the fifteenth narrative complex can be visualized thus:

I THE *TIME* AND THE *SIGN*	Mk. 13:1–6
Scene 1: How Will We Know When?	(vv. 1–4)
Scene 2: And What Will Be the Sign?	(vv. 5–6)
II HOW WILL WE KNOW WHEN?	Mk. 13:7–13
III AND WHAT WILL BE THE SIGN?	Mk. 13:14–18
III' WHAT ELSE WILL BE THE SIGN?	Mk. 13:19–27
II' AND HOW ELSE WILL WE KNOW WHEN?	Mk. 13:28–29
I' WHAT WILL BE THE *SIGN* AND THE *TIME*?	Mk. 13:30–37
Scene 1: Final Word on the True Sign	(vv. 30–32)
Scene 2: Final Word on How to Know When	(vv. 33–37)

The Central Motif

By way of farewell, Mark has Jesus describe the future as a time when he is absent and false claims are made about "the Christ's" presence that could even deceive "the elect." When they are "delivered up" to the authorities, they are to depend on the Holy Spirit to guide their response. As with many farewell discourses, it becomes a vehicle to warn the next generation to hold fast and keep guard of that which was delivered to them. Olivet, like Acts 20:13–36, is a call to "[B]e alert, remembering that for three years I did not cease night or day to warn everyone with tears" (Acts 20:31). Biographical conventions, whether the story of Jesus or the story of Paul, allowed for a traditional farewell speech addressed to the future need for vigilance in regard to the faith. But "farewell addresses" disturb precisely because they allow the written convention of biography to give way to the rhetorical conventions of composing *historia*.[3]

Much of this complex is heavily dependent on the apocalyptic book of Daniel for its imagery and allusions and the manner in which it melded the view of the determination of the times into a view of faith oriented to the present and the future rather than one rooted in the past.[4] The selective picture created by the juxtaposition of one citation or allusion with another depicts a divine judgment on Israel's faith. The phrase "desolating sacrilege" in verse 14 draws on the language of Daniel 11:31 and its description of a final desecration of the temple. Josephus drew on this same allusion to argue that the desolating sacrilege actually occurred during the events of 66–70. During the siege of Jerusalem (from November of 67 to the spring of 68) he describes a series of violations of the sanctity of the temple and temple precincts by the occupying Zealots (*Antiquities* 10.11.7). These heinous acts, for Josephus, were the final appalling sacrilege, far worse than any desecration that could ever come from the hands of foreigners.[5]

Mark's Jesus affirms that final judgment on the temple and temple-cult will occur within the generation of those listening to his words, but that the exact date is known only by the Father. When the time does come, however, followers should flee the vestiges of the Jerusalem temple-cult and await the return of the Lord to empower them as his elect. The important thing is not to be misled during the interim. The horror of this period is described and promises are made to the "elect" who are willing to listen. The fourth-century historian Eusebius states that,

> Before the war, the people of the Church of Jerusalem were bidden in an oracle by revelation to men worthy of it to depart from the city and to dwell in a city of Perea called Pella. To it those who believed in Christ migrated from Jerusalem. Once the holy men had completely left the Jews and Judea, the justice of God at last overtook them, since they had committed such transgressions against Christ and his apostles. (*Ecclesiastical History* III.5.3)

In the fifth narrative complex, Mark casts the reader of the parables as an insider who "understands" what Jesus' parables mean even when followers within the story misunderstand. With the parenthetical phrase, "Let the reader understand," Mark inserts his own voice parenthetically to invite the reader (third person singular) to again assume the role of one who understands.[6] This time the subject is the most catastrophic event of the century: the destruction of the temple as judgment on the temple-cult. The Greco-Roman historian Samuel captures something of the interpretive gulf we face today in arriving at such "understanding":

> It is difficult to imagine today the terrible impact of the destruction of the temple in August 70. Frightful though the losses were in life and freedom, the destruction of Herod's great second temple brought the end of a way of life for the whole Jewish people. No longer could the

> prescribed sacrifices be carried out; no longer would priests, garbed in the manner so lovingly spelled out by Philo or Josephus, carry out the people's duties to their God. Not only the inhabitants of Judea but Jews all over the world had lost the focus of their religious life. Since the religious life was indissolubly tied to the sense of the interaction of God with his people, whom he rewarded or punished as deserved, the events of 70 could only be interpreted as the will of God. For the great community of Jews in Alexandria as well as those in Judea, the destruction of the Temple was a statement about their situation in the world. The war which dragged to its end in 73 was a political event which might effectively terminate the view of God and God's country which Jews had held for a thousand years.[7]

It was a moment in time when a fundamentally different interpretation of Christian self-understanding became possible. Historically, the destruction of the temple became the watershed event that made the final separation of Christians from Jew culturally conceivable.[8]

Mark was willing to view the fall of the temple and Jerusalem as part of the predicted events of Daniel's prophetic outline, but beyond that, he invariably turns the focus of argument to the implications for discipleship in a post-temple world in which religious identity is in disarray and in which followers of Jesus will inevitably face betrayal, persecution, and deceit. What becomes clear in this reading is the way in which Mark's fictive argument shifts the focus away from an extensive outline of history (the "determination of times"). The previous ethical instructions concerning divorce, discipleship, and the distribution of goods, as well as the validation of the Gentile mission in the parable of the vineyard, suggest that Mark was committed to an interim ethic rather than a radical theology of imminence. The end, he argues, does not come until the gospel has been preached to all nations. He depicts Jesus as deeply vested in the apocalyptic view of understanding (cf. 13:14; 4:13) but not in the apocalypticist's lack of investment in the present moment. In fact, one could argue that Mark's Jesus purposefully puts a "pox" on those who try to calculate dates precisely because a fixation on dates tends to obscure the task of living in present vigilance. Those who only await the end tend to withdraw rather than taking up a cross to follow Jesus. To those in the "present" judgment, Mark has Jesus emphasize that the one who *stands firm* to the end, rather than the one who calculates it, will be saved. The emphasis in this challenge falls on "standing firm" more than "the end."

Mark confronts those who must have thought the fall of Jerusalem was the beginning of an imminent end, with the argument that passivity while awaiting the final denouement is unacceptable. If this Gospel was written shortly after the fall of Jerusalem, there must have been many who were prognosticating the imminent end and advocating that followers simply wait for it. One wonders if this may have been the first response of the oral community of the Twelve upon arriving in Pella. Whatever power this congregation had previously held in the first decades after Jesus' death and resurrection, their "voice" appears to have dissipated with the fall of Jerusalem.[9]

If the point of the parable collection in chapter 4 was to call disciples to listen, this collection of teaching calls them to watch how they live. They can no longer live rooted in the security of the past, as if the world has no end, no judgment—the day indeed will come. Nor can they wait passively for it to arrive. If one were to ask what this narrative complex requires of its "reader," the answer must come back quite simply: exercise faithful vigilance (Be alert!), flee from Jerusalem (and from the passivity of its oral leadership?) that stands judged, flee from deceivers, and place utter reliance on the Spirit to help one stand firm. Speak courageously as the end draws near. In addition, a reader who absorbed the subtext of Mark's fictive argument was also required to consider the unthinkable: that Jesus' life, death, and resurrection require an absolute rupture, a parting of company, with the church's Jewish past. By the middle of the second century, this unthinkable challenge to the reigning self-understanding of the church became a fait accompli.[10]

Mark 14:1–53
The Sixteenth Narrative Complex

I AUTHORITIES SEEK TO ARREST JESUS (Mk. 14:1–2)

{14:1}	A	It was two days before the Passover and the festival of Unleavened Bread.	FESTIVAL
	B	The chief priests and the scribes were looking for a way to arrest Jesus by stealth	ARREST
	B'	and kill him;	EXECUTE
{2}	A'	for they said, "Not during the festival, or there may be a riot among the people."	FESTIVAL

II DISCIPLES FAIL TO UNDERSTAND (Mk. 14:3–9)

{3}	A	While he was at Bethany in the house of Simon the leper, as he sat at the table, a woman came with an alabaster jar of very costly ointment of nard,	WOMAN ACTS
	B	and she broke open the jar and poured the ointment on his head.	POURED
{4}	C	But some were there who said to one another in anger, "Why was the ointment wasted in this way?	
{5}		For this ointment could have been sold for more than three hundred denarii, and the money given to the poor." And they scolded her.	POOR
{6}	D	But Jesus said, "Let her alone; why do you trouble her?	DEFENDED
	D'	She has performed a good service for me.	DEFENDED
{7}	C'	For you always have the poor with you, and you can show kindness to them whenever you wish; but you will not always have me.	POOR
{8}	B'	She has done what she could; she has anointed my body beforehand for its burial.	ANOINTED
{9}	A'	Truly I tell you, wherever the good news is proclaimed in the whole world, what she has done will be told in remembrance of her."	WOMAN REMEMBERED

III JUDAS AND THE POSSIBILITY OF BETRAYAL (Mk. 14:10–11)

{10}	A	Then Judas Iscariot, who was one of the twelve, went to the chief priests in order to betray him to them.	BETRAY HIM
{11}	B	When they heard it, they were greatly pleased,	PLEASED
	B'	and promised to give him money.	FINANCE
	A'	So he began to look for an opportunity to betray him.	BETRAY HIM

IV PASSOVER PREPARATION (Mk. 14:12–16)

{12}	1	On the first day of Unleavened Bread, when the Passover lamb is sacrificed, his disciples said to him, "Where do you want us to go and make the preparations for you to eat the Passover?"	
{13}		So he sent two of his disciples, saying to them, "Go into the city,	GO TO CITY
	2	and a man carrying a jar of water will meet you;	
{14}		follow him, and wherever he enters, say to the owner of the house, 'The Teacher asks, Where is my guest room where I may eat the Passover with my disciples?'	
{15}		He will show you a large room upstairs, furnished and ready.	PLANS
	3	Make preparations for us there."	PREPARED

			So the disciples set out and went to the city,	WENT TO CITY
		1'	and found everything as he had told them;	PLANS
{16}		2'	and they prepared the Passover meal.	PREPARED
		3'		

IV' PASSOVER PARTAKEN (Mk. 14:17–26)

{17} A   When it was evening, he came with the twelve.   COMES TO TWELVE
{18}   B   a   And when they had taken their places and were eating,
               Jesus said, "Truly I tell you, one of you will betray me,   AMEN AMEN
               one who is eating with me."
{19}   b   They began to be distressed and to say to him
               one after another, "Surely, not I?"
{20}   b' He said to them, "It is one of the twelve,
               one who is dipping bread into the bowl with me.
{21}   a' For the Son of Man goes as it is written of him,
               but woe to that one by whom the Son of Man is betrayed!
               It would have been better for that one not to have been
               born."
{22}   C   1   While they were eating, he took a loaf of bread,   BREAD
           2   and after blessing it
           3   he broke it, gave it to them,
           4   and said, "Take; this is my body."   MY BODY
{23}   C' 1' Then he took a cup,   CUP
           2' and after giving thanks
           3' he gave it to them, and all of them drank from it.
{24}   4' He said to them,
               "This is my blood of the covenant,   MY BLOOD
               which is poured out for many.
{25}   B' a   Truly I tell you,   AMEN AMEN
           b   I will never again drink of the fruit of the vine   WILL NOT DRINK
           b' until that day when I drink it new   WILL DRINK ANEW
           a' in the kingdom of God."   KINGDOM OF GOD
{26} A' When they had sung the hymn, they went out to the Mount of Olives.   TWELVE LEAVE

III' MORE POSSIBILITIES OF "BETRAYAL" (Mk. 14:27–31)

{27}   1   And Jesus said to them, "You will all become deserters;   YOU WILL ALL
           for it is written, 'I will strike the shepherd,   DENY ME
           and the sheep will be scattered.'
{28}   But after I am raised up,
           I will go before you to Galilee."
{29}   2   Peter said to him, "Even though all   I WILL NOT
           become deserters, I will not."   DENY
{30}   1' Jesus said to him, "Truly I tell you,
           this day, this very night,
           before the cock crows twice,   YOU WILL
           you will deny me three times."   DENY ME
{31}   2' But he said vehemently,
           "Even though I must die with you,   I WILL NOT
           I will not deny you." And all of them said the same.   DENY

II' DISCIPLES FAIL TO UNDERSTAND (Mk. 14:32–42)

Scene 1: Vigilance Required (14:32–34)

{32} A   They went to a place called Gethsemane;
         and he said to his disciples, "Sit here while I pray."   SIT HERE
{33}   B   He took with him Peter and James and John,
           and began to be distressed and agitated.   DISTRESS
{34}   B' and said to them, "I am deeply grieved, even to death;   GRIEF
       A' remain here, and keep awake."   REMAIN HERE

Scene 2: Accepting the Cup of Death (14:35–36)

{35} A   And going a little farther, he threw himself on the ground   OBEISANCE

		B	and prayed that, if it were possible,	
			the hour might pass from him.	HOUR PASS?
{36}		C	He said, "Abba, Father,	FATHER
		C'	for you all things are possible;	ALL THINGS
		B'	remove this cup from me;	CUP PASS?
	A'		yet, not what I want, but what you want."	OBEDIENCE

Scene 1': Vigilance Still Required (14:37–38)

{37}	A		He came and found them sleeping;	SLEEPING
		B	and he said to Peter, "Simon, are you asleep?	
			Could you not keep awake one hour?	KEEP AWAKE?
{38}		B'	Keep awake and pray that you may not	
			come into the time of trial;	KEEP AWAKE!
	A'		the spirit indeed is willing, but the flesh is weak."	TIRED

Scene 2': Accepting the Betrayal (14:39–42)

{39}	1		And again he went away and prayed, saying the same words.	
{40}			And once more he came and found them sleeping,	SLEEPING
			for their eyes were very heavy;	
	2		and they did not know what to say to him.	NO WORDS
{41}	1'		He came a third time and said to them,	
			"Are you still sleeping	SLEEPING
			and taking your rest? Enough! The hour has come;	
			the Son of Man is betrayed into the hands of sinners.	
{42}	2'		Get up, let us be going. See, my betrayer is at hand."	FATEFUL WORDS

I' AUTHORITIES SEEK TO ARREST JESUS (Mk. 14:43–53)

{43}	A			Immediately, while he was still speaking,	
				Judas, one of the twelve, arrived;	
				and with him there was a crowd with swords and clubs,	
				from the chief priests, the scribes, and the elders.	CHIEF PRIESTS
{44}		B	1	Now the betrayer had given them a sign, saying,	
				"The one I will kiss is the man;	KISS
			2	arrest him and lead him away under guard."	ARREST
{45}			1'	So when he came, he went up to him	
				at once and said, "Rabbi!" and kissed him.	KISS
{46}			2'	Then they laid hands on him and arrested him	ARREST
{47}		C		But one of those who stood near drew his sword	
				and struck the slave of the high priest, cutting off his ear.	ONE ATTACKS
{48}			D	Then Jesus said to them,	
				"Have you come out with swords and clubs	
				to arrest me as though I were a bandit?	SEIZE ME
{49}			D'	Day after day I was with you in the temple teaching,	
				and you did not arrest me.	ARREST ME
				But let the scriptures be fulfilled."	
{50}		C'		All of them deserted him and fled	ALL FLEE
{51}		B'	1	A certain young man was following him,	
			2	wearing nothing but a linen cloth.	NAKED
			1'	They caught hold of him,	SEIZE/ARREST
{52}			2'	but he left the linen cloth and ran off naked.	NAKED
{53}	A'			They took Jesus to the high priest; and all the chief priests,	
				the elders, and the scribes were assembled.	CHIEF PRIESTS

The Rhetorical Shape of the Narrative Complex

Critical scholars agree that Mark 14 onward represents a sustained meta-narrative concerning the passion of Jesus. Until recently, most critics believed that Mark's chief source was an earlier chronology of the events, and this view is still widely held.[1] Whichever view the interpreter assumes, critics still recognize that the meta-narrative breaks down into several functional narrative collections. However, these divisions are usually made based on thematic or theological assumptions rather than the rhetoric of Mark's inventional arrangement.[2] Based on the rhetoric of these internal cues, four collections are proposed here:

14:1–53	Eucharistic announcements of betrayal, death, and the promise of Galilee
14:54—15:20	The trial and Peter's failure
15:21–38	Crucifixion and death
15:40—16:8	Burial, resurrection divinely interpreted

Given the continuity between the structure of these four complexes and the previous material of this Gospel, it becomes obvious to any reader that the organizing technique and the nature of the fictive argument remains the same. Theories of a pre-Marcan passion narrative need to be reevaluated in light of how strongly this meta-narrative corresponds to the shape of meta-narrative collections already found in the Gospel. The older convention, that gospels are passion narratives with extended introductions, is clearly untenable based on the sustained nature of Mark's rhetorical invention sustained throughout the Gospel.[3]

In the stories before us, Judas betrays; a follower acts rashly; disciples quarrel, equivocate, and desert. Only Jesus and the unnamed woman respond with integrity. The juxtaposition of the faithfulness of Jesus in contrast with the faithlessness of his followers plays a major role in the episodes of this complex. This sense comes most readily if we read the narrative from its climactic center outward. Episode IV details the preparations for the Passover meal in a formulaic step parallelism stylistically reminiscent of the story of Jesus' sending disciples to secure the colt for his entry (Mk. 11:1–6). The center of the Passover story is also formulated in a simple step-progression.

    1 Jesus takes the element of provision
       2 gives thanks for it
          3 passes it among his disciples
             4 and by way of a pronouncement, metaphorically redefines the meaning of partaking

The event represents a level of redundancy that lacks the richness of detail characteristic of much of Mark's narrative technique.

Contrary to a previous generation's way of describing Mark's contribution, it may be the simple redundancy of this kind of story that represents the ring of an authentic pre-Marcan liturgical tradition.

On the other hand, Mark's voice may be found most definitively in the way in which he presents the betrayal. It represents the culmination of the fictive argument sustained throughout the Gospel. Accustomed as we modern readers are to Matthew's version of this same announcement of betrayal, we may need to look again to realize that Mark does not identify the culprit during the dinner. Like a kind of parlor room recital by the detective who has solved the crime, Mark depicts Jesus as knowing the identity of the perpetrator but as unwilling to reveal it just yet. Instead, he seems to be playing out the drama by cryptically hinting that "…one of you will betray me—one who is eating with me… one of the Twelve… one who dips his bread into the bowl with me." In good Alfred Hitchcock style, Mark has already alerted his readers in Episode III that the betrayer is Judas, so only characters within the narrative are at a loss to know the guilty party. What are we to make of this degree of after-the-fact narrative ambiguity? Rhetorically we are drawn to the parallel Episode III' for a resolution to the question, and given Mark's penchant of narrative juxtaposition, we would expect to return to a discussion of Judas' role as the betrayer. But Mark surprises readers by noting that Jesus charges all of the Twelve with their pending desertion. The narrative effect is to render the voiced question "Surely not I?" in the point-of-turning Episode IV' as an ironic counterpoint to Judas' prior decision. In effect, the narrative complex turns on an accusation that is *purposefully opaque*. Is a betrayer only the one who has made prior plans? Although Judas is narratively singled out, in balance we learn that the betrayer just as easily becomes any or all of the fleeing followers, any or all of the Twelve.

In Episodes II and II' the disciples are depicted as equally unseeing whether the issue is support of Jesus in his time of preparation and prayer (II') or in contrast with the woman who anointed him for his coming burial (II). The disciples are depicted as faithless by default, followers who too easily can "fall into temptation" since their spirit may be willing, but their resolve is undependable. In the story of the sleeping disciples, Mark juxtaposes their faithlessness with Judas' overt act of betrayal. Only the unnamed woman chooses to act with the faithfulness Mark's readers would have wished to have provided Jesus in his hour of need.

The boundary episodes I and I' present the stories of the chief priests and teachers of the law who were looking for a way to arrest Jesus during the feast. Mark frames Episode I by depicting the surreptitious attitude of the temple leadership, who desired to arrest Jesus when he was not in the spotlight. In the center of Episode I' Jesus demands, "Am I leading a rebellion...that you have to come out with swords and clubs to capture me? Every day I was with you in the temple courts, and you did not arrest me." Since the latter statement is rhetorically set in juxtaposition to the former scene, it is unimportant that Jesus expresses his outrage at emissaries rather than the actual temple authorities. It is, after all, the readers rather than the temple authorities who are intended to ponder how the manner of his arrest fulfills scripture.[4] The reference to the chief priests, the teachers of the law and the elders in the last verse of Episode I' (verse 53) not only balances the reference to the same group in the first segment of the episode, but it also brings to fruition the plot conceived by this same group in Episode I.[5]

The juxtaposition of the episodes in the sixteenth narrative complex can be visualized thus:

I AUTHORITIES SEEK TO ARREST JESUS	Mk. 14:1–2
II DISCIPLES FAIL TO UNDERSTAND	Mk. 14:3–9
III JUDAS AND THE POSSIBILITY OF BETRAYAL	Mk. 14:10–11
IV PASSOVER PREPARATION	Mk. 14:12–16
IV' PASSOVER PARTAKEN	Mk. 14:17–26
III' MORE POSSIBILITIES OF "BETRAYAL"	Mk. 14:27–31
II' DISCIPLES FAIL TO UNDERSTAND	Mk. 14:32–42
Scene 1: Vigilance Required	(vv. 32–34)
Scene 2: Accepting the Cup of Death	(vv. 35–36)
Scene 1': Vigilance Still Required	(vv. 37–38)
Scene 2': Accepting the Betrayal	(vv. 39–42)
I' AUTHORITIES SEEK TO ARREST JESUS	Mk. 14:43–53

The Central Motif

In Mark's narrative, Jesus has forced the inevitable by his outrageous conduct and his outright challenge to the temple leaders as authoritative interpreters of the Torah tradition. He humiliated their representatives: "You know neither the scriptures nor the power of God!" He actively repudiated their right to franchise the courtyards of the temple to vendors. He mocked their love of liturgical hierarchy, warning followers to beware of their craving of the adulation (12:38–40). He accused them of being merciless at the very point the Torah tradition had indicated as the measure of mercy: "They devour widows' houses" (cf. Ex. 22:22; Deut. 10:18). If one is not to take the cloak of a widow as pledge, how much more so her home (24:17–20). Painted into a corner because of Jesus' popularity, Mark portrays a group of leaders who must either capitulate to Jesus' authority or silence it. They chose the latter. The complex that begins with a plot to arrest Jesus could only end with the deed.

The story of the woman who anointed Jesus for burial has been shaped by Mark for his purpose. Matthew almost wholly appropriates Mark's chiastic telling. He maintains the same design and eliminates only what for his purpose were nonessential details. Unlike Luke or John's use of this story or a similar one (Lk. 7:36–50 and Jn. 12:1–8), Mark has quite purposefully stripped the episode of the detail that would allow us to draw a portrait of the woman or present a case for understanding her motives. She is an enigma. Like the naked man who comes later, she serves a purpose more than a person.[6] Her memorial is that she will forever be singled out as one person who responded in faithfulness to Jesus during his time of passion. She is the ideal disciple—the one who "gets it" and "gets Jesus" when everyone else is either confused or just dense. In contrast, the disciples are portrayed as dullards who fail to grasp what is happening. She brings testimony to his identity as the anointed one of God; they see only the momentary extravagance. Questions of who exactly she was (see Luke and John for suggested identities) or how she "knew" miss the point. At the outset of the passion narrative Mark makes it abundantly clear that the Twelve fundamentally did not "get" Jesus. Instead, they argue about expenses, sleep through his crucial hour of need, and then flee from him when he chooses not to resist.

Throughout this collection the disciples are depicted as those who should have understood but don't get it. They are continually depicted as obtuse. As indicated earlier, either Mark has created a narrative device by which the reader is co-opted into the story as one who knows the appropriate response better than the characters, or we must conclude that Mark's purpose is to suggest that faithlessness by default is little better than betrayal. Whichever intent, the outcome remains the same: The active conspiracy of the religious leadership in the framing episodes is matched internally by the passive torpidity of the Twelve. This growing body of evidence against the disciples in Mark leads Kelber to the disturbing conclusion that Gethsemane at the Mount of Olives marks Jesus' final attempt to resolve the conflict between himself and the disciples: "The conflict between Jesus and the disciples has been brought to a head and proven insoluble. Henceforth Jesus and his disciples will go different ways…He will die and through death enter into life. The disciples will abandon Jesus at the occasion of his arrest and thus forfeit their last chance for entering upon the way of the kingdom."[7] Kelber's reading of the Gospel's judgment concerning the disciples is bleak but not unwarranted based on the evidence of fictive argument presented in this study.

The only note of hope for Jesus' investment of himself in this chosen group of followers is voiced in the beginning of the episode that announces their desertion. In 14:27 the fleeing "sheep" are given the promise of being regathered when they meet Jesus in Galilee, "You will all fall away, for it is written: 'I will strike the shepherd, and the sheep will be scattered.' But after I have risen, I will go ahead of you into Galilee." This possibility of restored grace is extended once again at the climactic moment of the last narrative complex in the Gospel. But the present narrative ends on a solemn note of betrayal and desertion, both active and passive falling away.

The woe pronounced on those who would betray the Lord is significantly placed in the context of the eucharistic meal. It is the solemn responsibility of the disciple to examine him- or herself to discover whether they have become either an active or a passive betrayer of the Lord. And woe to that disciple who willfully betrays the Son of man (and his community). It would be better to never have been born. This fearful warning most certainly would resonate with Christian communities scattered throughout the Hellenistic world that found it necessary to live dependent on the sacred trust of the common eucharist.

While the Church Is Sleeping
A sermon by Ronald J. Allen

Sermon Text: Mark 14:1–9, 32–42

Not long ago, I got a new pair of bifocals. The new glasses enable me to see things I have not seen in a long time.

Just as I have lenses for my glasses, so I have lenses in my mind and heart through which I read the Bible. Recently, I also got a new pair of interpretive lenses with which to read the two passages on which this sermon is based. These new lenses enable me to see a relationship between the two texts that is new to me.

Mark sets up these narratives so that the attitude and behavior of the woman who anoints Jesus at Bethany contrasts with the attitude and behavior of the disciples who sleep while Jesus prays in Gethsemane. The contrast puts you and me on the spot.

From the very beginning of the Gospel of Mark, we know that Jesus is God's agent in manifesting the reign (NRSV: kingdom) of God (1:14–15). Through Jesus, God initiates a new phase in the renewal of the world. God is at work so that every relationship, every setting, every situation will mediate God's unconditional love for all and God's will for justice for all. Whereas the Jewish community has known that this was God's purpose since the days of Abraham and Sarah, Jesus Christ is an agent through whom this news comes to us Gentiles.

The divine rule comes to expression through the life, death, and resurrection of Jesus. When Jesus is crucified, it looks as if the powers of the old world defeat God. But the reader knows that the crucifixion is not a defeat but a revelation of how God exercises power in the world. God works through suffering, serving love.

By the time we get to Bethany, dinner is going on at the house of Simon the leper. A woman enters. We know almost nothing about her. In the ancient world, women were typically identified by the men to whom they were related. But we do not know this woman's male relationships. We do not know her history or her occupation. We do not know her name. In those days, women were seldom in company with men at formal occasions. We know that Jesus' presence prompts her to violate social custom by joining these men in the dining room. We know that she acts as an independent agent and on her own initiative. She breaks open an alabaster jar of nard and pours it on Jesus' head. Nard is a perfume from the Himalayans with a spicelike fragrance. Can you smell it?

Some of the other dinner guests get angry. They could have sold this perfume for 300 denarii and given the money to the poor. One denarius is a day's wage. Three hundred denarii is almost a year's salary! That would buy a lot of food for hungry people, furnish a lot of clothing, pay a lot of gas bills. I understand their frustration. Don't you?

But Jesus says, "She has performed a good service for me." Then he says something that calls for two comments. "For you always have the poor with you, and you can show kindness to them whenever you wish, but you will not always have me." First comment. Growing up, I heard this part of the story as a rationale for why we should not go out of our way to help the poor. Jesus quotes part of a verse from Deuteronomy. In Bible days, to quote from a piece of a verse was to call to mind the whole literary context. The larger context in Deuteronomy calls the community to *provide* for the poor. The whole verse reads, "Since there will never cease to be some in need on the earth, I [God] therefore command you, 'Open your hand to poor and needy in the land'" (Deut. 15:11).

Second comment. Poverty was not part of God's intention at creation. Poverty and other forms of social oppression result from the brokenness of the present age. In the great renewal, God intends to end poverty. The principles of Deuteronomy are a concession to this old age but are necessary now to demonstrate God's love for all. In the new world they will not be needed.

Back to the story. Why did the woman pour perfume on Jesus? "She has anointed my body beforehand, for burial." This woman understands that God's purpose through Jesus is the renewal of the world through suffering love. She does not flinch from this fact. She knows that Jesus will die. She knows that in the Jewish community, proper burial is one of the highest forms of respect. An improper burial is cause for deepest regret. Proper burial requires anointing. "She did what she could" to join the movement toward renewal.

Unnamed women—both figuratively and literally—still recognize God's renewing activity in the world and do what they can to join it. And sometimes their witness takes them the way of suffering love. I think of women who are abused at home or in the workplace and who step forward to say that God wants people to relate in ways that are respectful, encouraging, and supportive. Sometimes these women lose jobs, even homes and husbands, but they feel the wind of renewal.

Recently we spent the summer in Jamaica I taught in a program for theological students. The students are bright and immensely hard working. They could have high-paying careers in business, law, government, medicine. The church is short of money and pays only a subsistence wage. But they believe that God is working to redevelop their land. Some of them will spend their whole lives in ramshackle houses that cling to the sides of the mountains, miles from the nearest village, without a car or phone. Climbing up and down the mountains on foot, their bodies will ache. But what I remember most is their energy, their hopefulness, their confidence that God can use their sacrifice for the renewal of their communities.

Juxtapose the attitude and actions of the unnamed woman with those of Peter, James, and John in the garden of Gethsemane. Jesus asks them only to wait and to stay awake while he prays alone.

As Jesus speaks with God, he begins "to be distressed and agitated." This language is the same language with which writers in Mark's day describe the suffering of the world in the tribulation—the last days before the end of the old age and the beginning of the new. Jesus feels this distress in his own body. He throws himself on the ground—a gesture of abject pleading. "Remove this cup from me; yet, not what I want, but what you want." Can you feel the tension within Jesus?

Jesus is locked in the struggle for the renewal of the world. But what are the disciples doing? Sleeping. Quadruple entendre. (a) By sleeping they fail to support Jesus when he needs them most. (b) By sleeping, they fail to do the very thing he has asked them to do: keep awake. (c) By sleeping, they turn away from the renewal of the world that is coming through Jesus. The term "keep awake" is the same Greek word that is elsewhere translated "Watch," as in "Be alert for the coming of the new age." Instead, they sleep. (d) In Mark's day, the dead are sometimes described as sleeping. The struggle for the regeneration of the world is taking place, and they are the same as dead to it.

Mark says things three times when Mark wants to indicate their importance. Three times Jesus predicts his suffering, death, and resurrection. Three times he comes to the disciples in the garden and asks them to "keep awake." This failure is the kind that leaves you hanging your head in disbelief.

The struggle for the regeneration of the world is taking place in their very presence, and they are asleep. And yet, when the betrayer comes with a crowd to arrest Jesus, we know that the processes of renewal continues, even when we sleep. And the disciples will be the same as asleep when Jesus is before the council, when Pilate hands Jesus over to be crucified, when Jesus is nailed to the cross, and even when Jesus is buried.

It grieves me to say, but often I think that the disciples are a picture of the church—sleeping while the struggle for the renewal of the world takes place in our presence. The European American church slept through generations of racism and awoke only when the African American church shook us so hard we could not continue our slumber. How many European American congregations do you know today who are ready to call an African American pastor?

Many congregations are sleeping through the change in the church's relationship to the larger world. We used to be on the mainline of society. Now, we're moving toward the margins. The world is changing, but we maintain many of our services of worship, our church structures, and our mission strategies as if it were business as usual in 1959 instead of 1999. In 1959, people may have joined the church in order to serve on a committee, but not today.

Many congregations appear to be sleeping through the current call of the gay and lesbian community to reconsider their relationship with God and their place in the church. Then the son or daughter of a congregational leader comes down with HIV/AIDS contracted through a homosexual practice. And the congregation's "eyes are very heavy." And, like the disciples, they "do not know what to say."

The attitude and behavior of the woman who anoints Jesus at Bethany contrasts with the attitude and behavior of the disciples who sleep in Gethsemane. The contrast puts you and me on the spot. An unnamed woman is faithful. She epitomizes how to respond to the renewal of the world coming through Jesus. The disciples—senior students in Jesus' traveling seminary—cannot even keep their eyes open.

While the church is sleeping, unnamed women are breaking open alabaster jars and pouring nard on Jesus. Which would you rather join?

Compositional Comments

This sermon is based on the narrative analysis of Mark 14:1–53 in which Professor Reid regards the story of the anointing at Bethany (Mark 14:3–9) and the story of the disciples sleeping (Mark 14:32–42) as parallel elements in the chiastic structure of the larger sixteenth narrative complex. The two stories exist in a contrasting, or antithetical, relationship. Mark regards the unnamed woman as a model of faithful response to Jesus. The disciples exhibit an imperceptive, unfaithful response to Jesus.

I take Mark's rhetorical purpose in developing this contrast as pressing the listeners to consider whether to identify with the woman (and so to do what we can to join the movement toward God's reign) or with the disciples (and so to misperceive, and even resist, the movement toward God's reign). In the sermon I attempt to help the congregation realize this rhetorical strategy and to consider for themselves whether they would like to join the unnamed women or the disciples.

Surprise and irony are related subthemes of this material. Popular Christian piety in North America leads us to expect the disciples to be exemplars of the faithful life. They have been with Jesus for fourteen chapters. Jesus has repeatedly taken them aside for private tutoring sessions into the nature of the reign of God. They have names. Since they were independent operators in the fishing industry, we expect them to have stature, insight, and leadership ability at least comparable to today's independent business people. However, they exemplify how conventional, old-world patterns of perception and acting are so deeply rooted that they can manifest themselves in the very presence of Jesus. On the other hand, we expect the woman to be subservient, marginal, victimlike. However, in the presence of Jesus, she becomes the exemplar of faithful discipleship. The Gospel of Mark, of course, is thoroughly apocalyptic and reversal is a basic conviction of apocalypticism. As Jesus says earlier, "Many who are first will be last, and the last will be first" (Mk. 10:31). In the sermon, I try to help the congregation sense this irony.

A subtheme in the rhetorical strategy of the sermon is to encourage the congregation to be alert to persons and situations in our setting that are marked by the unexpected. Who around us unexpectedly leads us in the movement toward God's reign? Whom do we expect to lead us in that direction? And who actually models resistance (active or passive) to that reign?

Mark 14:54—15:20
The Seventeenth Narrative Complex

I PETER THE FOLLOWER (Mk. 14:54)

54}	1		Peter had followed him at a distance,	FOLLOWED
		2	right into the courtyard of the high priest;	COURTYARD
	1'		and he was sitting with the guards,	SAT
		2'	warming himself at the fire.	COURTYARD

II SANHEDRIN ACCUSATIONS LEVELED (Mk. 14:55–59)

{55} 1 Now the chief priests and the whole council
were looking for testimony against Jesus
to put him to death; but they found none.
{56}   For many gave false testimony against him,   FALSE TESTIMONY
     2 and their testimony did not agree.   DID NOT AGREE
{57} 1' Some stood up and gave false testimony   FALSE TESTIMONY
against him, saying,
{58} "We heard him say, 'I will destroy this temple
that is made with hands, and in three days
I will build another, not made with hands.'"
{59} 2' But even on this point their testimony did not agree.   DID NOT AGREE

III CONDEMNATION PRONOUNCED (Mk. 14:60–64)

{60} A Then the high priest stood up before them
and asked Jesus, "Have you no answer?
What is it that they testify against you?"   HOW DO YOU PLEAD?
{61}   B But he was silent and did not answer.   SILENCE
       C Again the high priest asked him,
"Are you the Messiah, the Son of the Blessed One?"   ARE YOU THE
                                                       MESSIAH-SON?
{62}   C' Jesus said, "I am; and 'you will see the Son of Man   I AM
seated at the right hand of the Power,'
and 'coming with the clouds of heaven.'"
{63}   B' Then the high priest tore his clothes and said,
"Why do we still need witnesses?
{64}   You have heard his blasphemy! What is your decision?"   BLASPHEMY!
     A' All of them condemned him as deserving death.   GUILT PRONOUNCED

IV THE BRUTAL MOCKERY (Mk. 14:65)

{65} 1 Some began to spit on him, to blindfold him   SPIT/BLIND
     2 and to strike him,   STRIKE HIM
    1' saying to him, "Prophesy!"   PROPHESY
    2' The guards also took him over and beat him.   BEAT HIM

I' PETER THE BETRAYER (Mk. 14:66–72)

{66} **1** 1 While Peter was below in the courtyard,   PETER
one of the servant-girls of the high priest came by.   CHALLENGED
{67}   When she saw Peter warming himself,
she stared at him and said,
"You also were with Jesus, the man from Nazareth."
{68}   2 But he denied it, saying,   DENIES
"I do not know or understand what you are talking about."
And he went out into the forecourt.
         3 Then the cock crowed.   COCK CROWS
{69} **2** 1 And the servant-girl, on seeing him,
began again to say to the bystanders,   PETER
"This man is one of them."   CHALLENGED

{70}			2 But again he denied it.		DENIES
	1'	1'	Then after a little while the bystanders again said to Peter, "Certainly you are one of them; for you are a Galilean."		PETER CHALLENGED
{71}			2' But he began to curse, and he swore an oath, "I do not know this man you are talking about."		DENIES
{72}			3' At that moment the cock crowed for the second time.		COCK CROWS
	2'	1'	Then Peter remembered that Jesus had said to him, "Before the cock crows twice, you will deny me three times."		PETER REMEMBERS
			2' And he broke down and wept.		DENIER

II'   ACCUSATIONS LEVELED IN THE GENTILE COURT (Mk. 15:1–5)

{15:1} 1   As soon as it was morning, the chief priests   CHIEF PRIESTS
            held a consultation with the elders and scribes
            and the whole council. They bound Jesus,
            led him away, and handed him over to Pilate.
{2}   2   Pilate asked him, "Are you the King of the Jews?"   QUESTION
         3   He answered him, "You say so."   RESPONSE
{3}   1'   Then the chief priests accused him of many things.   CHIEF PRIESTS
{4}   2'   Pilate asked him again, "Have you no answer?   QUESTION
             See how many charges they bring against you."
{5}   3'   But Jesus made no further reply,
             so that Pilate was amazed.   RESPONSE

III'   THE CRY OF CONDEMNATION (Mk. 15:6–15)

{6}   A   Now at the festival he used to release   PRISONER RELEASED
            a prisoner for them, anyone for whom they asked.
{7}   B   Now a man called Barabbas
             was in prison with the rebels
             who had committed murder during the insurrection.   BARABBAS
{8}   C   So the crowd came and began to ask Pilate   CROWD REQUEST
               to do for them according to his custom.
{9}   D   Then he answered them,   KING OF THE JEWS
                 "Do you want me to release for you the King of the Jews?"
{10}   E   For he realized that it was out of jealousy
                   that the chief priests had handed him over.   CHIEF PRIESTS
{11}   E' But the chief priests stirred up the crowd
                   to have him release Barabbas for them instead.   CHIEF PRIESTS
{12}   D' Pilate spoke to them again,
                 "Then what do you wish me to do
                 with the man you call the King of the Jews?"   KING OF THE JEWS
{13}   C' They shouted back, "Crucify him!"   CROWD REQUEST
{14}   Pilate asked them, "Why, what evil has he done?"
               But they shouted all the more, "Crucify him!"
{15}   B' So Pilate, wishing to satisfy the crowd,
             released Barabbas for them;   BARABBAS
       A'   and after flogging Jesus,
             he handed him over to be crucified.   PRISONER RETAINED

IV'   THE SECOND BRUTAL MOCKERY (Mk. 15:16–20)

{16}   A   Then the soldiers led him into
            the courtyard of the palace
            (that is, the governor's headquarters);   COHORT COMES IN
            and they called together the whole cohort.
{17}   B   And they clothed him in a purple cloak;   PURPLE CLOAK
             and after twisting some thorns into a crown, they put it on him.
{18}   C   And they began saluting him,   HOMAGE
               "Hail, King of the Jews!"

{19}		C' They struck his head with a reed, spat upon him, and knelt down in homage to him.	STRIKE/SPAT HOMAGE
{20}	B'	After mocking him, they stripped him of the purple cloak and put his own clothes on him.	PURPLE CLOAK
	A'	Then they led him out to crucify him.	COHORT LEADS OUT

The Rhetorical Shape of the Narrative Complex

Mark begins this narrative with a cliffhanger! The introductory statement about Peter's entry into the courtyard at verse 54 is quite brief. The story does not resume until verse 66, where it continues almost as if it had not been interrupted.[1] Narratively, this serves to create a sense of simultaneity between Peter's story and that of Jesus. By interrupting and resuming the story in this abrupt fashion, Mark has indicated that the complex is organized as a step-progression. The symmetry is obvious. After each of the episodes concerning Peter come parallel episodes in which accusations are leveled against Jesus, followed by parallel episodes of condemnation, and concluding with episodes in which brutal indignities are enacted.

In the final episode of the first half of the collection, Jewish guards mock the purported prophet by playing a pitiful version of blind-man's bluff: "If you're such a prophet who hit you that time: Prophesy! Tell us!" In the parallel section, Gentiles are depicted as mocking the supposed king: "How can we worship a true king without the royal accoutrements? Try these on for size!" Although one might note other parallel possibilities for this collection, the symmetry between the first and final episodes of each half of this collection provide a forceful case that this complex is organized as a step-progression.

The juxtaposition of the episodes in the seventeenth narrative complex can be visualized thus:

```
  I  PETER THE FOLLOWER                              Mk. 14:54
     II  SANHEDRIN ACCUSATIONS LEVELED               Mk. 14:55–59
        III  CONDEMNATION PRONOUNCED                 Mk. 14:60–64
           IV  THE BRUTAL MOCKERY                    Mk. 14:65
  I' PETER THE BETRAYER                              Mk. 14:66–72
     II' ACCUSATIONS LEVELED IN THE GENTILE COURT    Mk. 15:1–5
        III' THE CRY OF CONDEMNATION                 Mk. 15:6–15
           IV' THE SECOND BRUTAL MOCKERY             Mk. 15:16–20
```

The Central Motif

Commentators come to this narrative and instead of sensing its rhythms they become consumed with establishing historical detail. "Would the Sanhedrin actually meet at night?" "Is this how they conducted trials?" "Wouldn't suborned witnesses have been schooled in advance to have testimony that agreed?" "Would a high priest seek to lead a witness in self-incrimination?" "Is there any record of the Roman custom of releasing a prisoner?" "Since none of the Twelve were present, how does Mark know what was said in either trial?" Apart from this, critics who notice the obvious parallels between the two cycles question whether "doublets" have crept into the tradition.[2] Commentaries rightly struggle over such issues but too often miss that Mark tells *the story*: Roman condemnation and execution came about because Jewish religious leadership demanded his death "out of envy" (15:10). Nothing would stop them; not Peter, nor any of the other disciples. Divided and fearful, they had fallen. Most religious leaders had been offended by Jesus early on, so few, if any, would risk support for one who so openly offended the established Torah leadership. Even the crowds, which had previously cheered him, now jeered at the comeuppance for his arrogance to challenge the status quo. The Roman officials (here and at the foot of the cross) are depicted as helpless in the face of this overwhelming Jewish hostility. In the end, Mark depicts Jesus as utterly abandoned. His followers flee and his captors mock. The canvas is bleak. The players are either merciless or helpless. Jesus had become a pariah.

Mark, the craftsman, tells his story twice over. Rejection comes in the mouth of two witnesses: the court of the religious and the court of the crowds. He is at pains to establish that Jesus was not judged guilty of sedition by the Gentile authorities. Rather, he was politically sacrificed to quell Jewish hostilities. Jesus states his truth only once in each court (cf. Isaiah 53:7–12). They are his last words until the cry of "God-forsakenness" on the cross.

At the head of each of these cycles is the story of Peter. Mark's fictive argument against the understanding of the community of the Twelve finds its denouement in this collection. Peter's story should be read without the color of Matthew, Luke, and John, each of whose gospels clearly took issue with this portrayal of the leader of the Twelve.[3] All agree that it is both Jesus and Peter who are on trial. All include this story. However, the other gospels all describe the redemption of Peter after the resurrection, while in Mark's Gospel, this is the last of Peter. Mark contrasts Jesus as victim and Peter as one whose failure leads him to join those about the fire—people who mimetically stand in for the mob that calls for Jesus' death (15:13–14).[4] Even as Jesus finally acknowledges that he is indeed "Christ," "the son of the Blessed One," and the great "Eschatological Judge," Mark depicts Peter as repudiating his association with Jesus by invoking a curse on himself, the eschatological equivalent of exclaiming, "God dammit, I said I don't know him!"[5]

Many contemporary readings of the Gospel present Peter as a flawed hero, but Mark's depiction would have shocked Christian readers in the seventh decade of the first century. At best, he is presented as a tragic figure—a man who comes to inevitable *recognition* of his own "fallibility." In true dramatic form, the *reversal* of his commitment as a disciple is made apparent in his own denials and this, in turn, brings about the *recognition* of his final failure as a disciple. This is classic Greek tragedy. In the *Poetics*, Aristotle argues that the finest and most complex form of *recognition* arises at the moment when a character moves from ignorance to knowledge concerning his or her own fallibility (*hamartia*).[6] The result of this *recognition* produces fear for the character and pity for those watching or reading of the reversal of fortune (*Poetics* 11).

Kim Dewey reads Peter's story in this collection as the culmination of a trajectory of denial, with Mark picturing Peter as a failed, dysfunctional leader who presents the final negative model of discipleship.[7] Burton Mack writes, "The narrative of Peter's denial was composed when the Gospel was composed. Peter's denial does not throw light on the circumstances of 30 C.E., but upon the circumstances of 70 C.E. Mark's community must have been under considerable duress."[8] Rhoads and Michie conclude, "the narrator leads the reader to face squarely the harsh failures of the disciples and also to care about them and how they will fare in the future of the story world."[9] Without question, the depiction of Peter as having both denied Jesus and invoking a curse on himself represented a crucial issue for Mark's church as witnessed by the circumstances of betrayal, rejection, and repudiation described by Jesus in the farewell address in Mark 13. To invoke a curse and deny being a follower was the essence of apostasy (Mk. 8:38). Disciples in Mark's community would want to stand firm to the end, not be caught sleeping or denying even once, let alone three times. They would want to trust the Holy Spirit to give them words and courage to confess Christ as Lord if they were brought before the courts or into the courtyards of the law.

The only glimmer of redemptive seed in this story comes from Jesus' quotation of Zechariah 13:7 at Mark 14:27. With the striking of the shepherd the sheep would, indeed, flee, but it was the Lord who would strike, not the betrayers and rejecters, "*I will strike* the shepherd and the sheep will be scattered" (14:27). Mark makes it clear that behind all the schemes and actions lies the controlling hand of God. It appears that the crowds, who in his teaching ministry once looked like sheep without a shepherd (Mk. 6:34), fleeing followers now appear the same. While he is tried and executed they are simply "scattered sheep." Still, the possibility of redemption exists for all who will continue to follow, looking for him even after death. Immediately after citing the Zechariah passage, Mark's Jesus tells his disciples (whom he knows will fall away) that restoration awaits them when they meet him in Galilee (Mk. 14:28). Thus, Mark's story of Peter is only tragic if Peter remains committed to Jerusalem and never calls the believers to gather with Jesus again in Galilee.

Mark 15:21–39
The Eighteenth Narrative Complex

I A HELLENISTIC JEW CYRENEAN BEARS HIS CROSS (Mk. 15:21)
{21} They compelled a passer-by, who was coming in from the country to carry his cross;
it was Simon of Cyrene, the father of Alexander and Rufus.

II THE CRUCIFIXION (Mk. 15:22–24)
{22} A   Then they brought Jesus to the place called Golgotha   THEY BRING
            (which means the place of a skull).
{23}   B   and they offered him wine mixed with myrrh;   THEY OFFER WINE
                but he did not take it.
{24}   B'   And they crucified him,   THEY CRUCIFY
          A'   and [they] divided his clothes among them,
                casting lots to decide what each should take.   THEY TAKE

III "SUBJECTS" MOCK THEIR "KING" (MK. 15:25–33)
{25} A   It was nine o'clock in the morning when they crucified him.
{26}   The inscription of the charge against him read,   NINE O'CLOCK
            "The King of the Jews."
{27}   B   And with him they crucified two bandits,   TWO BANDITS
                one on his right and one on his left.
{28–29}   C 1   Those who passed by derided him,   PASSERSBY INSULT
                 2   shaking their heads and saying, "Aha!
                     You who would destroy the temple
                     and build it in three days,
{30}   3   save yourself, and come down from the cross!"
{31}   C' 1' In the same way the chief priests, along with the   LEADERS INSULT
                     scribes, were also mocking him among
                     themselves and saying,
                 2' "He saved others; he cannot save himself.
{32}   3' Let the Messiah, the King of Israel,
                     come down from the cross now,
                     so that we may see and believe."
          B'   Those who were crucified with him also taunted him.   TWO BANDITS
{33} A'   When it was noon, darkness came over   NOON 'TIL
            the whole land until three in the afternoon.   THREE O'CLOCK

II' THE "KING" DIES (Mk. 15:34–38)
{34} A   At three o'clock Jesus cried out with a loud voice,   LOUD CRY
            "Eloi, Eloi, lema sabachthani?" which means,
            "My God, my God, why have you forsaken me?"
{35}   B   When some of the bystanders heard it, they said,
                "Listen, he is calling for Elijah."   ELIJAH
{36}   B'   And someone ran, filled a sponge with sour wine,
                put it on a stick, and gave it to him to drink, saying, "Wait,
                let us see whether Elijah will come to take him down."   ELIJAH
{37} A'   Then Jesus gave a loud cry and breathed his last.   LOUD CRY
{38}   And the curtain of the temple was torn in two, from top to bottom.

I' A GENTILE ROMAN WITNESS INTERPRETS THE DEATH (Mk. 15:39)
{39} Now when the centurion, who stood facing him,
      saw that in this way he breathed his last,
      he said, "Truly this man was God's Son!"

The Rhetorical Shape of the Narrative Complex

Two stories of Hellenists at the cross, Simon of Cyrene and the Roman centurion, form the stark boundaries for this narrative. They stand as witnesses from two different continents, each of whom in his own way participates (one by conscription and one through duty) in the execution of Jesus.[1] One acts out discipleship by taking up the cross, the other acts out discipleship by confessing Jesus as the Son of God. They serve as Hellenistic bookends to the central message of Jewish rejection and repudiation.

By placing the crucifixion and death in Episodes II and II', respectively, Mark subordinated the aspects of the story in order to emphasize the mockery in the central episode from bystanders and from the religious leaders. The spotlight is directed away from the death of Jesus to focus on the way in which he had been "delivered over to the hands of men." Only in Episode II' does the narrator's eye settle on Jesus in anything more than an incidental way. In this episode Jesus cries out alone in his experience of God-forsakenness. Yet for most of Episodes II and II' the focus is on the actions of others; for example, in Episode II the attention is directed to the soldiers: "They brought…they offered…they crucified…they cast lots." In Episode II' the words and actions of bystanders are portrayed: "Listen, he's calling Elijah…" and "Let's see if Elijah comes to take him down." Thus, in Episodes I, II, and II', I', Mark alternately focuses on the actions of the soldiers, the sightseers, the helpless participant, the awe-inspired centurion, and even, briefly, on the relationship between Jesus and God as Son and Father. However, in the central narrative (III) the focus is singularly on those who reject and repudiate Jesus.

Segments A and A' of the point-of-turning Episode III provide the time, the setting, and the circumstance. The two crucified robbers who also "heap insults" on him are depicted in B and B'. But the central segment C shifts style, developing the point-of-turning portion of the episode in the balanced symmetry of a step-progression. Those who insult and mock take center stage. They rail their accusations against him and scoffingly demand that he prove himself by "coming down" from his cross of death. If Jesus' can overturn this fate, then their words are depicted as self-condemning. By placing a step parallelism in the center of an inversion, Mark forces his audience to focus lingering attention on the final line of the point of turning, "Let this Christ…come down…*that we may see and believe.*"

The juxtaposition of the episodes in the eighteenth narrative complex can be visualized thus[2]:

```
I   A GENTILE CYRENEAN BEARS HIS CROSS         Mk. 15:21
  II  THE CRUCIFIXION                          Mk. 15:22–24
    III "SUBJECTS" MOCK THEIR "KING"           Mk. 15:25–33
  II' THE "KING" DIES                          Mk. 15:34–38
I'  A GENTILE WITNESS INTERPRETS THE DEATH     Mk. 15:39
```

The Central Motif

The author has composed a masterful theological commentary on the crucifixion rather than a simple physical description of what happened. Scene by scene his cast of characters act out a series of events that had already been fixed in the consciousness of Israel by her inspired poets. The entire narrative is formulated as a midrash on the promise of a suffering king. During the first century before Christ an interpretive revolution had occurred as faithful Jews had come to attribute the authorship of much of the "psalms" to King David. The interpretive tradition had then reasoned that, if these were the words attributable to King David, then they could also be attributed, allegorically, to the coming Davidic king. Mixed with apocalyptic expectation, this became the basis of much of the messianic expectation fostered in first century Israel.[3]

In this interpretive tradition, Psalm 22:16–18 came to be understood as the words of a Davidic king who had been utterly delivered over to the hands of his mocking enemies, utterly given over to those who cast lots for his garments at his feet. The taunt that "he saved others but is unable to save himself" is clearly a variation on Psalm 22:8, "Commit your cause to the Lord; let him deliver—let him rescue the one in whom he delights!" The cry of dereliction in 15:34 is merely an echo of the psalmist's king who cries out his sense of abandonment in Psalm 22:1. Similarly, Psalm 69:19–21 speaks of the gall and vinegar offered to the despised and scorned Davidic king, who is parched even as he experiences a sense of drowning in personal rejection. Those who scorn him put gall in his food and offer him vinegar for his thirst (Mk. 15:23, 36). Allusions such as these lead the readers to the fated silence of the suffering Davidic king before his accusers in Psalm 38. In this prayer the king has been deserted by his friends and stands mute before his accusers offering no reply to their accusations. And, of course, the suffering servant of Isaiah 53 then comes quickly to hand: he does "not open his mouth" either, but was "pierced for our transgressions." The list of allusions goes on, but the reader grasps that he or she has been called to view this story as a series of allusions that serve as cues to its interpretive meaning.

Biblical tradition was not alone in depicting the tragic figure of the true king who suffered on behalf of his people. The Greco-Roman ideal easily intermingled with this Jewish concept of the Davidic king who would even die in order to serve his people. This notion of the sacrificially suffering king as the authentic shepherd of the people over whom he has domain was an ideal well known in the Hellenistic world of the first century. So Jesus' cry of forsakenness, though it may seem astonishing as a messianic entreaty, was an indication to members of the larger Hellenistic world that Jesus understood this kind of death and rejection as what Robbins calls "a necessary route to true kingship."[4] Mark's story of Jesus' death simultaneously fulfills all that was most noble in the Jewish conception of the King-Messiah, and the Greco-Roman conception of the true Caesar-Lord, Son of Zeus.[5] The centurion is presented to Mark's readership as grasping that Jesus virtuously fulfilled the role of the suffering king on behalf of "his people." But Mark's rhetorical juxtaposition of his confession set against the utter rejection of the Jewish leaders in the center of the narrative serves another, more significant purpose.

From the very beginning of the passion narrative, Mark has created a story with an increasing sense of forsakenness, intensified by every scene. Jesus goes to the cross abandoned by all and understood by none. Pilate still *wonders* even after he's dead. The Praetorium guards *debase* him. Simon the Cyrene is *coerced*. The soldiers at the cross are *indifferent*. Those passing by *taunt*. Temple authorities *ridicule*. Those crucified with him are *contemptuous*. The darkness from the sixth to the ninth hour is punctuated only at the end by his final cry of anguish in the face of abandonment and misunderstanding. His being "delivered up" (14:10, 11, 18, 21, 41, 42, 44; 15:1, 10, 15) occurs not merely into the hands of the Roman-Jewish power structure but, as Kelber has concluded, "into demonic darkness and God-forsakenness." Even in this heartfelt cry, Jesus is depicted as conducting himself with nobility to the end. God's nonintervention and apparent abandonment "constitutes the ultimate depth of Jesus' suffering. With his last question left unanswered, Jesus utters the cry of derelicion and dies."[6]

Mark has fashioned a dark story of isolation and alienation as the Gospel concludes. It seems the very forces of darkness have conspired to bring hope to despair. The tragedy is unremitting. Then at the moment in which one would expect an exclamation of the deepest grief come the words of the centurion proclaiming the only full confession of Jesus' true identity offered by a character within the

Gospel, "Surely this man was the Son of God!"⁷ In his death comes the acclamation of life. In his death comes the invitation to the audience who has known from the day that John the Baptist was "delivered up" (Mk. 1:14) that the Son of man would also be delivered up to the hands of men. The curtain barring entrance to the temple is now severed. Gentiles everywhere can stand before the Son of God and, like the centurion, find in the manner of his death reason to claim that he is vindicated by God. In fact, Gentiles no longer need to come through the temple courts of Judaism to claim Jesus as Son of God. Confessing the Son, Jesus, as Lord and taking up Jesus' cross to follow him is sufficient to stake one's citizenship in the kingdom-come.

Mark 15:40—16:8
The Nineteenth Narrative Complex

I THE WOMEN ARE WITNESSES OF THE CRUCIFIXION (Mk. 15:40–41)

{40} 1   There were also women looking on from a distance;   WOMEN SAW THE DEATH
       2   among them were Mary Magdalene,   THREE WOMEN NAMED
           and Mary the mother of James the younger
           and of Joses, and Salome.
{41} 1' These used to follow him and provided for him   WOMEN SAW THE MINISTRY
           when he was in Galilee;
       2' and there were many other women   OTHER WOMEN INDICATED
           who had come up with him to Jerusalem.

II JESUS IS OFFICIALLY PRONOUNCED DEAD (Mk. 15:42–46)

{42} A   When evening had come,
          and since it was the day of Preparation,   PREPARATION
          that is, the day before the sabbath,
{43}   B   Joseph of Arimathea, a respected member of the council,
             who was also himself waiting expectantly for the kingdom of   JOSEPH AND
             God, went boldly to Pilate and asked for the body of Jesus.   THE BODY OF JESUS
{44}   C   Then Pilate wondered if he were already dead;
                and summoning the centurion, he asked him whether
                he had been dead for some time.   IS HE DEAD?
{45}   C' When he learned from the centurion that he was dead,   PRONOUNCED DEAD
     B' he granted the body to Joseph.   JOSEPH AND JESUS' BODY
{46} A' Then Joseph bought a linen cloth,   PREPARATION
          and taking down the body,
          wrapped it in the linen cloth, and laid it in a tomb
          that had been hewn out of the rock.
          He then rolled a stone against the door of the tomb.

I' THE WOMEN ARE WITNESSES OF THE EMPTY TOMB (Mk. 15:47—16:8)

{47} A   Mary Magdalene and Mary the mother of Joses   WOMEN SAW THE BURIAL
          saw where the body was laid.
{16:1}   B   When the sabbath was over, Mary Magdalene,   WOMEN WENT IN
             and Mary the mother of James, and Salome bought spices,
             so that they might go and anoint him.
{2}   And very early on the first day of the week,
             when the sun had risen, they went to the tomb.   THEY CAME TO THE TOMB
{3}   C   They had been saying to one another,   WHAT THEY SAID TO
                "Who will roll away the stone for us   ONE ANOTHER
                from the entrance to the tomb?"
{4}   D   When they looked up, they saw that the stone,   LOOKING UP THEY BEHELD
                   which was very large, had already been rolled back.
{5}   E   As they entered the tomb, they saw a young   YOUNG MAN PRESENT
                      man, dressed in a white robe, sitting on
                      the right side;
                  F   and they were alarmed.   ALARMED
{6}   F' But he said to them, "Do not be alarmed;   ALARMED
                  E' you are looking for Jesus of Nazareth,   JESUS ABSENT
                      who was crucified. He has been raised;
                      he is not here.
             D' Look, there is the place they laid him.   LOOK! (BEHOLD!)
{7}   C' But go, tell his disciples and Peter   TELL DISCIPLES
                that he is going ahead of you to Galilee;
                there you will see him, just as he told you."

{8}   B'   So they went out and fled from the tomb,   WOMEN FLED IN
             for terror and amazement had seized them;   FEAR
       A'   and they said nothing to anyone, for they were afraid.   WOMEN AFRAID OF
                                                                     WHAT THEY SAW
  II' ???

The Rhetorical Shape of the Narrative Complex

The four complexes that compose the meta-narrative collection known as the passion narrative are symmetrically related in a step-progression like the beginnings meta-narrative (Mk. 1:1—4:1).

```
  I  Mk. 14:1–53        The Sixteenth Narrative Complex
 II  Mk. 14:54—15:20    The Seventeenth Narrative Complex
  I' Mk. 15:21–39       The Eighteenth Narrative Complex
 II' Mk. 15:42—16:8     The Nineteenth Narrative Complex
```

The parallels within this meta-narrative are particularly important, because the arrangement of the seventeenth narrative complex provides the pattern for the present narrative complex. Just as the story of Peter was interrupted and then resumed halfway through that collection, the story of the three female witnesses (Mary Magdalene, Mary the mother of James and Joses, and Salome) is similarly interrupted in the present narrative. Episode I' resumes the story begun in Episode I as if the story concerning Joseph's request for the body and Pilate's confirmation of the death (Episode II) had not interrupted it. The intervening episode functions to establish and officially confirm Jesus' death and burial. But the continuity of the story between Episodes I and I' clearly define this narrative as a step-progression. In other words, something is amiss. Where form dictates the necessity of four episodes we possess only three plus a number of textual variants that lay claim to be the final episode of the Gospel.

The rhythm of parallels demands that a balance to the official pronouncement of the death in Episode II should occur after Episode I'. The expected arrangement would thus have been:

```
  I  WITNESSES OF THE DEATH
 II  OFFICIAL PROCLAMATION OF THE DEATH
  I' WITNESSES OF THE EMPTY TOMB
 II' [UNQUALIFIED PROCLAMATION OF THE RESURRECTION]
```

The controlling theme of the complex alternates between *witness* and *proclamation*. Of course, the problem is that there is no final proclamation. The last episode is not there.

The scandal of Mark's Gospel has always been its enigmatic conclusion of women fleeing in fear.[1] The modern reader who resists harmonizing the story by filling in the details of the other gospel writers (who first read and reacted "resistingly" to this narrative) must account for the text much as did its first audience.² After having read the Gospel to this point, with form always creating the sense of expectation of what is next, readers would undoubtedly suspect why Mark left such a gaping whole at the end. By resisting modern genre conventions in favor of the conventions of the *finished* narrative style of composition, the final narrative complex can be read as a further example of Mark's manipulation of the audience's expectation of narrative conventions. As in the second narrative complex, this collection demands that the *aporia* concerning the missing *proclamation* be resolved. Someone needs to be willing to step forward, fill the void, and proclaim, without qualification, their own testimony that Jesus is alive! Mark's arrangement demands closure and his audience members, well versed in resolving such textual ambiguities, know what action is expected.³

This is narrative as fictive argument, with argument a function of arrangement.⁴ The multiple endings that were eventually attached to the Gospel of Mark simply testify that from the outset Mark's audience experienced the rhetorical *aporia* of his narrative art.⁵ The fact that others felt compelled to compose whole gospels in response can even be counted as further evidence of the power of this kind of argument.⁶ The reconstruction of the Marcan arrangement presented in this study clearly indicates that this literary complex was intended to end precisely on the disconcerting note found in verse 8. All other endings may be formally rejected.⁷

The juxtaposition of the episodes in the nineteenth narrative complex can be visualized thus:

I THE WOMEN ARE WITNESSES OF THE CRUCIFIXION	Mk. 15:40–41
II JESUS IS OFFICIALLY PRONOUNCED DEAD	Mk. 15:42–46
I' THE WOMEN ARE WITNESSES OF THE EMPTY TOMB	Mk. 15:47—16:8
II' [*WILL JESUS BE PROCLAIMED ALIVE?*]	

The Central Motif

In this Gospel's final narrative collection life overturns death. Mark portrays the judgment, condemnation, and mockery of Jesus as vindicated by God. Jesus was not abandoned. Yet questions remain. Even if the conclusion was meant to elicit the active response of a reader who would choose to fill the gap, why such a dark, enigmatic conclusion? Given the record of the other gospels, one is also led to ask, why is there no record of actual appearances?

Taking up these questions in reverse order, readers naturally wonder "Why is there only an empty grave and an angelic explanation?"

In Matthew's Gospel, after the promise of a Galilean appearance, Jesus is portrayed as appearing in the vicinity of the tomb. This is followed by a record of "the" Galilean appearance. Luke has no gravesite appearances, but records appearances in several other situations. John seems to follow a tradition not unlike that of Matthew for the gravesite and records other appearances as well. Mark stands alone with no record of post-resurrection conversations with the risen Lord. Harmonizing efforts aside, it is disturbing. In this Gospel, the resurrection *event* is utterly dependent on its interpretation by a heavenly agent.

Strange as this may seem to modern readers, this dependence on the interpretive word is consistent with the prophetic patterns of ancient revelation stories. It was always the inspired prophet of God, who spoke on behalf of the Lord, interpreting the divine significance of a particular set of events. It was primarily by means of this interpretive word that Israel ever understood her own destiny as providentially guided by Yahweh. So Mark chose *interpretive word* over *eyewitness stories* of resurrection appearances that were clearly available in the oral tradition (cf. 1 Cor. 15:3–8). What he provides is not only an *interpretive* story, but a story about *interpretation* itself. Without interpretation, the women would have fled heartsick at the evidence of grave-robbery rather than fear of God. In Mark's Gospel, theophanies are exclusively word-of-interpretation events; for example, both the voice at the baptism and the voice at the transfiguration were interpretations of the event offered in the name of God. Compositionally, the final event of the Gospel had already been implicated in the death-resurrection imagery of baptism in the first narrative complex and reimplicated in the central narrative complex. Commentators have regularly argued that the transfiguration story is a misplaced resurrection narrative, but such a suggestion assumes that the Gospel is organized as rectilinear biography rather than a topically organized *historia*.[8] Kelber describes this intersignifying effect as the "interior retrospectivity" of the plot. Symmetries can occur across the *finished* style of composition, because such plots are constructed backward from the end, with the conclusion determining and framing the beginning.[9]

In light of this, the voice heard by Jesus in the first complex, heard by several selected disciples in the central complex, and in the message delivered to the women in the final story is more important than stories of appearances. It is the *interpretation* that creates the reality. For Mark, a message interpreting the meaning of an empty tomb defines reality more clearly than the evidence of eyewitness stories. In Mark's radical rhetoric, *interpreted event* is more persuasive than *eyewitness testimony*. As for the resurrection, Mark has already implicated and reimplicated it in the baptismal and transfiguration stories. These stories are neither "misplaced" nor are they out of sequence. They are *narrative synonyms* of one another and function as the most important witness—the interpretive one.

The second question emerging from reading the text is "Why *silent, fleeing* women?" Some interpreters contend that it was an attempt to justify the fact that testimony concerning the empty tomb had not been more forthcoming early in the movement. Bornkamm states, "We may also take it from the phrase at the end, that the women 'said nothing to anyone' (Mk. 16:8), that it appeared only later in the tradition."[10] Yet, even if this is true, Mark's narrative artistry suggests that he has created much more than a poor attempt at after-the-fact verifications. Other critics question whether there may have been an original ending now lost, or they attempt to reconstruct how this relates to the original pre-Marcan passion tradition.[11] These suggestions are less than satisfying because they are too caught up in the a priori criteria of their own critical method to adequately respond to the text as a serious narrative creation.

Recent Marcan scholarship has leaned heavily toward Kelber's polemical interpretation that the fleeing, fearful women bring the tragic story of the disciples who were the bearers of the oral tradition to its logical conclusion. Because the community of the Twelve fail to respond to the interpretive message, they stay in Jerusalem instead of meeting Jesus in Galilee.[12] Kelber marshals a powerful argument that by *writing* a gospel, Mark offered an alternative to the *oral* authority of the Jerusalem church. He functionally reshaped the sacred actuality of Jesus from an orally controlled presence to a "textually recoverable actuality."[13] In addition, Mark effectively undermined the authority of the Jerusalem church's ability to "understand" its own present circumstance by telling the story in a way that consistently juxtaposed the story of the failure of the religious leadership to grasp who Jesus was with the similar failure of the disciples to understand. Mark's revolutionary contribution, according to Kelber, was to *write* Jesus' story. In doing so, he bypassed and displaced the oral authority of the community of the Twelve.[14] His witness to Jesus' ministry, message, and motives offered a deeply frustrated response to the unacceptable silence that had remained huddled too long in Jerusalem. His voice is added to that of Paul, who also had problems with the contrariness of the Jerusalem church (Gal. 2), and the efforts of Judaizing Christians, who sought to overturn the gains of the

Gentile mission. Many of the readers of Mark's Gospel were undoubtedly sympathetic to the author's frustration with the Jerusalem leadership and their resistant support of the Gentile mission.

If Mark had intended his readers to be shocked by his ending, he was enormously successful. A variety of endings were appended to it early in its life. In fact, we could argue that Luke, John, and Matthew each responded resistingly by composing his own written gospel interpretation of what happened. Each fills the lacuna and presents his own version of the response of the Jerusalem community.

Whatever conclusions the reader makes concerning Mark's fictive argument, the choice to act cannot be escaped. Whether to dismiss or embrace, accept or reject, the narrative demands decision and action. The reader is forced to respond to silent witnesses who say nothing to anyone. From the outset, this controversial Gospel caused many to feel impelled to take up its unfinished task of sharing the good news. Mark calls followers to keep the failed appointment in Galilee, to get the gospel out the door and communicated to a world desperate to hear the message proclaimed that life has meaning if one is willing to make the confession of faith that Jesus is Lord and believe in one's heart that he has been resurrected from the dead (Rom. 10:9–10).[15] In the manner in which Mark concludes this collection, his fictive argument simultaneously depicts a crisis of silence and summarily ends it.

Tell All to Everyone
A sermon by Lucy Lind Hogan

Sermon Text: Mark 15:40—16:8

How can it be that on Easter Sunday, the most glorious feast in the year, we read Mark's account of the resurrection? There are no angel choruses with trumpets and timpani. No one is singing the "Hallelujah Chorus" from Handel's *Messiah*. Instead, to paraphrase T. S. Eliot, Mark seems to end, not with a bang, but with silence.

Mark tells us that the women ran out of the empty tomb, "and they said nothing to anyone, for they were afraid." Even though the young man had told them the good news that Jesus was raised, they said nothing to anyone.

I have a friend who always reads the ends of mysteries first. Before she reads the whole book she wants to know if it is worth investing the time and the effort. I have never been able to understand that. I love the mystery and suspense. Don't you love the unbearable tension of waiting to find out what happens, who did it? I am afraid that, if she had picked up Mark's Gospel, that ending would have driven my friend away. Why would you want to read a story that seems to end in fear and silence?

We must understand two things about Mark's Gospel. First, you can't read the end without first reading the *whole* story. And second, if you do read the *whole* story you will know that this is not the end! Alleluias, trumpets, drums, and joyful rejoicing only have meaning if we have journeyed from life, to death, and then to life.

Silence plays an important part in Mark's Gospel, and we would know that if we went back to the beginning and read the whole story. Unfortunately, time does not permit, so let me remind you.

On the very first morning of his ministry, Jesus walked into his home synagogue and began to teach and heal. People were astounded and spread the good news that here was a preacher we can listen to and trust, he teaches with authority and he drives out demons. The news spread quickly to everyone, and soon Jesus could not go anywhere without attracting a crowd—a crowd of hurting, desperate people. Not long after, a leper came to Jesus filled with great faith. "If you will, you can make me clean" (1:40b). Jesus touched the man and told him to go to the priests who would pronounce him clean and welcome him back into the community. But Jesus also said a curious thing. Mark tells us that Jesus, with a stern voice, told the man, "See that you say nothing to anyone" (1:44a). Say nothing to anyone—do you hear the connections between the beginning and the end of the story? Say nothing to anyone.

But that is not the only time that Jesus made this same command. He healed a deaf man who could not hear and could not speak. Jesus put his fingers in the man's ears and spat on his tongue. When the man could finally hear and speak, Jesus told him, "tell no one." Again, think of the healing of the blind man. Mark tells us that, after Jesus put his fingers on the man's eyes, he could see. But Jesus told the man go right home—don't go to your village where you might tell people and they might see you.

Why all the silence? If you or I had been cured of leprosy, deafness, or blindness, wouldn't we want to tell people? Of course we would, and so did those people. Mark not only tells us of Jesus' commands to silence but also tells us how they disobeyed those commands. In fact, Mark tells us that the more Jesus told people to keep silent, "the more zealously they proclaimed it."

They went into the villages and homes telling all to everyone. Telling their family and friends, even strangers, about the teacher who taught with authority and who had healed them. He gave them new life, lifting them out of darkness and silence into light and sound. Wouldn't we shout that from the rooftops? Of course we would—and indeed they did.

Why, then, did Jesus command silence? Perhaps to keep the crowds down? Or maybe he did not want to attract leeches and jackals who would attempt to exploit him.

Mark offers the key in two moments that come at the center of his Gospel. Jesus asked the disciples who people said that he was. After the always zealous Peter proclaimed that Jesus was the Christ, Jesus again demanded silence—"He charged them to tell no one about him" (8:30). Jesus then went on to teach about what it meant to be his disciple. Telling the good news was not enough. A true disciple was one who would be willing to pick up the cross and, like Jesus, die on that cross for the sake of the world. This is followed immediately by Jesus' transfiguration. After seeing the glory that awaited Jesus, Peter, James, and John were told that they "should tell no one what they had seen, until the Son of man should have risen from the dead."

After this there are no more commands to keep silent, but there are also no more zealous proclamations. Not, that is, until this final moment, the end of Mark's Gospel. But who is it that tells all to everyone?

Think again about the final moments of the story. Slowly, over the course of the book, Mark has been telling us who this Jesus is. And now the story has come to an end. But has it? At the end, we are told, the women were the witnesses to his death on the cross. They had traveled with him, cooked his food, washed his clothes, laughed at his jokes, comforted him when people would not understand. And now, from a distance, they watched in agony as he, in agony, died. And make no mistake, Mark stresses the fact that Jesus was dead. In verses 44 and 45 he uses the word *dead* three times. A centurion tells Pilate that Jesus was dead, and Joseph of Arimathea claims the body of Jesus and buries it in a tomb. It is over. Finished.

But the story is not over, nor finished. The women, who had witnessed the death, now become witnesses of the empty tomb. Early in the morning they went about their sad task. Even though the body of their beloved teacher and friend had been wrapped in a linen cloth and put into the tomb, there had not been enough time to apply the spices before the coming of the Sabbath. Finally, as the religious celebrations were over and the work week began, they would finally be able to do this one last, final thing. But the body was not there. "He has been raised; he is not here" (15:6).

Is it over? Is it finished? No, of course not, Mark tells us. It is, in fact, only beginning. Remember how Jesus told us that we should not say anything "until the Son of man should have risen from the dead"? Well, this is the day, the Son is risen.

Therefore, this Jesus, who makes the blind to see, the deaf to hear, and the dumb to speak, has opened our eyes and ears and tongues so that we all can speak.

The women said nothing so that Mark could inspire us to become the proclaimers of the good news. Because the women said nothing to anyone, we are called to zealously proclaim all to everyone. And we do this, knowing the whole story, knowing that *we* are the disciples.

There are trumpets and timpani at the end of Mark's Gospel —and it is we who play them. There are loud alleluias at the end of Mark's Gospel. We sing alleluia and we shout "HE IS RISEN." Mark wants to remind us that no one will do it if we do not. We cannot sit idly by and think that the testimony of the leper, or the blind man, or the man who was deaf, will be enough to spread the good news. Mark wants to convince each one of us that we must climb up on the rooftop to shout of new life for all. You and I are the ones who carry the word of the empty tomb to a world filled with pain and sorrow. We go ahead, reminding everyone that Jesus of Nazareth, who was crucified, has been raised, and that you will see him. You will see him when the sick are healed, when the oppressed are lifted up, when the hungry are fed, when the naked are clothed.

Go, Mark tells us, and tell all the world what you have seen. Go, you are God's messengers. Do not be anxious "about what you are to say;...for it is not you who speak, but the Holy Spirit" (13:11). Alleluia, he is risen, the Lord is risen indeed!

Compositional Comments

Easter services, while usually grand and glorious, often run the risk of becoming spectator events. We have a tendency to stress remembering. We lift up what God did in the past, without thinking about what God is doing now and in our future. We must also draw people who have a tendency to come only at Christmas and Easter, the "beginning" and "end" of the story, into the middle of the story so they can hear not only the good news but the claim that good news has on their lives. The challenge for preachers, therefore, is how to draw people into the whole story and to present them with the realization that the story is not yet finished. Rather, the wonderful story of God's gracious gift continues to unfold daily in our lives.

The argumentative structure of Mark's Gospel draws the preacher/reader into just such a format. This becomes particularly evident when one reads the end of his Gospel. What at first seems to be a tentative, hesitant ending filled with fear and uncertainty is, upon reflection, an open-ended challenge. The women did not speak after they had seen and heard; therefore, we who have seen and heard must become the witnesses.

To see this connection between new life and proclamation it was necessary to go back into the Gospel and point to a pattern that Mark develops. That pattern is a healing, the command to be silent, and the disobeying of that command. Leaving the resurrection story and going back into the Gospel gave me the opportunity to both demonstrate the pattern and also provide Christmas/Easter Christians with the middle of the story. When the transfiguration story is included, with its command to tell the story after the Son of man had been raised, Mark's intention becomes clear. Now is the time, he tell us, and we are the ones who must spread the story. Mark's structure allows the preacher to preach both doxology and discipleship. Not only do we rejoice about what God has done, we see that we must continue to hear the claim in our lives.

Conclusion

The Design of the Overarching Meta-Narrative

Throughout this analysis, relationships between the complexes have been discussed where they would enhance the argument for construing a specific complex in the manner proposed. The moment has come to draw those arguments together and propose an overarching meta-narrative. In the visualization suggested here, thematic relationships are summarized as a means of visualizing the Gospel's fictive argument as a whole. The Roman numerals attempt to indicate the relationship within a meta-narrative block. For example, the beginnings meta-narrative and the passion meta-narrative are both internally developed as a step-progression, but in the over-arching meta-narrative they are thematically construed as an inversion with one another; that is, the first and last narrative collections are parallel, the second and the eighteenth narrative complexes are parallel, and so forth. Similarly the Galilean ministry meta-narrative (4:35—9:29) is construed in its relationship with the ethics of servanthood meta-narrative (9:30—12:44). The following is a summary construal of the meta-narratives:

```
I   THE BEGINNINGS META-NARRATIVE (1:1—4:1)
 II  THE FIRST SAYINGS COLLECTION: KINGDOM PARABLES (4:2–34)
  III  THE GALILEE MINISTRY JOURNEYS META-NARRATIVE (4:35—9:29)
  III' THE ETHICS OF SERVANTHOOD META-NARRATIVE (9:30—12:44)
 II' THE SECOND SAYINGS COLLECTION: KINGDOM ESCHATOLOGY (13:1–36)
I'  THE PASSION META-NARRATIVE (14:1—16:8).
```

Mark has upset the expectation of parallelism between the central meta-narrative collections. Meta-narrative III' begins with a lengthy narrative complex that functions as a central statement of Jesus' kingdom ethics in Mark's Gospel (what I have called Mark's

Sermon on the Servant). This is followed by a series of three narrative complexes that are not in parallel with the Marcan ethics collection and represent a return to the themes raised in the first half of the Galilean ministry meta-narrative: the challenge to "have faith" (4:35—5:43 and 10:46—11:25), the concern for the church-in-prospect/Gentile-mission (6:1–52 and 11:27—12:12), and the confrontational debate collections (6:53—7:30 and 12:13–44). Construed in this way, it is surprising that Mark appears to have developed the material of the tenth of nineteen narrative complexes as the outer narrative complex of the Galilean ministry meta-narrative (8:26—9:29). This forces the complex to carry two roles, to conclude the Galilean ministry meta-narrative while also functioning as the central collection that is in echo balance with the first and last narrative complexes of the gospel.

In the outline below, it becomes quickly obvious that Mark does not offer simple symmetry in the arrangement of the whole. He plays by the rules in ways that create firm expectations for readers, but just when the pattern seems too pedantic, he upsets the expectations. He does this with the expected parallels within a specific episode (2:13–14), at the level of a narrative complex (15:40—16:8), and, here, in the presentation of the whole as well. The effect of allowing the central narrative to conclude the Galilean ministry narrative, followed by the unconventional way in which the ethic of servanthood meta-narrative privileges its first collection, poses a tantalizing question worthy of a study of its own. In effect, the *Sermon on the Servant* collection vies with the transfiguration collection for centrality. Such questions must be left for another inquiry. It is enough here to sketch the apparent outlines of Mark's arrangement and invite modern readers to join the conversation concerning the purposes of his fictive argument.

A Chiastic Presentation of the Overarching Meta-narrative of the Gospel

A   THE BEGINNINGS META-NARRATIVE—Mk. 1:1—4:1
   Narrative Complexes 1–4
1:1–15   I   The Beginning: Ministry Credentialed by God
1:16—2:14   II The Temptation: Responding to Calling and Expectations
2:15—3:6   I' The Conflict: Ministry Rejected by Religious Leaders
3:7—4:1   II' The Affirmation: Responding to Calling and Confrontation

   B   THE KINGDOM PARABLE COLLECTION—Mk. 4:2–34
      Narrative Complex 5

    C **THE GALILEAN MINISTRY META-NARRATIVE**—Mk. 4:35—9:29
         <u>Narrative Complexes 6–10</u>
4:35—5:43   I The Miracle Narrative: A Call to Faith
6:1—52   II The Feeding of the Five Thousand Narrative: The Church in Prospect
               Framed by Doubt and Misunderstanding
6:53—7:3   III Public Confrontation Narrative: Jesus' Repudiation
               of the Tradition of the Elders
7:32—8:27   II' The Feeding of the Four Thousand Narrative: The Gentile Mission
               Framing Misunderstanding and Incomprehension
8:27—9:29   I' THE CENTRAL CLIMACTIC NARRATIVE
               A Radical Call to Discipleship and The Miracle of the Transfiguration
               Narrative

    C' **THE ETHIC OF SERVANTHOOD META-NARRATIVE**—Mk. 9:30—12:44
         <u>Narrative Complexes 11–14</u>
         First Grouping: THE MARCAN ETHICS
9:30—10:45   The *Sermon on the Servant*—Servanthood as the Essence of Kingdom Conduct
         Second Grouping: THE JERUSALEM DEBATE NARRATIVES
         (Strong Parallels to Complexes 6–8, Mk. 4:35—7:30)
10:46—11:26 I' Triumphal Entry Narrative: Challenge to Have Faith in God
11:27—12:12 II' Parable of the Vineyard Narrative: The Validity of the Gentile Mission
12:13–44   III' Public Debate Narrative: Jesus Rejects the Authority of
                the Leaders of the Temple-Cult.

  B' **GATHERED ESCHATOLOGICAL TEACHING COLLECTION**—Mk.13:1–36
       <u>Narrative Complex 15</u>

A' **THE PASSION META-NARRATIVE**—Mk. 14:1—16:8
     <u>Narrative Complex 16–19</u>
14:1–53   I The Betrayal: The Arrest and Apostasy
14:54—15:20 II The Trial Narrative: Condemnation by Religious Powers
15:21–39   I' The Death Narrative: Rejection Complete—Death as Calling
15:40—16:8 II' The Vindication: The Empty Tomb and Gospel Message

On Mark's Textuality

Mark wrote. His carefully crafted composition commands readers who will contemplate its textuality. He states this explicitly at 13:14 by addressing his audience directly, "Let the reader understand." In preaching to his community, he took the existing Jesus story and shaped it to his purposes, allowing the form of his storytelling to carry the burden of his argument. Thus, apart from occasional asides, it is my thesis that Mark's voice is conveyed primarily in the argument to be found in discovering his arrangement, in determining which stories belong together and unpacking the resulting intersignification. I have referred to this element of Mark's textuality as his fictive argument.

Zahava McKeon maintains that all argument is fictive in that it creates its own world by constituting the subject matter, the ideas, the movement, that which can be known about the author's concerns and, as all argument should, its audience.¹ In this study, I have appropriated this notion, bringing it back to narrative, but applying it specifically to the *world* that is created in the way Mark tells his story fraught with implications for his own community. Gospel, in light of this, is a kind of fictive history, or historicized prose fiction much like that which Alter suggests as a way of understanding the nature of the Hebrew biblical texts. Alter maintains that the Hebrew "historians" could manipulate "inherited material with sufficient firmness of authorial purpose to define motives, relations, and unfolding themes…with the kind of subtle cogency we associate with conscious artistry of the narrative mode designated prose fiction."² Mark is heir to this tradition of narrativity and displays an artistry to match that of the best of master composers in the Hebrew tradition. This description is not meant to suggest that Mark's Gospel does not represent history, but rather as Alter states, "fiction was the principal means which the biblical authors had at their disposal for realizing history."³ These are *plausibly* reconstructed narratives around a core of tradition with a goal "to reveal the enactment of God's purposes in historical events."⁴

In the rhetorical analysis of the prose economy (*oikonomia*, "God's plan for salvation") of Mark's arrangement offered in this study, the relationship of the form to the central motif of each section has been the core of the presentation. The evidence adduced throughout sustains the theory that Mark composed his gospel to be *read*. Read aloud publically, of course, but nonetheless, *read*. Mark preaches in ways that move readers with an urgency that cannot be ignored. Critic Vincent Taylor finds that Mark succeeded on an "unimaginable scale" in effecting "the compulsion and maintenance of belief," and this, according to literary theorist and novelist Reynolds Price, is the first aim of all narrative.⁵ There is no question that Mark preaches, but apart from recognizing the potential of recovering his voice in the form of his presentation, we are left with an enigma. As good a story as this is—and it is good—it is also a strange story that in Frank Kermode's words, jostles us "from one puzzle to the next—immediately, again, *euthus, palin*—as if the purpose of the story were less to establish a comfortable sequence than to pile one crux on another, each instituting an intense thematic opposition. [The episodes] differ in detail; they do not fit. But one is, as it were, deposited on top of the other, as if to form a sort of aniconic figure for meditative interpretation."⁶ All of which strongly suggests that the only way we can hear that voice today is in the rhetoric of the form of the textualized remains of his preaching. It can be heard as a story, but to attend to Mark's *voice* in the story it must be read.

On Mark's Voice—The Thrust of His Fictive Argument

The evidence presented here also leads to a clear confirmation of part of Werner Kelber's thesis, that, through its overt textuality, Mark's Gospel functions to disestablish the oral authority of the Jerusalem church.[7] The fact that Mark composed his Gospel according to the principles of what counts as a *finished* narrative text supports Kelber's thesis that Mark chose writing as a medium to convey his message in order to distance himself from the standard-bearers of the oral tradition in Jerusalem.[8] It is the conclusion of this study that Mark used his own formulation of a topically organized *historia* to persuade followers of Jesus to seize the moment and unite around a new authority other than the failed oral authority of the community of the Twelve.[9]

At the climax of the central narrative in this Gospel, when Jesus returns from an absence in which he was transfigured in a resurrectionlike experience, Mark depicts the "would-be leaders of the church" arguing with the scribes about their powerlessness to effect miracles in his absence. If we accept that this is the *culminating story* of the step-progressive construction on the central complex, then this episode should somehow function as the climax of his fictive argument.[10] Accepting Kelber's thesis that the Gospel of Mark is written as a polemic against the ineffective leadership of the Jerusalem church, Jesus' cry of dereliction, "You faithless generation, how much longer must I be among you? How much longer must I put up with you?" (Mk. 9:19) becomes an indictment of the Jerusalem church's decision to cling to the failed policy of being accepted as a sect of Judaism.

At the conclusion of his survey analysis of *Mark's Story of Jesus*, Kelber opts for a postwar date for its composition (Jerusalem fell to the Roman siege ca. A.D. 70).[11] He finds that Mark's preoccupation with the judgment and destruction of the temple justifies the harshness with which he speaks concerning the revered leaders of the Jerusalem church, because it appears that whatever leadership they had exercised came to an end with that "judgment." Thus, Mark's Gospel provides an answer for the demise of the Jerusalem church in much the same manner that Augustine's *City of God* attempted to explain the fall of Rome to a later generation of believers who could not understand why God would allow such a thing to happen to that "holy city." According to Kelber, by retelling the Jesus story in a way that depicts the original disciples as missing the "way into the kingdom," it would have dawned on Mark's Greco-Roman readers that they must break with the dissipating authority of the leaders of the oral tradition. Time and again, as became obvious in the reading, "these guys don't get it." Readers, living after the fall of Jerusalem, would interpret the demise of the temple and the temple-cult as a vindication of the ministry of Jesus and, by default, the demise of the Jerusalem church could be seen as a consequence of the unwillingness of the oral leadership to disentangle itself from this judgment. As Kelber argues, "Having undergone the gospel therapy, that is knowing the cause of the crisis, they can turn from passive readers of the gospel of the Kingdom, to active participants in the Kingdom of God."[12] This *sitze im leben* for the Gospel accords with the rhetorical analysis presented in this study and is actually strengthened by it, since Kelber tends to view the Gospel as lacking in compositional elegance and is unaware of how this presentation of Mark's rhetorical technique consistently lends credence to his thesis.

In proposing an overarching organizational structure for Mark, the rhetorical technique of parallelism has been demonstrated to be intrinsic to the way in which Mark preached to his own community. Mark told the story of Jesus with a clear eye on the need to challenge a new generation of disciples to "take up their cross" and follow. The subtext of the relationship between the Twelve and the Gentile mission after the fall of Jerusalem has been consistently implicated in the nature of Mark's juxtaposition of his stories through the use of the rhetorical devices of inversion and step-parallelism. The content of Mark's argument cannot be separated from his form. In the tradition of good *historia* and in the historical tradition of the Hebrew narratives, Mark argued his case for directing the allegiance of his audience to Jesus' call to radical discipleship through the medium of telling the story. As an author, he was in complete control of his tradition. Mark's rhetorical mastery of his material is such that earlier form-critical, redaction-critical, as well as more recent narrative and composition criticism presuppositions, need to be reevaluated in light of this demonstrated control of technique.

On Preaching Intentions and Mark's Intention

This study reaffirms the validity of Muilenburg's insistence that inquiry into the rhetorical technique of the biblical author allows the critic and the student of the text to make substantive assumptions and assertions concerning the author's *intentions*. But here, arriving at *intention* is controlled by the exigency of audience expectation as dictated by the rhetoric of what counted as a *finished* narrative design. This design clarifies the nature of much of Mark's fictive argument and the circularity of so much of what otherwise appears as rectilinear narrative. If we are to understand the kind of arguments Mark makes as he tells the story, if we are to understand the nature of the persuasive task that he set before himself, it is essential that Mark be evaluated in light of the rhetorical shape of his text.

Bibliography

Unless otherwise noted, references to the Bible are from the *New Revised Standard Version* and references to ancient works other than biblical texts are to the editions in the Loeb Classical Library.

Alter, Robert. *The Art of Biblical Narrative*. New York: Basic Books, 1981.
Anderson, Janice Capel, and Stephen D. Moore, eds. *Mark and Method: New Approaches in Biblical Studies*. Minneapolis: Fortress Press, 1992.
Aune, David. *The New Testament in Its Literary Environment*. Library of Early Christianity. Ed. Wayne Meeks. Philadelphia: Westminster, 1987.
Bailey, Kenneth. *Poet and Peasant* and *Through Peasant Eyes*. Combined edition. Grand Rapids: Eerdmans, 1983.
Bengel, J. A. *Gnomon of the New Testament*. Trans. A. R. Fausett, Edinburgh: T & T Clark, 1863. First published in 1742.
Best, Ernest. *Following Jesus: Discipleship in the Gospel of Mark*. Journal for the Study of the New Testament. Supplement Series, 4. Sheffield: JSOT Press, 1981.
———. *Mark: The Gospel as Story*. Edinburgh: T & T Clark, 1983.
Betz, Hans Dieter. *Galatians: A Commentary on Paul's Letters to the Churches in Galatia*. Hermeneia Commentary. Philadelphia: Fortress Press, 1979.
———. *2 Corinthians 8 and 9: A Commentary on the Two Administrative Letters of the Apostle Paul*. Hermeneia Commentary. Philadelphia: Fortress Press, 1985.
———. *The Sermon on the Mount*. Hermeneia Commentary. Minneapolis: Fortress Press, 1995.
Booth, Wayne. *The Rhetoric of Fiction*. 2d ed. Chicago: University of Chicago Press, 1983.
Bornkamm, Gunther. *Jesus of Nazareth*. Trans. Irene and Fraser McLuskey. New York: Harper Brothers, 1960.
Bowersock, G. W. "Philostratus and the Second Sophistic." *The Cambridge History of Classical Literature*. Vol. 1, Part 4: *The Hellenistic Period and the Empire*. Ed. P. E. Easterling and B. M. W. Knox. Cambridge, Eng.: Cambridge University Press, 1989.
Brett, Laurence F. X. "Suggestions for an Analysis of Mark's Arrangement." Appended to the "Introduction" in Mann, *Mark*, 174–90.
Brown, Colin. *Miracles and the Critical Mind*. Grand Rapids: Eerdmans, 1984.
Brown, Raymond. "The Gospel Miracles." *New Testament Essays*. Garden City, N.Y.: Doubleday, 1968.
Bruce, F. F. *New Testament History*. Garden City, New York: Doubleday, 1971.
Brueggemann, Walter. *Old Testament Theology: Essays on Structure, Theme, and Text*. Minneapolis: Fortress Press, 1992.
Bruns, Gerald. *Hermeneutics: Ancient and Modern*. New Haven: Yale University Press, 1992.
Burke, Kenneth. *The Rhetoric of Religion: Studies in Logology*. Berkeley: University of California Press, 1961.
———. *Language as Symbolic Action: Essays on Life, Literature, and Method*. Berkeley: University of California Press, 1966.
Buttrick, David. "On Doing Homiletics Today." *Intersections: Post-Critical Studies in Preaching*. Ed. Richard Eslinger, Grand Rapids: Eerdmans, 1994.

Cairns, Francis. *Generic Composition in Greek and Roman Poetry*. Edinburgh: Edinburgh University Press, 1972.
Collins, Adela Yarbro. *The Beginning of the Gospel: Probings of Mark in Context*. Minneapolis: Fortress Press, 1992.
Cranfield, C. E. B. *The Gospel According to St. Mark*. Cambridge: Cambridge University Press, 1959.
Crossan, John Dominic. *In Parables: The Challenge of the Historic Jesus*. New York: Harper and Row, 1973.
Depew, David J. *The Greeks and the Good Life*. Proceedings of the Ninth Annual Philosophy Symposium, California State University, Fullerton. Fullerton: California State University Press, Fullerton, 1980.
Dewey, Joanna. "The Literary Structure of the Controversy Stories in Mark 2:1–3:6," *Journal of Biblical Literature* 92 (1973): 394–401.
———. *Markan Public Debate: Literary Technique, Concentric Structure, and Theology in Mark 2:1–3:6*. The Society of Biblical Literature Dissertation Series 48. Chico, Calif.: Scholars Press, 1980.
———. "Oral Methods of Structuring Narrative in Mark." *Intersections: Post-Critical Studies in Preaching*. Ed. Richard Eslinger. Grand Rapids: Eerdmans, 1994, 23–41.
Dewey, Kim. "Peter's Curse and Cursed Peter." In Kelber, *The Passion in Mark*, 110–19.
Donahue, John R., S.J. (1976). "Introduction: From Passion Traditions to Passion Narrative." In Kelber, *The Passion in Mark*, 1–20.
———. *The Gospel in Parable*. Minneapolis: Fortress Press, 1988.
Drury, John. *The Parables in the Gospels: History and Allegory*. New York: Crossroad, 1985.
Drury, John. "Mark." *The Literary Guide to the Bible*. Ed. Robert Alter and Frank Kermode. Cambridge: Harvard University Press, 1987, 402–17.
Dunn, James D. G. *Jesus' Call to Discipleship*. Cambridge: Cambridge University Press, 1992.
Eagleton, Terry. *Literary Theory: An Introduction*. Minneapolis: University of Minnesota Press, 1983.
Epicurus. "Letter to Menoeceus." In *Epicurus: The Extant Remains*. Trans. Cyril Bailey. Oxford: Clarendon Press, 1926.
Farmer, W. R. *The Last Twelve Verses of a Mark*. New York: Cambridge University Press, 1974.
Farris, Stephen. "Limping Away with a Blessing: Biblical Studies at the End of the Second Millenium." *Interpretation* 51 (Oct. 1997): 358–70.
Fishbane, Michael. *Text and Texture: Close Readings of Selected Biblical Texts*. New York: Schocken Books, 1979.
Fowler, Robert M. *Let the Reader Understand: Reader Response Criticism and the Gospel of Mark*. Minneapolis: Fortress Press, 1991.
———. "Reader-Response Criticism: Figuring Mark's Reader." In Anderson and Moore, eds. *Mark and Method*, 50–83.
Gadamer, Hans-Georg. *Truth and Method*. 2d, rev. ed. New York: Continuum, 1991.
Girard, René. *The Scapegoat*. Baltimore: Johns Hopkins University Press, 1986.
Greidanus, Sydney. *The Modern Preacher and the Ancient Text: Interpreting and Preaching Biblical Literature*. Grand Rapids: Eerdmans, 1988.
Halliwell, Stephen. *The Poetics of Aristotle: Translation and Commentary*. Chapel Hill: University of North Carolina Press, 1987.
Hammerton-Kelly, Robert G. *The Gospel and the Sacred: Poetics of Violence in Mark*. Minneapolis: Fortress Press, 1994.

Handcock, John. "The Boston Massacre Oration—March 5, 1774." In Ronald F. Reid, ed., *American Rhetorical Discourse*. 2d ed.
Havelock, Eric. *The Muse Learns to Write: Reflections on Orality and Literacy from Antiquity to the Present*. New Haven: Yale University Press, 1986.
Heinemann, Joseph. "The Nature of Aggadah." *Midrash and Literature*. Ed. Geoffrey Hartmann and Sanford Budick, trans. Marc Bergman. New Haven: Yale University Press, 1986.
Hendrickx, Herman. *The Miracle Stories of the Synoptic Gospels*. San Francisco: Harper and Row, 1987.
Hengel, Martin. *Judaism and Hellenism*. Trans. John Bowden. Philadelphia: Fortress Press, 1974.
Hogan, Lucy Lind. "The Squint: Critical Reflexivity and the Homiletic Process." *Sewanee Theological Review* 41:3 (1998): 253–60.
Hooker, Morna. *The Message of Mark*. London: Epworth Press, 1983.
Jackson, Jared and Martin Kessler, eds. *Rhetorical Criticism: Essays in Honor of James Muilenburg*. Pittsburgh: Pickwick Press, 1974.
Kealy, Sean. *Mark's Gospel: A History of Its Interpretation from the Beginning Until 1979*. New York: Paulist Press, 1982.
Kelber, Werner. *Mark's Story of Jesus*. Philadelphia: Fortress Press, 1979.
———. *The Oral and the Written Gospel: The Hermeneutics of Speaking and Writing in the Synoptic Tradition, Mark, Paul, and Q*. Philadelphia: Fortress Press, 1983.
———, ed. *The Passion in Mark: Studies on Mark 14–16*. Philadelphia: Fortress Press, 1976.
Kennedy, George A. *Greek Rhetoric under Christian Emperors*. Princeton, N.J.: Princeton University Press, 1983.
———. *New Testament Interpretation through Rhetorical Criticism*. Chapel Hill, N.C.: University of North Carolina Press, 1984.
———. *A New History of Classical Rhetoric*. Princeton, N.J: Princeton University Press, 1994.
Kermode, Frank. *The Genesis of Secrecy: On the Interpretation of Narrative*. Cambridge, Mass.: Harvard University Press, 1979.
Kugel, James. "Poets and Prophets: An Overview." *Poetry and Prophecy: The Beginnings of a Literary Tradition*. Ed. James Kugel. Ithaca, N. Y.: Cornell University Press, 1990.
Lane, William. *The Gospel According to Mark*. New International Commentary. Grand Rapids: Eerdmans, 1974.
Long, Thomas. *Preaching and the Literary Forms of the Bible*. Philadelphia: Fortress, 1989.
———. *The Witness of Preaching*. Louisville: Westminster/John Knox Press, 1989.
———. "The Preacher and the Beast: From Apocalyptic Text to Sermon." *Intersections: Post-Critical Studies in Preaching*. Ed. Richard Eslinger. Grand Rapids: Eerdmans, 1994.
Lord, Albert Bates. *Epic Singers and Oral Tradition*. Myth and Poetics Series. Ed. Gregory Nagy. Ithaca, N.Y.: Cornell University Press, 1991.
Mack, Burton. *A Myth of Innocence: Mark and Christian Origins*. Philadelphia: Fortress Press, 1988.
———. *Rhetoric and the New Testament*. Guides to Biblical Scholarship. Minneapolis: Fortress Press, 1990.
Malbon, Elizabeth Struthers. "Narrative Criticism: How Does the Story Mean?" *Mark and Method: New Approaches to Biblical Study*. Ed. Janice Capel Anderson and Stephen Moore. Minneapolis: Fortress, 1991, 23–49.
Mann, C. S. *Mark: A New Translation with Introduction and Commentary*. The Anchor Bible Commentary. Garden City, N.Y.: Doubleday, 1986.

Marrou, H. I. *A History of Education in Antiquity*. Trans. George Lamb. New York: New American Library, 1964.
McKeon, Richard. *Introduction to Aristotle*. New York: Random House, 1947.
McKeon, Zahava Karl. *Novels as Arguments: Inventing Rhetorical Criticism*. Chicago: University of Chicago Press, 1982.
Meijering, Roos. *Literary and Rhetorical Theories in Greek Scholia*. Gröningen: Egbert Forsten, 1987.
Metzger, Bruce, *A Textual Commentary on the Greek New Testament*: *A Companion Volume to the United Bible Societies' Greek New Testament*. New York: United Bible Societies, 1971.
Meye, Robert. *Jesus and the Twelve: Discipleship and Revelation in the Gospel of Mark*. Grand Rapids, Mich.: Eerdmans, 1968.
———. "Psalm 107 as 'Horizon' for Interpreting the Miracle Stories of Mark 4:35—8:26." *Unity and Diversity in the New Testament: Essays in Honor of George E. Ladd*. Ed. Robert A. Guelich. Grand Rapids, Michigan: Eerdmans, 1978, 1–13.
Moore, Stephen D. *Poststructuralism and the New Testament*. Minneapolis: Fortress Press, 1994.
Muilenburg, James. "Form Criticism and Beyond." *Journal of Biblical Literature* 88 (1969): 1–18.
Nineham, Dennis. *Saint Mark*. Pelican New Testament Commentaries. Middlesex: Penguin Books, 1963.
Nussbaum, Marth C. *The Fragility of Goodness: Luck and Ethics in Greek Tragedy and Philosophy*. New York: Cambridge University Press, 1986.
Patterson, Annabell. "Intention." *Critical Terms for Literary Study*. 2d ed. Ed. Frank Lentricchia and Thomas McLaughlin. Chicago: University of Chicago Press, 1995, 135–46.
Piper, Otto. "Gospel." *The Interpreters Dictionary of the Bible*. Vol. 2. Ed. George Buttrick. Nashville: Abingdon Press, 1962.
Price, Reynolds. "Foreword." In Rhoads and Michie, *Mark as Story*.
Reid, Robert S. "When Words Were a Power Loosed: Audience Expectation and Finished Narrative Technique in the *Gospel of Mark*." *Quarterly Journal of Speech* 80 (1994): 427–47.
———. "Rhetorical Criticism and Gospel Narratives: The Power of Preaching Fictive Argument." *Papers of the Annual Meeting*. The Academy of Homiletics, Nov. 30–Dec. 2, Atlanta, Ga., 1995. 102–11.
———. "Dionysius of Halicarnassus' Theory of Compositional Style and the Theory of Literate Consciousness." *Rhetoric Review* 15 (1996): 46–64.
———. "'Neither Oratory Nor Dialogue': Dionysius of Halicarnassus and the Genre of Plato's *Apology*." *Rhetoric Society Quarterly* 27 (Fall 1997): 63–90.
———. "Hermagoras' Theory of Prose *Oikonomia* in Dionysius of Halicarnassus." *Advances in the History of Rhetoric: Disputed and Neglected Texts in the History of Rhetoric*. Ed. Richard Leo Enos. Fort Worth: Texas Christian University Press/American Society for the History of Rhetoric, 1997, 1:9–24.
———. "Proper 10 for July 13, 1997, Year B." *Word & Witness: A Lectionary Resource*, Year B, vol. 97. New Berlin, Wis.: Liturgical Publications, 1997.
Reid, Ronald F., ed. *American Rhetorical Discourse*. 2d ed. Prospect Heights, Ill: Waveland Press, 1995.
Rhoades, David and Donald Mitchie. *Mark as Story: An Introduction to the Narrative of a Gospel*. Philadelphia: Fortress Press, 1982.
Ricoeur, Paul. "Biblical Hermeneutics." *Semeia* 4 (1975): 27–148.
———. *Interpretation Theory: Discourse and the Surplus of Meaning*. Forth Worth: Texas Christian University Press, 1976.

———. *Time and Narrative*. 3 vols. Trans. Kathleen McLaughlin (Blamey) and David Pellauer. Chicago and London: University of Chicago Press, 1984–1988.

———. "Philosophy and Religious Language." *Figuring the Sacred: Religion, Narrative, and Imagination*. Ed. Mark I. Wallace. Minneapolis: Fortress Press, 1995.

Rivkin, E. "Pharisees." *The Interpreters Dictionary of the Bible: Supplementary Volume*. Ed. Keith Crim. Nashville: Abingdon Press, 1976, 657–63.

Robbins, Vernon. *Jesus the Teacher: A Socio-Rhetorical Interpretation of Mark*. Philadelphia: Fortress Press, 1984.

Rudd, Niall. *Lines of Enquiry: Studies in Latin Poetry*. Cambridge: Cambridge University Press, 1976.

Sacks, Kenneth. *Diodorus Siculus and the First Century*. Princeton, N. J.: Princeton University Press, 1990.

Schweizer, Eduard. *The Good News According to Mark*. Trans. Donald H. Madvig. Atlanta: John Knox Press, 1970.

Svenbro, Jesper. *Phrasikleia: An Anthropology of Reading in Ancient Greece*. Trans. Janet Lloyd. Myth and Poetics Series. Ed. Gregory Nagy. Ithaca, N.Y.: Cornell University Press, 1993.

Talbert, C. H. *Literary Patterns, Theological Themes and the Genre of Luke-Acts*. Society of Biblical Literature Monograph 20. Missoula, Mont.: Scholars Press, 1974.

———. *What Is a Gospel?* Philadelphia: Fortress Press, 1977.

Tannehill, Robert C. *The Sword of His Mouth: Forceful and Imaginative Language in Synoptic Sayings*. SBL Semeia Supplements, no. 1. Philadelphia and Missoula, Mont.: Fortress Press and Scholars Press, 1975.

Taylor, Vincent. *The Gospel According to St. Mark*. 2d ed. London: Macmillan, 1966.

Tolbert, Mary Anne. *Sowing the Gospel: Mark's World in Literary-Historical Perspective*. Minneapolis: Fortress Press, 1989.

Tompkins, Jane P. "The Reader in History: The Changing Shape of Literary Response." *Reader Response Criticism: From Formalism to Post-Structuralism*. Ed. Jane P. Tompkins. Baltimore: Johns Hopkins University Press, 1980.

Toynbee, A. J., trans. *Greek Historical Thought: From Homer to the Age of Heraclitus*. New York: The New American Library, 1952.

Trible, Phyllis. *God and the Rhetoric of Sexuality*. Philadelphia: Fortress Press, 1978.

Weber, Max. *Economy and Society: An Outline of Interpretive Sociology*. 2 vols. Ed. Guenther Roth and Claus Wittich, trans. Ephraim Fischoff, et al. Berkeley: University of California Press, 1978.

Welch, Kathleen. *The Contemporary Reception of Classical Rhetoric: Appropriations of Ancient Discourse*. Hillsdale, N. J.: Lawrence Erlbaum Associates, 1990.

Williams, Gordon. *Figures of Thought in Roman Poetry*. New Haven: Yale University Press, 1980.

Woodman, Tony and David West, eds. *Quality and Pleasure in Latin Poetry*. Cambridge: Cambridge University Press, 1974.

Worthington, Ian. "Greek Oratory, Revision of Speeches and the Problem of Historical Reliability." *Classica Et Mediaevalia* 62 (1991): 55–74.

———. *A Historical Commentary on Dinarchus: Rhetoric and Conspiracy in Later Fourth-Century Athens*. Ann Arbor, Mich.: University of Michigan Press, 1992.

Notes

Introduction

[1] Talmudic tradition distinguishes between halakah and aggadah midrash with the former being that which provides an account of the binding issue at stake in a legal text and the latter an interpretation or expression of the moral ideal of any nonlegal text. Although technically an anachronistic use of the terms, these rabbinic distinctions were already implicit in the oral tradition. Most of Jesus' teaching was pronouncement of a moral ideal rather than casuistic argument in the tradition of halakah. In this sense, Jesus is depicted by the gospel writers as the "rabbi" who remained true to the intent of the interpretive tradition, as opposed to those who had become enmeshed in making legal distinctions that would have the force of law (see Mk. 12:24). As Heinemann reminds us,

> While rabbinic creators of the Aggadah looked back into Scripture to uncover the full latent meaning of the Bible and its wording, at the same time they looked forward into the present and the future. They sought to give direction to their own generation, to resolve their religious problems, to answer their theological questions, and to guide them out of their spiritual complexities...The aggadists do not mean so much to clarify a difficult passage in the biblical texts as to take a stand on burning questions of the day, to guide the people and to strengthen their faith. (Heinemann, "The Nature of Aggadah," 48–49)

[2] Kennedy, *New Testament Interpretation Through Rhetorical Criticism*, 9–10. Cf. Marrou, 267–81.

[3] Cf. Havelock, *The Muse Learns to Write*.

[4] See Kugel, "Poets and Prophets," 11.

[5] Tompkins, "The Reader in History," 201–6.

[6] Welch has recently challenged the presuppositions of objectivist historians of the discipline who "interpret the concepts available in classical rhetoric as a series of writings that exist in a more or less objective world of artifacts, knowledge, and retrievable reality" (*The Contemporary Reception of Classical Rhetoric*, 9).

[7] References in commentaries are ubiquitous and need no citation. See Long, *Preaching and the Literary Forms of the Bible*, 81–86 and Greidanus, *The Modern Preacher and the Ancient Text*, 58–67.

[8] For Papias see Eusebius, *Church History*, III.39.15; for Justin see *1 Apology* 66.3, 67.3 and *Dialogue with Trypho* 106.3. Cf. the discussion of this issue in Aune, *The New Testament in Its Literary Environment*, 65–67. Note especially Aune's fine rhetorically sensitive translation of Papias. Most contemporary scholars question the motives of Papias in detracting from Mark's role in composing the Gospel. On this see Kelber, *The Oral and the Written Gospel*, 212.

[9] For a more extended presentation of the argument that follows see Reid, "When Words Were a Power Loosed," 427–47. On the rhetoric of *koinê* as an expression of Asianist rather than Atticist compositional practice see Kennedy, *Greek Rhetoric Under Christian Emperors*, 45–46.

[10] Reid, "When Words Were a Power Loosed"; cf. Sacks, *Diodorus Siculus and the First Century*, 14 and 15, n. 23.

[11] Lord, *Epic Singers and Oral Traditions*, 32.

[12] Dionysius makes clear what he means by this compositional strategy in the organization of his own essays; see Reid, "Neither Oratory Nor Dialogue." For additional study of the use of this phenomenon as an aspect of arrangement theory in Greek oratory see Worthington, "Greek Oratory," 55–74, and *A Historical Commentary on Dinarchus*; Svenbro, *Phrasikleia*, 204–14.

[13] Toynbee's translation, 177.

[14] Woodman and West, eds., *Quality and Pleasure in Latin Poetry*, 133.

[15] Rudd, *Lines of Enquiry*, 144; Cairns, *Generic Composition*, 7. For additional clarification see Cairns's chapter on "Inversion"; 127–37. See also the discussion of the prevalence of ring-composition as "thematic anticipation, repetition, and echo" in Williams, *Figures of Thought in Roman Poetry*, 95–161.

[16] On the Second Sophistic as a distinct period of Greek rhetorical theory under Roman rule see Bowersock's discussion of "Philostratus and the Second Sophistic" and Kennedy's recent discussion in *A New History of Classical Rhetoric*, 230–56.

[17] For an extended discussion of the significance of the concept of *prose economy* (*oikonomia*) as the technical principles of prose composition in the first centuries before and after Christ see Reid, "Hermagoras' Theory of *Prose Oikonomia* in Dionysius of Halicarnassus."

[18] On this argument for a self-consciously literate compositional style see Reid, "Dionysius of Halicarnassus' Theory of Compositional Style and the Theory of Literate Consciousness," 46–64.

[19] Kermode, *The Genesis of Secrecy*, 127.

[20] Bengel, *Gnomon of the New Testament*, I:491–96. On contemporary options see J. Dewey, *Markan Public Debate* and Tolbert, *Sowing the Gospel*.

[21] For an accessible introduction to this compositional technique see Bailey, *Poet and Peasant* and *Through Peasant Eyes*. For a critical introduction see Talbert, *Literary Patterns, Theological Themes and the Genre of Luke-Acts*.

[22] Fowler, *Let the Reader Understand*, 151–52.

[23] Dewey, *Markan Public Debate*. The irony here is that Dewey has recently capitulated to those who reject the notion that texts like Mark can be radically literate in their compositional technique; Dewey, "Oral Methods," 23–41.

[24] Fowler, 152.

[25] Reid, "Dionysius of Halicarnassus's Theory of Compositional Style," 55–60.

[26] Two books that came to my attention after this manuscript was sent to the publisher are worth noting. The first, John Breck, *The Shape of Biblical Language: Chiasmus in the Scriptures and Beyond* (Crestwood, N.Y.: St. Vladimir's Seminary Press, 1944) is an impressive study of Chiasmus by one of the contributors to the NRSV version of the New Oxford Annotated Bible. Breck offers an extensive proposal for the construal of Mark's Gospel that has important points of agreement as well as offering alternatives to the argument presented here (see pp. 143–75). Those interested in finding additional literature on chiastic readings of biblical texts and in other ancient literature are directed to recently published bibliography by John Welch and Daniel McKinlay, eds. *Chiasmus Bibliography* (Provo, Utah: Research Press, 1999). Of particular interest is the textual index directing readers to books, dissertations, and journal essays analyzing specific chiastic structures found in the Bible and related religious literature.

[27] Wimsatt and Beardsley declared that any effort to get at such authorial meanings commits the *intentional fallacy*. These literary theorists were opposed to the reigning hegemony of reading psychologically biased interpretations into a written text as if the interpreter can know the actual "meaning" the author intended in composing a text (*Sewanee Review*, 1946). Originally, the critical effort was designed to undermine the dominating conception of an "author" as a construct in literary criticism, as if biographical information concerning who wrote the text was somehow necessary to understand and interpret the meaning of a text. Eventually, in this battle over the notion of "author" and "intent" new divisions arose, still arguing at one end for some historicist role for interpretation (i.e., that there is a need to understand the sociopolitical context in which a text participates as conversation) as opposed to accepting only the environment of textuality itself. In practice, the effort to wholly banish all interest in the intentional has failed—texts are born of contexts. But the debate has forever changed our assumptions about the hermeneutics of reading texts, and preachers need to be aware of this. On the subject see the important essay by Patterson, "Intention," 135–46; cf. Eagleton, 67–88.

[28] See Ricoeur, *Interpretation Theory*, 92.

[29] See Gadamer's discussion of legal and theological hermeneutics in *Truth and Method*, 324–41.

[30] Buttrick, "On Doing Homiletics Today," 99.

[31] See Long, "The Preacher and the Beast," 3–10.

[32] Buttrick, "On Doing Homiletics Today," 99. See Long, *Preaching and the Literary Forms of the Bible*, 50, and *The Witness of Preaching*, 84. Hogan finds

> The postmodern critique has attempted to relocate the production of meaning away from the exclusive domain of the writer or speaker. The reader/listener is not to be understood as a passive vessel into which the ideas and arguments of the text/speech/sermon are poured. One may not be willing to go as far as some in arguing that there is no meaning until it is produced by the reader/listener. Nevertheless, reception and the role of the reader/listener are not understood to have an important place in the production of meaning. ("The Squint," 256–57)

[33] Ricoeur, *Time and Narrative*, II:88-99; III: 160–64. On point-of-view in the Gospel of Mark see Rhoads and Michie, *Mark as Story*, 35–44. On voice as part of the rhetoric of fictive argument see Booth, *The Rhetoric of Fiction*, 170–266.

[34] Moore, *Post-Structuralism and the New Testament*, 6. There are, of course, critical problems with this approach. For example, Moore argues that the most significant problem is that "reader-response criticism enacts and reenacts the collapse of critical 'metalanguage'—the pretensions of one form of language (criticism) to pronounce on another form of language (literature) from a position safely outside or above it" (Moore, 6). I concede Moore's point but do not feel compelled to abandon my ability to make reasonable wagers concerning meaning and the way in which issues of form and genre help clarify the expectations of an *originary* audience for the language of this text.

[35] Ricoeur asks, "What is it that interpreters try to offer when they have explored the implications of the mode(s) of discourse by which a text is arranged?" He responds, "If we can no longer define hermeneutics as the search for another person and psychological intentions that hide behind a text, and if we do not want to reduce interpretation to the identification of structures, what remains to be interpreted? My response is that to interpret is to explicate the sort of being-in-the-world unfolded in front of the text" ("Philosophy and Religious Language," 42–43). "Structures" referred to in this statement is a reference to the codes of structuralist analysis concerning which an author is wholly unaware in the composition of a text. This is different from the kind of structures of parallelism discussed in this study that are assumed as intentional aspects of the author's compositional process.

[36] Ricoeur, *Time and Narrative*, III:174.

[37] Ricoeur, *Time and Narrative*, III:175.

[38] For an explanation of the distinction in these four strategies of preaching see Reid, "Faithful Preaching."

[39] Farris, "Limping Away with a Blessing," 364.

[40] Muilenburg, "Form Criticism and Beyond," 1–18. Fishbane, *Text and Texture: Close Readings of Selected Biblical Texts*; Trible, *God and the Rhetoric of Sexuality*; Tolbert, *Sowing the Gospel*.

[41] Kennedy, the leading historiographer of the classical rhetorical tradition, produced three key works, *The Art of Persuasion, The Art of Rhetoric in the Roman World,* and *Greek Rhetoric Under Christian Emperors*, all of which have recently been synthesized and updated in his *A New History of Classical Rhetoric* .

[42] Hermeneia commentaries by Betz, *Galatians*; *2 Corinthians 8 and 9*; and *The Sermon on the Mount*; Mack, *A Myth of Innocence* and *Rhetoric and the New Testament*; Collins, *The Beginning of the Gospel*.

[43] Muilenburg originally proposed that "rhetorical criticism" could be applicable to all of Israel's scriptures and that focus was certainly maintained in the early efforts to pursue his challenge. See Jackson and Kessler, eds., *Rhetorical Criticism: Essays in Honor of James Muilenburg*.

[44] Booth, *The Rhetoric of Fiction*, 112.

[45] McKeon, *Novels as Arguments*, 20–25.

[46] This is a departure from McKeon's use, but one intended to highlight the function of argument as conducted in the form of composing a fictive account.

Mark 1:1–15: The First Narrative Complex

[1]For much of the second half of the twentieth century, the standard English commentary on the Gospel of Mark has been that of Vincent Taylor. Using a form critical methodology, Taylor divided the book into discrete "literary complexes" (90–113). For example, in this collection he includes verse 1 but concludes the narrative complex at verse 13. Taylor, *The Gospel According to St. Mark*, 90.

[2]On "intersignification" see Ricoeur, "Biblical Hermeneutics," 104–5.

[3]The birthday of Caesar Augustus was hailed as being "for the world the beginning of good news" in an inscription dated 9 B.C.; Piper, "Gospel," 443. See also Cranfield, *The Gospel According to St. Mark*, 36–37.

[4]Cranfield, 45.

[5]Kennedy, *New Testament Interpretation Through Rhetorical Criticism*, 104. Kennedy observes, "There are [arguments] in Mark, but they are usually of a very simple sort, offering an obvious explanation and usually in his own voice" (106–7).

[6]Kennedy, *Classical Rhetoric*, 127.

Mark 1:16—2:14: The Second Narrative Complex

[1]Nineham, *Saint Mark*, 91.

[2]Schweizer, *The Good News According to Mark*, 59.

[3]A more developed analysis of this collection is found in my essay, "When Words Were a Power Loosed," 427–47.

[4]For a provocative alternative chiastic construal of Mk. 1:22–45 see Hendrickx, *The Miracle Stories*, 39–40.

[5]Ernest Best has examined the compositional design of both sets of stories and finds them all to be cut from the same redactional cloth. Best is led to ask, "Given that Mark knew one such incident in the tradition has he created two more of a similar pattern? Did all three come to him in the tradition already constructed according to this pattern? Did all three come in the tradition but the pattern has been imposed by him?" (*Following Jesus*, 166). Taylor suggests that the similarity of these episodes is dependent on the fact that they are "biographical apothegm [Bultmann's term] told and retold until [they have] been reduced to its barest essentials" (201). What all seem to miss is the rhetorical effect of these stories in bracketing the material between them.

[6]See Tompkins, "The Reader in History," 201; See also Booth's chapter on "Beliefs and the Reader" in which he illustrates how a reader's emotions and responses are always involved in the reading of a narrative text; *The Rhetoric of Fiction*, 119–47.

[7]This limerick and its illustrative use in this capacity originates with my friend and colleague Dr. Alvin Lustie who, in years past, colabored with me in the recovery of Mark's chiastic strategy of composition.

Mark 2:15—3:6: The Third Narrative Complex

[1]The following piece of text does not fit: "but one puts new wine into fresh wineskins" (NRSV). It has no echo balance in the prior parable. The UBS editors only rate this phrase at the {C} level of authority.

[2]Booth, 105ff.

[3]This proposal is in contrast to that of J. Dewey, *Markan Public Debate*, 48–49, Tolbert *Sowing the Gospel*, 144, and Hendrickx, 106–12, who all appear to allow the form critical assumption that there are five consecutive conflict stories (re: Dibelius and Albertz) to control their presentation of this material. For the latter see Taylor, 91.

[4]Rivkin summarizes its effect, "The Pharisees were teachers of salvation for the individual through a community of true believers in the twofold law [the written law and oral law], and not nationalists focusing on the land, or on the temple, or on the sovereign state. Their kingdom of God was an internalized kingdom of those who affirmed God's unity (cf. M. Ber. 2.5) and adhered to its laws wherever they were living—Jerusalem, Corinth, Ephesus, or Rome—and under whatever conditions prevailed" (Rivkin, "Pharisees," 661).

[5]Ibid., 660.
[6]Again, Rivkin notes, "Because all Biblical writings were believed to be divinely inspired, every verse was regarded as saturated with divine insight. Each could be detached from its context and freely joined to other verses from other books to support or elucidate either a *halachic* or *haggadic* dictum" (660).
[7]Hengel, *Judaism and Hellenism*, 173. Hengel finds that "Pharisaism is based on the unhistorical, 'ontological' conception of the law, which was alien to the Old Testament itself…Old Testament history writing finds its continuation *not* in the casuistic legal collections of the Mishnah, Tosefta or the Talmuds, nor even in the Rabbinic *midrashim* with their unhistorical thought, but—albeit in the alien garb of Hellenism—in the work of the Palestinian priestly aristocrat and Hellenist Jew, Josephus" (114–15).

Mark 3:7—4:1: The Fourth Narrative Complex

[1]Cf. J. Dewey, *Debate*, 148.
[2]Cf. Booth, 105ff.
[3]On the use of metaphor in Jesus' argument to "disclose truth by using words which when taken literally, are false" see Tannehill, *The Sword of His Mouth*, 177–85.
[4]The A-B-A' structure of Episode II' is one of seven instances of Mark's use of intercalation to thematically juxtaposed material he wants to put in counterpoint (Mk. 3:20–35; 5:21–43; 6:7–33; 11:12–25; 14:1–11; 14:53–72; 15:6–32).

Mark 4:2–34: The Fifth Narrative Complex

[1]In the previous complexes, I used the term *scene* to separate multiple parallel structures within a particular episode. I use the term *section* to divide an episode in this sayings collection.
[2]Drury, "Mark," 402–3; cf. Drury, *The Parables in the Gospels*, 25.
[3]Drury, "Mark," 404–5.
[4]Ibid., 405. Drury draws the phrase from Rimbaud's "Illuminations."
[5]Crossan, *In Parables*, 50–52.
[6]See Drury, *The Parables in the Gospels*, 54.

Mark 4:35—5:43: The Sixth Narrative Complex

[1]Taylor, 94. See Best, *Mark*, 16; Malbon, "Narrative Criticism," 36–47. However, see Mack, *Myth*, 216–18; Fowler, *Let the Reader Understand*, 67–68.
[2]Rhoades and Mitchie, *Mark as Story*, 51.
[3]Meye, "Psalm 107 as 'Horizon,' 1–13. Meye applies Psalm 107 in the following manner: (1) Deliverance from hunger and thirst in the wilderness (Ps. 107:4–9; cf. Mk. 6:30–44; 8:1–10, 14–21). (2) Deliverance from darkness and distressing bondage (Ps. 107:10–16; cf. Mk. 5:1–20; 6:13; 7:24–30). (3) Deliverance from sickness (Ps. 107:17–22; cf. Mk. 5:21—6:5, 13, 53–56; 7:31–37; 8:22–26). (4) Deliverance from peril at sea (Ps. 107:23–32; cf. Mk. 4:35–41; 6:45–52). Meye's thesis is amazingly strong when dealing with the material in Mk. 4:35—5:43, but is less helpful outside of the collection. Cf. Malbon, 38.
[4]"Most of the miracles were actions whereby the dominion of God was actually established over man and nature. A few of the miracles were more symbolic in purpose, teaching men about the kingdom rather than directly bringing this kingdom about…Thus the miracle stories were part of the *kerygma* and *didache* of the Synoptic tradition" (R. Brown, "The Gospel Miracles," 231).
[5]C. Brown, *Miracles and the Critical Mind*, 306.

Mark 6:1–52: The Seventh Narrative Complex

[1]The reference may be an allusion to YHWH as the I AM who "passed by" both Moses (Exodus 33:17–23) and Elijah (1 Kings 19:11). Cf. Job 9:5–11, in which God is described as the one who does great things beyond understanding: "Look he passes by me, and I do not see him; he moves on but I do not perceive him."
[2]Most exegetes have found thematically connected material only at the end of this portion of Mark. Taylor is indicative when he writes, "Before…[the small complex of Mk. 6:30–56] there are three isolated stories: the Rejection at Nazareth (6:1–6a), the Mission

Charge to the Twelve (6:6b–13, and Herod's Fears (6:14–16); and as a pendant to the third, the account of the Death of the Baptist (6:17–29). These narratives do not form a complex, for there are no connecting-links and there is no common theme" (95).

³This discussion is adapted from my "Commentary" in *Word and Witness*, "Proper 10 for July 13, 1997."

⁴Girard, "The Beheading of John the Baptist," 147.

⁵Kelber, *Mark's Story of Jesus*, 34.

⁶Pastoral metaphors were in vogue throughout the ancient world and *shepherd* was an honorary title that had been applied to divinities and rulers for centuries. Ezekiel 34 presents an extended example of this term's metaphorical usage (cf. 1 Kings 22:17, 36; 2 Chr. 18:16), but it is Numbers 27:15–17 that provides the full horizon.

⁷As he instructs the disciples to have the crowd "sit down in groups [of hundreds and fifties] on the green grass" the reader is quickly reminded of the "green pastures" and promise of provision from the Lord found in Psalm 23. Chasing one more allusion, the division of the people into groups of hundreds and fifties evokes the same numbering of the organizational hierarchy established by Moses in Deuteronomy 1:15–18. Deuteronomy outlines the job description for the pastor-shepherd and provides an interpretive horizon that unlocks the focus of the feeding miracle story. It is the disciples as undershepherds who take the proleptic eucharistic meal out to the people, and in the climax of the step-progression they pick up twelve basketfuls of broken pieces. In the post-resurrection ministry, church leaders are called to mediate the eucharistic provision of table fellowship with the Lord.

⁸Taylor, 324.

Mark 6:53—7:31: The Eighth Narrative Complex

¹This verse is omitted from the NRSV. According to Metzger, it has a strong witness in the majority of extant texts but is absent from the important Alexandrian witness. For this reason, the UBS committee concluded that it was a scribal gloss derived perhaps from 4:9 or 4:23 and "introduced as an appropriate sequel to verse 14" (*A Textual Commentary on the Greek New Testament*, 94–95). The present study offers an equally strong argument that this verse should be reincluded as the necessary echo balance of verse 14.

²In Jesus' day, the practice of pious Jewish casuistry, labeled as the traditions of the elders, allowed its most prominent citizens a tax loophole in regard to provision for parents. Not only were those who claimed the loophole no longer responsible for the care of their aging parents, but the individual who declared his assets as "gift devoted to God" was able to appear as if it was all done in the name of honoring God. Jesus finds that the commands of God were being nullified by such actions both permitted and even encouraged by the institutional religious leadership. Their casuistry had become the very evil it was supposed to prevent.

³Booth, *The Rhetoric of Fiction*, 107. Note that I am arguing for a third kind of rhetorical strategy, one created by arranging the material elements of a story in a manner that an argument is sustained in the juxtaposition of the carefully construed narrative.

⁴Bruce, *New Testament History*, 283–85.

⁵Reid, "John Hancock: Commentary," 99.

⁶For Hancock's mastery of inflammatory rhetoric see "The Boston Massacre Oration—March 5, 1774," 99–108.

⁷Nineham evidences sensitivity to the connection between this complex and the one that follows when he notes that Mark 7:1–23 presents a message of "emancipation from Jewish particularism" and provides "a fitting prelude to the account which follows of Jesus' ministry on Gentile soil (7:24ff)" (188).

Mark 7:32—8:27: The Ninth Narrative Complex

¹For a discussion of the journeys by boat as part of the organization of Mark 4:35—8:21 [26] see Meye, *Jesus and the Twelve*, 63–73.

²Taylor, 368.

³Mark appears willing to draw limits on Jesus' knowledge and abilities for narrative effect in ways that made the other evangelists uncomfortable. Here it takes two attempts to heal the blind man. In Mark 6:1–6 the texts state that he could do no miracles because of their unbelief. Matthew says that he chose to do no miracles because of their

unbelief (Mt. 13:58) and Luke avoids the dilemma by having Jesus miraculously escape from an angry mob (Lk. 4:30). Matthew also appears uncomfortable with Jesus' apparent lack of knowing who it was who touched him in the crowd (Mt. 9:21–22), but Luke follows Mark at this point (Mk. 5:30; Lk. 8:45).

⁴As Robert Meye notes, "One is struck with a contrast in reading the Marcan narrative: the disciples, having eyes to see, could not see (8:18); the blind man, also confronted with Jesus' works, was made to see clearly. Mark 8:22–26 demands connection to 8:14–21" (*Jesus and the Twelve*, 70).

⁵Note these are clues that demand readers. Having listened to Mark's Gospel is not sufficient to solve this puzzle. The interpreter must be able to go back and ponder previous allusions. Mark assumes literate readers, not listeners.

⁶Drury, "Mark," 415.

Mark 8:27—9:29: The Tenth Narrative Complex

¹Taylor, 98.

²E. g., both J. Dewey (*Debate*, 23) and Kelber suggest an additional framing of the central discipleship section using the stories of the healing of the blind man of Bethsaida in 8:27–26 at one end and the healing of blind Bartimaeus (10:46–52) at the other. Kelber writes, "As the frame conditions the contents, so do the framing stories cast interpretive light on the purpose of the journey. The opening of the eyes is what Jesus does at the beginning and at the end of the way, and this is also what characterizes his relation with the disciples all along the way. To open the eyes of the disciples and make them see is the overriding purpose of the journey from Caesarea Phillipi to Jerusalem" (*Mark's Story*, 44).

³Mark 9:35–50 and 10:42–44 represent other similar sets of condensed formulations as instruction in following Jesus. See Mack, *Myth*, 341–6.

⁴Prior instances are at Mk. 3:28 and 8:12. Latter occurrences: 9:41; 10:15, 29; 11:23; 12:43; 13:30; 14:9, 18, 25, 30.

⁵E.g., Mk. 10:29–30 and Mk. 14:25.

⁶The story of Elijah's ascension is recorded in 2 Kings 2 and the popular legend of Moses' ascension is found in the noncanonical *Assumption of Moses*.

⁷Dunn, *Jesus Call to Discipleship*, 127–28.

"Who Is He—And So What If He Is?"

¹Cited from printed materials on Mark used in Robert Reid's teaching ministry in his capacity as scholar-in-residence at University Place Presbyterian Church.

Mark 9:30—10:45: The Eleventh Narrative Complex

¹Mack, *Myth*, 342–43.

²On "the good life" see the essays in Depew, *The Greeks and the Good Life* and Nussbaum, *The Fragility of Goodness: Luck and Ethics in Greek Tragedy and Philosophy*.

³See Houlden, *Ethics and the New Testament*, 41–46.

⁴In his *Introduction to Aristotle*, 298, R. Mckeon notes that in Aristotle, there is no agreement concerning what happiness is and therefore "it must be defined…in terms of activity of the soul in accordance with perfect virtue."

⁵Translation by Samuel in *The Promise of the West*, 153. I have also followed Samuel's summary of Aristotle's ethics in this discussion.

⁶*Letter to Menoeceus* in *Epicurus: The Extant Remains*, 91. Schematization mine.

⁷This is a play on K. Burke's definition of humankind: "Man is [1] the symbol-using (symbol-making, symbol-misusing) animal; [2] inventor of the negative (or moralized by the negative); [3] separated from his natural condition by instruments of his own making; [4] *goaded by the spirit of hierarchy* (or moved by the sense of order); [5] and rotten with perfection." In discussing the fourth part of his definition, Burke regularly speaks of "mounting the hierarchy" as that which we who are "rotten with perfection" are prone to do; *Language as Symbolic Action*, 16.

Mark 10:46—11:25: The Twelfth Narrative Complex

[1]Critics regularly suggest that the episode of the fig tree has been inserted into a more primitive tradition by Mark, (e.g., "as an example of faith and prayer," Nineham, 298–9; or intended as a didactic illustration of the fate that awaited Jerusalem and the Jewish people, Cranfield, 355). Because of the unusual nature of this miracle story, form critics regularly suggest that the original story may have been a parable that became an event in transmission. Arguments of this kind assume that Mark was not master of his material, that he was merely an organizer of pieces of tradition. But Mark's masterful control of his material, amply demonstrated by this point in the gospel, should suggest that many form and redaction critical assumptions that have shaped Marcan studies for half a century need to be reconsidered in light of the Marcan artistry demonstrated in his control of rhetorical form.

Mark 11:27—12:12: The Thirteenth Narrative Complex

[1]Most critics of the Jerusalem debate section of the Gospel of Mark begin a new complex at this juncture but carry it into the material that follows. On the other hand, J. Dewey believes that 12:1–40 forms an inverted narrative complex (p. 162), but recognizes that she fights against the tide, which sees this complex begin at 11:27 (*Debate* 216, n. 87). Most critics tend to group the seven episodes after 11:27 as the public debate portion of the second half of Mark's gospel. See J. Dewey for a survey of options, *Debate*, 55–63.

[2]The use of Psalm 118 placed on the lips of Jesus has provoked a great deal of critical comment. Clearly, this psalm helped forge part of the post-Pentecost sense of identity for the church (e.g., Acts 4:11; Eph. 2:20; 1 Pet. 2:6). Many critics assume that this self-understanding is being read back onto the lips of Jesus in the gospels and attempt to discover what, if anything, might be the original pre-Pentecost parable uttered by Jesus. The critical question is important, but from a rhetorical perspective, the interpretive allusion to the Gentile mission in vv. 9–10 cannot simply be treated as a Marcan addition to an existing parable. As schematized, it is intrinsic to the rhetorical balance of the whole. This kind of form critical urge to separate the "sheep" from the "goats" in sayings of Jesus demonstrates a lack of sensitivity to the rhetorical dimensions of how Mark has made use of the tradition.

[3]Drury, *The Parables in the Gospels*, 68; cf. Donahue, *The Gospel in Parable*, 56–57, who makes a similar connection to the function of the parable of the sower.

[4]Drury, *The Parables in the Gospels*, 64–65.

[5]E.g., Mann, 463. For other attempts to recover a pre-Marcan parable, see Crossan, *In Parables*, 86–96.

[6]Mack, *Myth*, 168. Mack argues that "Those who are to be instructed by Jesus' teaching are not those to whom he speaks in the story, but those who read the story in Mark's time. Mark addressed his readers by attributing his message to Jesus and letting them overhear Jesus' instructions to others" (169).

[7]Max Weber, *Economy and Society*, 1:244. The reference and its implications are drawn from Bruns, *Hermeneutics: Ancient and Modern*, 71ff.

Mark 12:13–44: The Fourteenth Narrative Complex

[1]Mann, 481.

[2]To put enemies under one's foot in a Middle Eastern society is beyond humiliation, since feet are considered the filthiest portion of the body. This is especially true in cultures where animal waste is commonly part of the mud that accumulates on feet shod only in sandals.

[3]Weber, Vol. 1, 244. See the larger quotation from which this reference is drawn in the discussion of the motif in the thirteenth narrative complex.

[4]Tannehill, *Sword of His Mouth*, 176–77.

[5]See the discussion of this text and its control of the shape of the meta-narrative collection in the twelfth narrative complex.

⁶This discussion is adapted from Reid, "Epiphany 6."
⁷Brueggemann, *Old Testament Theology*, 270–95.
⁸Mark's radical ethic, commitment to the Gentile mission, and his use of the stories to cast the leadership of the Jerusalem church as too accommodating, may be some of the reasons he depicts a complete abrogation of the temple cult and relationship of Christianity with Judaism. One must examine the context that might have led Mark to frame his story in this manner, before assuming that this irreconcilability is of the essence of Christianity.
⁹Hooker, *The Message of Mark*, 84.

Mark 13:1–37: The Fifteenth Narrative Complex

¹See Brett, "Mark's Arrangement," 187; Mack, *Myth*, 317; and Tolbert, *Sowing the Gospel*, 314.
²Bornkamm is representative when he finds, "Undoubtedly traditional matter which has its origin in late Jewish apocalypticism has been taken over during transmission of the synoptic material and set down as the sayings of Jesus…[with only] two genuine sayings of Jesus interwoven" (93). However, based on the evidence adduced thus far in the gospel, the criterion traditionally used to distinguish actual sayings of Jesus and those created by either Mark or the tradition need to be reevaluated. When there is little difference in the rhetorical configuration of those stories that redaction and form critics attribute to Jesus and those they attribute to Mark or the tradition, theories of the Marcan purpose predicated on the distinctions are not tenable (93). For an overview of other approaches see Kealy who discusses the apocalyptic theories of Marxsen, 160–65; Pesch, 195–97; Perrin, 223–25; and Kee, 229–30.
³Talbert, *What Is a Gospel?* 120–21, 134.
⁴Based on an extensive chart of citations covering more than four pages of text, Mann declares Mark 13:5–27 to be a freely composed, ahistorical pastiche of allusions and quotations from the Hebrew scriptures (500–4).
⁵Lane, *The Gospel According to Mark*, 468–69.
⁶I have assumed that the parenthetical explanation is an interpretive clue that "the reader" is suppose to see that scripture was fulfilled in the destruction of the temple. For a careful analysis of alternative readings of this parenthetical note see Fowler, *Let the Reader Understand*, 82–87.
⁷Samuel, *The Promise of the West*, 327–28.
⁸Ibid., 342.
⁹This is not to suggest that literate authority replaced oral; cf. the testimony of Papias, "And again, on any occasion when a person came (in my way) who had been a follower of the Elders, I would inquire about the discources of the elders…. For I did not think that I could get so much profit from books as from the utterances of a living and abiding voice" (Eusebius, *Hist. Eccl.* 3.39). However, in Papias' list of apostolic voices, he presents them as individuals rather than the single voice of the community of the Twelve or the leadership of the Jerusalem church. It was the dissipation of the latter's authority that gave rise to the possibility of "books" contending with "voices."
¹⁰Samuel, *The Promise of the West*, 343.

Mark 14:1–53: The Sixteenth Narrative Complex

¹Donahue notes that the view that Mark is a passion narrative with an extended introduction was almost dogma in gospel research until recently ("From Passion Traditions to Passion Narrative," 1). In *The Oral and the Written Gospel*, Kelber notes that the collection of essays he edited concerning *The Passion in Mark* (in which Donahues's essay is the first) represented the first clear consensus that the passion narrative was part of the internal narrative logic of the whole gospel rather than a preexisting narrative for which the Gospel was composed as an extended introduction (xvii). However, Childs maintains that, "There is still a widespread consensus (*contra* Kelber) that Mark found the passion story in a largely completed form with the major components already established. Nevertheless, Mark left his redactional stamp on the material in chaps. 14ff, which brings to completion his original purpose" (*The New Testament as Canon*, 91).

²For example, Taylor suggests three natural breaks in the text at 14:1–52;14:53—15:47; and 16:1–8; (526). More recently, Mann has proposed only two major blocks at Mk. 14:1–52 and 14:53—16:8 (543).
³*The Passion in Mark*, 1.
⁴Luke appears to have felt the need to clarify the allusion by citing Isaiah 53:12, "He was numbered with the transgressors" (Lk. 22:37).
⁵*Contra* Taylor and Mann, I argue that Marcan parallelism demands that 14:53 rounds out this collection rather than initiating the next narrative complex.
⁶Scholarly puzzlement about the identity of the naked young man abounds, but the schematization presented in this complex demonstrates that he also serves a purpose more than a person. Jesus was "seized" to be led away in segment B. He is depicted as a proud leader offering no resistance, but indignant over being treated as a common criminal. In the similar attempt to "seize" the anonymous young man, the follower is depicted as escaping with great indignity. He "fled naked." Nakedness and running are both great humiliations to men in the Middle-Eastern culture. See Bailey, who notes that, "An Oriental nobleman with flowing robes never runs anywhere. To do so is humiliating. Ben Sirach confirms this attitude. He says, 'A man's manner of walking tells you what he is'"; *Poet and Peasant*, 181.
⁷Kelber, *Mark's Story*, 75–77.

Mark 14:54—15:20: The Seventeenth Narrative Complex

¹Cranfield, 446.
²Cf. Nineham, 410ff.
³Mark was not the first to use the figure of Peter as an example of failure. Paul had already told the story of Peter's unwillingness to stand by the "true meaning of the gospel" in Galatians 2:11–14. Peter was an important figure in the early church, but the clarity of his advocacy of the Gentile mission gets mixed reviews. Apparently Peter saw that the future lay with Gentile believers, but he is variously depicted as torn between the implications of this vision and his role as a central figure in the establishment of Jewish Christianity in the Jerusalem church.
⁴On the opposition between Peter and Jesus as victim and victimizer see Hammerton-Kelly, *The Gospel and the Sacred*, 52–54.
⁵Mack, *Myth*, 305–6.
⁶In the New Testament, *hamartia* is a classic word for "sin," the *fallibility* of missing the mark. However, *hamartia* in Aristotle is the word used to describe the human *fallibility* that causes the transformation of fortune in the ideal tragic plot. On the latter see Halliwell, *The Poetics of Aristotle: Translation and Commentary*, 128–30.
⁷See K. Dewey, "Peter's Curse and Cursed Peter," 113–14.
⁸Mack, *Myth*, 306.
⁹Rhoades and Michie, *Mark as Story*, 129.

Mark 15:21–39: The Eighteenth Narrative Complex

¹Because of the way in which he is identified, we cannot know whether Simon, the first character identified in this tragedy, was a Gentile God-fearer, or a Diaspora Jew in Jerusalem for the holy days. Rhetorically, the Greek names of his sons are indicated in such a manner that we are left to presume that they are people known by name among the Hellenistic constituents of Mark's audience.
²For a similar construal see Tolbert, *Sowing the Gospel*, 279.
³Cf. Robbins, *Jesus the Teacher*, 187.
⁴Ibid., 190–91.
⁵Ibid., 191.
⁶Kelber, *Mark's Story*, 81.
⁷Ibid., 83.

Mark 15:40—16:8: The Nineteenth Narrative Complex

¹See Kermode, *The Genesis of Secrecy*, 64–73.
²Cf. Fowler, "Reader-Response Criticism: Figuring Mark's Reader," 75–81.

³Werner Kelber has arrived at a similar conclusion by means of a different methodological approach to the text: "One reason the Gospel ends in this 'incomplete' fashion is because the failure of the women is indeed not the last word on the story of the Kingdom. While the disciples' fate is sealed [with the collapse of the oral community in the temple destruction of A.D. 70] the readers in Mark's time, who understand the nature of the crisis, are invited to complete the journey of Jesus left incomplete by the disciples. In this sense reading the gospel is but the beginning of the gospel's actualization in real life"; *Mark's Story*, 94.

⁴Z. McKeon would refer to Mark's history as a text that makes a fictive argument and that "What is important is that fictive arguments, whether street signs or histories, are not 'about' experience. Rather, any one of them will constitute an experience; fictive arguments invent not only statements, but also what is involved in statements: their subject matters, their authors and audiences, the ideas they express, and the things they present" (*Novels as Arguments*, 25).

⁵Cf. Farmer, *The Last Twelve Verses of a Mark*.

⁶See Kelber, *The Oral and the Written Gospel*, 90–139.

⁷For further discussion, see Reid, "When Words Were a Power Loosed," 439–41.

⁸On the argument that the transfiguration as a misplaced resurrection narrative see Mann, 357. The transfiguration is no more a misplaced resurrection story than is the baptism. This kind of form-criticism comment misses the narrative point. Viewing the gospel narratively, one might assume that certain stories begin to imply one another tautologically; events become synonyms in their symmetry even as they exhibit the semblance of chronology. Kenneth Burke notes this phenomenon of circularity in ostensibly rectilinear narratives and states, "We don't usually realize how often we use the quasi-successiveness of narrative when actually we are but giving a synonym" (*The Rhetoric of Religion: Studies in Logology*, 225).

⁹Kelber, *The Oral and the Written Gospel*, 108.

¹⁰Gunther Bornkamm, *Jesus of Nazareth*, 183.

¹¹Cf. Mann, 659–63.

¹²Kelber, *Mark's Story*, 87.

¹³Kelber, *The Oral and the Written Gospel*, 116.

¹⁴Ibid., 130.

¹⁵For Romans 10:9–10 as an early baptismal confession of faith see Martin, *Worship in the Early Church*, 60.

Conclusion

¹Z. McKeon, *Novels as Arguments*, 25.

²Alter, *The Art of Biblical Narrative*, 32.

³Ibid., 32.

⁴Ibid., 33.

⁵Price, "Foreword," xi.

⁶Kermode, *The Genesis of Secrecy*, 141.

⁷Kelber argues that Mark's depicts the Twelve as the oral heirs of the paradigm of Jesus' life and death, but that "theirs is a failing discipleship." Mark portrays them simultaneously as the intended tradition-bearers (a *mimetic* function) and as a failing, dysfunctional group. "This leads us to suggest that the dysfunctional role of the disciples narrates the breakdown of the mimetic process and casts a vote of censure against the guarantors of tradition. Oral representatives and oral mechanisms have come under criticism. If the foremost oral authorities are depicted as failing to perceive the message and mission of Jesus, the conclusion is inevitable, that as far as Mark is concerned, mimesis malfunctioned and did so at a crucial juncture"; Kelber, *The Oral and the Written Gospel*, 97.

⁸Kelber, *The Oral and the Written Gospel*, 130. Kelber's description of the Marcan argument as "parable" (131) has not been examined, but it is also not critical to the argument cited here. What Kelber and others call a "parabolic logic" for connecting the medium (form) and the message (content) is, in my opinion, actually the narrative operation of the Hebrew and Greek rhetorical convention of parallelism demonstrated in this study. Unlike Kelber, I would argue that the shift to conceiving a literate reading audience as recipients for this Gospel is radical precisely because this choice constructs a Greco-Roman

rather than a Hebrew audience. By *writing* the Gospel in this radically literate fashion, Mark conforms his medium to the particularity of his message.

[9]On the genre of the Gospel of Mark as *historia*, see my introduction above, pp. 4–7.

[10]For an elaboration of this use of the rhetorical term *oikonomia* see Meijering, *Literary and Rhetorical Theories in Greek Scholia*, 134–225 and Reid, "Hermagoras' Theory of Prose *Oikonomia* in Dionysius of Halicarnassus" and "Neither Oratory Nor Dialogue."

[11]Kelber, *Mark's Story of Jesus*, 91–96.

[12]Ibid., 94.